2021 年第 1 辑

新市場財政學研究

The Journal of Neo-Public Finance

李俊生 主编

01

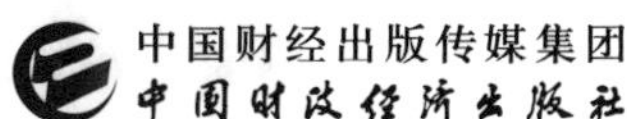

中国财经出版传媒集团
中国财政经济出版社

图书在版编目（CIP）数据

新市场财政学研究 = The Journal of Neo-Public Finance. 2021 年 . 第 1 辑：汉英对照/李俊生主编 . — 北京：中国财政经济出版社，2021. 7

ISBN 978 - 7 - 5223 - 0620 - 9

Ⅰ. ①新… Ⅱ. ①李… Ⅲ. ①财政学 - 研究 - 汉、英 Ⅳ. ①F810

中国版本图书馆 CIP 数据核字（2021）第 116076 号

责任编辑：闫 娟
封面设计：陈宇琰

新市场财政学研究
XINSHICHANG CAIZHENGXUE YANJIU

中国财政经济出版社 出版
URL：http：//www. cfeph. cn
E - mail：cfeph @ cfeph. cn

社址：北京市海淀区阜成路甲 28 号 邮政编码：100142
营销中心电话：010 - 88191537
北京财经印刷厂印刷 各地新华书店经销
成品尺寸：185mm × 260mm 16 开 13. 5 印张 215 000 字
2021 年 7 月第 1 版 2021 年 7 月北京第 1 次印刷
定价：68. 00 元
ISBN 978 - 7 - 5223 - 0620 - 9
（图书出现印装问题，本社负责调换）
本社质量投诉电话：010 - 88190744
打击盗版举报热线：010 - 88191661 QQ：2242791300

新市場財政學研究
The Journal of Neo-Public Finance

主办单位

中国财政发展协同创新中心
http://icfd.cufe.edu.cn/
中央财经大学新市场财政学研究所
http://datacenter.cufe.edu.cn/inst/home

中国财政发展协同
创新中心

目录

市场经济环境下的财政基础理论建设问题
——范式与理念

李俊生

摘　要： 本文在辨析财政学学科属性问题、介绍新市场财政学学科定位的基础上，阐述了《新市场财政学研究》的办刊宗旨。首先，笔者认为，当前经济学范式对财政学研究范式的“垄断”导致了财政理论缺乏足够解释力和预测力。因此，建议探索构建一套复合型财政科学分析范式，为人类社会科学探索本地区和世界性的财政问题提供一套科学系统的财政理论体系与分析工具。其次，针对有些学者和学生混淆财政学与政治经济学之间关系的现象，笔者从学说史的角度论证了财政学与政治经济学之间的关系，指出财政学在性质上与政治经济学完全不同，建议学术界从满足社会共同需要的角度对“公共机构”财务活动深入探索，共同推进科学的财政理论体系建设与完善。再次，笔者强调指出了“新市场财政学”与“公共财政论”（即“旧市场财政学”）之间的共同特征在于两者都是以市场经济作为科学研究的时代背景的，而两者之间的主要区别在于：新市场财政学除了以“社会共同需要”取代“市场失灵”作为财政学的核心概念以外，同时还从“经济体制”和“价值观”两个“维度”解释市场经济作为财政学科时代背景的意义，指出中国社会历史上早已存在基于市场经济的“价值观”，因而具备了以市场经济为背景基础构建财政科学理论的条件。最后，文章还就如何构建中国的财政基础理论向读者和撰稿者提出了三点建议。

关键词： 财政基础理论　新市场财政学　学科属性

［中图分类号］ F810　**［文献识别码］** J

［作者简介］：李俊生，中央财经大学教授、博士生导师，主要从事财政税收理论与政策等领域的教学研究工作。

2016 年 11 月 12 日，中央财经大学中国公共财政与政策研究院和中国财政发展协同创新中心联合举办了“新市场财政学理论创新学术研讨会暨新市场财政学研究所成立大会”，在这次会议上，我向来自中国社会科学院财经战略研究院、中国财政科学研究院以及北京大学、中国人民大学、美国佐治亚州立大学（Georgia State University）等国内外高校、科研院所、学术期刊编辑部的学术界同仁介绍了“新市场财政学”理论框架的构想①，获得了与会同仁的积极响应；与此同时，我也萌生了创办一本杂志作为学术界研讨财政基础理论问题的学术交流平台的想法。在学术同仁的有力支持和热情帮助下，中国财政发展协同创新中心及其“新市场财政学研究所”的相关同事经过四年多的筹备，今天这本杂志终于和大家见面了。作为杂志的创刊人、主编和从事财政基础理论研究与教育工作的财政学人，我想结合我个人在财政基础理论研究方面的体会，就创办本杂志的宗旨、财政科学与其他相关学科之间的关系、财政基础理论研究方法等问题谈点看法，求教于学术界同仁。

一、突破经济学对财政学的范式垄断，构建科学的财政理论体系——为什么要创办《新市场财政学研究》杂志

《新市场财政学研究》杂志主要刊载财政基础理论研究领域的稿件，其目的是为财政基础理论研究者提供一个学术交流平台，通过这个平台，学术界可以相互坦诚交流学术批评观点，共同分享理论创新成果。我们搭建这个财政基础理论学术交流平台的长期目标则是希望财政学术界同仁通过这个平台集思广益、共同努力，探索构建一套从多学科交叉融合的角度（而不仅仅是从经济学的角度）研究市场经济条件下中国和世界财政问题的复合型财政科学分析范式，打破当代“公共财政论”② 用“经济学”范

---

① “新市场财政学”理论创新学术研讨会举行［EB/OL］. 光明网，2016 - 11 - 21.

② 本文用“公共财政论”一词代表英美财政理论，该理论实际上构成了我国当代主流的财政理论的核心内容。在 20 世纪 40 年代，我国学术界曾经出版了一大批教材和学术著作，全面引进和阐述自凯恩斯主义经济学诞生以后形成的英美财政理论；20 世纪 90 年代中期以来，我国财政学术界再次从西方国家全盘引进了这个理论。

式对财政科学范式[①]的垄断，为人类社会科学探索本地区和世界性的财政问题提供一套科学系统的财政理论体系与分析工具。

财政学术界为什么必须破除经济学对财政学的范式垄断？我想从财政学研究对象的特殊性和财政理论的科学性两个不同的角度回答这个问题。

首先，作为财政学研究对象的财政现象绝不是单纯的经济现象，而是集经济、政治、社会、文化、道德等因素于一体的综合体，在市场经济中，这些因素的作用集中体现在公共机构[②]的财务活动中，如果仅仅用经济学的方法分析公共机构的财务活动，是无法科学准确地解释财政活动规律的。因此，在财政科学研究中，不能用经济科学范式替代财政科学范式。

财政活动的内容之所以庞杂，其主要原因在于财政活动是以满足一定范围内社会共同需要为目标的、非营利性质的社会现象，所以，如果仅仅使用经济学范式（以分析牟利性质的经济现象为主要功能）研究财政问题，其结果只能是得出片面的结论。这里我只想以当代最典型的财政活动之一“政府预算”为例予以说明。在当代世界，当打开任何国家或者地区的年度政府预算时都会发现，政府预算绝对不是一部什么企业的财务账本，更不是一个什么家庭的收支流水账，而是一个集政治、经济、社会、文化、道德伦理等因素于一体的法律文本，是经过不同的利益集团博弈、行政和立法机构协商，最后由立法机构通过立法程序批准生效的、具有法律效力的法律文件。这样一部政府预算，从其讨论起草、形成预算方案（草案）呈送立法机构、征询民意、在立法机构中的民意代表之间讨论（甚至争论），到完成立法程序、形成立法文件、送交行政机构（政府）执行的全过程，无处不充斥着不同利益群体之间的博弈、不同文化认知者之间的交流和不同行政机构之间对财政资源配置的争夺与妥协，直到最后所有争议都落脚在满足社会共同需要目标上，正是基于满足社会共同需要

① “科学范式”是决定一门科学的学科属性及其归属的主要因素。美国科学史学家与哲学家库恩（Thomas Samuel Kuhn，1922—1996）曾经在其划时代的著作《科学变革的结构》（The Structure of Scientific Revolutions）一书中用“科学范式（scientific paradigm）”一词定义特定时期的“学科（scientific discipline）”，他是这样为“科学范式”下定义的：科学范式是在一定的时期内被普遍接受的、用于解释现实世界特定现象的模型和解决相应问题的方案（universally recognized scientific achievements that，for a time，provide model problems and solutions for a community of practitioners）。参见 Kuhn，Thomas S. The Structure of Scientific Revolutions，3rd edition. Chicago：University of Chicago Press，1996. pp. 10。我认为，目前“公共财政论”实际上是用经济学范式替代财政学范式。当前财政学界的重要使命就是总结百余年来全球财政科学发展的成果，探寻和梳理财政科学范式，进而恢复财政科学的本来面目。

② 本文用“公共机构”代表政府、准政府组织和其他财政行为主体。

的目标，由行政机构起草提供的预算方案，经过讨论、修改后，才能够完成立法程序，形成年度立法文件。对这个过程的复杂内涵，如果仅仅用经济学的方法研究、分析，所得出的结论只能是局部的，而不可能是全面的、客观的。因此，财政学作为专门研究财政问题的复合型社会科学，如果仅仅用经济学的范式研究财政问题，是无法揭示财政活动在满足社会共同需要目标方面的内在规律的。

其次，经济学对财政科学范式的垄断严重削弱了财政科学的解释力和预测力。经济学范式垄断财政科学范式对财政科学解释力和预测力的损害直接体现在经济学范式对财政学的垄断使财政科学矮化为经济学科的一个小小的组成部分，使得财政科学仅仅可以被用来解释和揭示财政活动的经济特征与经济规律，揭示财政活动对经济目标的满足状况（或者程度），而无法观察财政活动的全貌，无法揭示财政活动对社会共同需要目标的满足状态，因而也无法了解财政现象的实质。

在市场经济条件下，财政活动首先表现为“公共机构”的财务收入、财务支出和财务管理等财务活动形式，因此，从表现形式上看，财政活动似乎与一般性的微观经济活动相同。在这种情形下，如果运用微观经济学的方法研究政府财政问题的话①，就会把财政学变成了微观经济学的一个组成部分；然而，微观经济学属于研究个体或者单个企业有关稀缺资源配置及其个体或者单个企业之间经济关系的经济科学；微观经济学在财政领域中的应用目的则是研究个别公共机构财政行为的经济特征及其对单个企业等市场行为主体行为的微观经济影响。因此，微观经济学范式被运用于财政分析的目的就是服务于企业等市场行为个别的需要，而不是服务于社会共同需要的满足目标；如果将微观经济学范式作为财政科学范式的话，其结果就是将财政科学变成了微观经济学的一个分支。

在当代市场经济条件下，特别是自 20 世纪 30 年代凯恩斯主义经济学诞生以来，宏观经济学的范式也被英美学者引入财政学，进而使得财政学在实质上

① 例如，美国财政学家哈维·罗森（Harvey Rosen）就将财政学定位在微观经济学范围内。他提出用微观经济学的方法研究政府财政活动：Our focus is on the microeconomic functions of government, the way government affects the allocation of resources and the distribution of income. 参见 Harvey Rosen and Ted Gayer, Public Finance, 10th Edition, ISBN10: 0078021685, ISBN13: 9780078021688, 2014, pp. 4.

变成了宏观经济学的一个分支。宏观经济学的研究领域主要分布在对区域范围内（中观）、国家范围内（宏观）或者全球范围内（国际）的经济运行、经济结构、经济政策研究方面，例如，宏观经济学研究政府（包括中央银行）运用货币政策、财政政策、产业政策等调控经济的方法与效果等就属于当代宏观经济学的一个重要的研究领域，许多关系国计民生的热点经济问题，诸如GDP问题、失业率问题、国民收入问题、价格指数以及通货膨胀问题、宏观投资环境问题、能源问题、国际贸易问题和国家与区域金融问题等都属于宏观经济学的研究主题。当代“公共财政论”以“市场失灵”问题为切入点，研究政府通过财政政策（包括税收政策、预算政策、政府债务等）调控经济问题，实质上就是宏观经济学研究范式在财政领域的运用；斯蒂格利兹关于财政学的四个核心问题①更是属于宏观经济问题，而不是财政问题本身。因为回答这四个所谓的财政学“核心问题”实质上是要解决宏观经济学关于政府宏观财政调控的时机（何时）、方法（如何）、干预的理由（为何）以及干预的效果（影响）等问题，而没有回答财政学所应当回答的关于满足社会共同需要的财政方法、决策规律、满足效果等问题。

综上所述，经济学范式垄断财政科学范式的结果是将财政学变成了经济学的一个分支，以当代“公共财政论”为代表的英美财政理论所具有的所谓“解释力”和“预测力”只能满足人类社会从经济角度探索财政规律的部分要求，而无法满足人类社会从经济、社会、政治、伦理道德等多方面全面了解财政运行规律、预测财政发展趋势的要求。与此同时，经济学范式对财政科学范式的垄断还造成了财政科学体系本身的混乱，例如，在当代“公共财政论”教科书中，“财政学”教科书作者在关于财政学究竟是属于“宏观经济学”还是属于“微观经济学”的问题上一直没有给出明确的答案。

二、关于财政学与政治经济学的关系问题——《新市场财政学研究》杂志的学术交流主题

近年来，常常有学生问我财政学与政治经济学之间有什么关系？财政学是

① 斯蒂格利兹提出的财政学的四个核心问题是：a. 何时是政府干预市场的恰当时机？b. 政府应当如何对市场进行干预？c. 政府干预市场的影响是什么？d. 政府为什么采用财政手段干预市场？参见Joseph E Stiglitz，Economics of The Public Sector，W. W. Norton & Company；Third Edition，2000。

否就是经济学中的政治经济学？我估计许多学者都在关心这个问题，搞清楚这个问题对于学术界有针对性地参与《新市场财政学研究》杂志关于财政基础理论问题的讨论大有裨益。

从学科交叉的角度来看，财政学与政治经济学之间的关系确实十分密切，财政学的确采用了许多经济学（政治经济学）的研究方法，财政学与政治经济学也的确都具有学科交叉的共同特点。一般认为，政治经济学的研究方法分别来自于经济学、政治科学和社会学；而财政学的研究方法同样也来自于经济学、政治科学和社会学等学科。然而，财政学的研究对象与政治经济学是不同的，财政学针对其研究对象和研究目的所采用的研究范式和理论基础、财政学理论体系的构成方式等与政治经济学完全不同。因此，财政学与政治经济学虽然都具有学科交叉的特点，甚至共享学说源头史，但是财政学与政治经济学却是两种性质完全不同的社会科学学科。

从学说发展历史渊源的角度来看，财政学与政治经济学似乎是同宗同种的两个社会科学学科，共同构成了当代经济学的源头。从欧洲政治经济学说发展的历史来看，政治经济学作为研究个人与社会、政府与市场之间关系的一门社会科学，主要源于古希腊的柏拉图（Plato，公元前 428/427 年至公元前 348/347 年）和亚里士多德（Aristotle，公元前 384 年至公元前 322 年）等思想家的学说，据说政治经济学的英文表述方法“Political economy”也源于希腊文“polis”和“oikonomos”，其中，polis 的意思是英文的 city（城市）或者 state（国家或者城邦）；而 oikonomos 的英文意思是“家庭或者国家管理者”。如果按照古希腊思想家们的学说，政治经济学可以被理解为主要从政治和经济的角度研究家庭或者国家管理的学问。从这个角度来看，早期政治经济学所研究的主要问题（管理国家）与财政学所研究的主要问题（政府财政）已经非常接近了，甚至可以认为财政学所研究的问题是政治经济学所研究的国家管理问题的一个组成部分——正是从这个意义上说，政治经济学和财政学具有相同的学说源头史。不过，在柏拉图和亚里士多德时代，政治经济学并没有形成系统的理论，同样，财政学在那个时代也没有形成系统的理论。因此，我们只能说，只是在这个时期，政治经济学和财政学作为社会科学学说，其讨论的主题是相近的，特别是由于在古希腊时期的思想家们可能更关心城邦或者国家的管理问题，因此，我们可以把柏拉图和亚里士多德等古希腊思想家的学说同时视为财政学说和政治经济学学说的先驱[①]——在这个意义上，财政学和政治经济学是同宗同种的社会科学学科。

然而，当财政学和政治经济学各自的理论体系基本形成后，我们发现财政学与政治经济学实际上是两个完全不同的社会科学学科——政治经济学所研究的问题实际上就是经济领域的问题，政治经济学所关注的“国家”或者“政府”经济行为的侧重点是“国家”或者“政府”对经济的影响，并且主要是从生产关系的角度研究经济问题（马克思主义政治经济学）；而财政学主要研究“公共机构”财务活动形成的政治、经济、社会和伦理道德方面的动因及其政治、经济和社会影响等问题，其研究的领域涉及政治、经济、社会和伦理道德之间的交叉领域，财政学所关注的“国家”或者“政府”财政行为的侧重点是其对社会、经济和政治的综合性影响。

欧洲政治经济学发展历史也充分证明了政治经济学与财政学分属于不同学科的观点。凡是关注欧洲经济学说史的人都知道，大约在16世纪到18世纪之间，欧洲盛行重商主义学派（mercantilist school）的经济理论，重商主义者主张建立强有力的政府以便管制经济。当时以英语作为学术语言的重商主义学派的重要代表人物是苏格兰经济学家詹姆斯·斯图亚特爵士（Sir James Steuart，1712—1780），他在1767年出版的《政治经济学原理》（Inquiry into the Principles of Political Economy，1767）一书被认为是英语世界第一部系统阐述政治经济学理论的学术著作，比同为苏格兰人的亚当·斯密的《国富论》还早出版了9年。斯图亚特认为，人类自私的行为导致人类社会不可能实现人类社会的共同目标（他用public good来表述人类社会的共同目标），这一点充分表露了斯图亚特高度重视政府在经济生活中的作用的重商主义观点，这种观点与亚当·斯密的观点完全不同，因而按照斯图亚特的观点是不可能得出斯密的“看不见的手”的结论的。因此，学术界通常认为，当代政治经济学系统的理论体系形成于18世纪中叶，以苏格兰哲学家亚当·斯密（Adam Smith，1723—1790）、大卫·休谟（David Hume，1711—1776）和法国经济学家弗朗西斯·魁奈

① 与古希腊思想家生活年代相当或者稍早一些的中国古代思想家诸如老子（约生于公元前571年）、孔子（约生于公元前551年）和墨子（约生于公元前468年）等，也都是以国家、君主的统治之道作为主题进而形成了道家和儒家的思想。由此可以推断，在我国古代，财政学说与政治经济学说也是同源的。

（François Quesnay，1694—1774）为代表的学者们在批判重商主义经济学的同时，开始系统地研究政治经济学问题，他们采取了世俗的方法，研究政治、经济、技术、自然和社会等因素在财富形成过程中的相互作用，进而构建了当代政治经济学理论体系；特别是亚当·斯密在其具有划时代意义的著作《国富论》（An Inquiry into the Nature and Causes of the Wealth of Nations，1776）中首次综合系统地阐述了政治经济学理论，进而创建了政治经济学理论体系。而在亚当·斯密的政治经济学理论体系中，“政府”已经退居“守夜人”的地位，亚当·斯密在《国富论》第五卷[①]讨论财政问题时也明白无误地采用了政治经济学的范式，其目的是探寻政府的经济作用——至此，我们可以看到，政治经济学与财政学已经彻底分道扬镳了[②]。

反观 18 世纪的财政学，则采取了与政治经济学完全不同的范式。我们以 1650—1850 年肇始于德国，并且以当时的德国为中心发展起来的德国官房学派财政理论为例[③]，在这一时期形成的财政理论把获取“共同利益（common good）”作为财政学的研究对象，将政府预算作为市场经济条件下私人财产向公共财产转移过程中的资金池，社会通过这个资金池为公共服务提供资金[④]。由此可见，在官房学派财政理论中，其研究范式已经开始朝着以财政公共资金池（The Fiscal Commons）、公共选择（The Public Choice）等为核心概念的范式转变；而这里的共同利益已经远远超出了经济领域范围，除了经济方面的内容以外，当时的官房主义财政学还将社会安全、维护社会秩序、人口规模等领域的问题纳入财政学的研究范围，这些问题实质上都属于当代财政活动涉及的

---

① 参见亚当·斯密《国富论》英文版第五卷（An Inquiry into the Nature and Causes of the Wealth of Nations（1776），Book V，of the Revenue of Sovereign or Commonwealth），该卷共分为三章：第一章“支出”，第二章“收入”，第三章“债务”。

② 尽管亚当·斯密创建了当代政治经济学理论体系，但是其中的重要思想和方法则是来源于斯密之前的思想家和著作家，例如，《国富论》中的个人主义思想主要来源于英国政治哲学家托马斯·霍布斯（Thomas Hobbes，1588—1679）和约翰·洛克（John Locke，1632—1704）及意大利政治理论家尼古拉马基阿维力（Niccolò Machiavelli，1469—1527），其著作中采用的科学归纳法则来自于英国哲学家弗朗西斯·培根（Francis Bacon，1561—1626）。

③ 参见 Backhaus J. G.，Wagner R. E.（2005）Society，State，and Public Finance：Setting the Analytical Stage. In：Backhaus J. G.，Wagner R. E.（eds）Handbook of Public Finance. Springer，Boston，MA. https：//doi. org/10. 1007/1 -4020 -7864 -1_ 7.

④ 参见 Alexandre Mendes Cunhal，Polizei and the system of public finance：tracing the impact of Cameralism in eighteenth-century Portugal，Kurz，Heinz；Nishizawa，Tamotsu；Tribe，Keith.（Org.）. The dissemination of economic ideas. Cheltenham：Edward Elgar，2011，pp. 65 -83.

领域。

财政学说史是财政科学宝库，是我们探索和构建科学的财政理论体系的重要理论和思想源泉。“大胆探索、小心求证”这个史学箴言对财政学界研究财政学说史、从核心概念体系入手总结梳理财政科学范式同样具有重要借鉴意义。因此，我在此特别建议财政史学界（包括财政学说史和财政理论史）的同仁关注本刊，向本刊投稿。

三、从“经济体制”和“价值观”两个“维度”理解市场经济对财政活动的意义——新市场财政学“新”在哪里

对于本杂志和我个人来说，学术界同仁可能希望了解的另一个问题就是“新市场财政学”为什么以“新市场”作为财政理论的限定词。实际上，这是相对于当代“公共财政论”以市场经济为时代背景的情况而提出来的：“公共财政论”实际上就是以市场经济为时代背景研究财政问题的“市场财政学”，“新市场财政学”也是以市场经济为时代背景研究财政问题的“市场财政学”。在这里，我把仅仅从市场经济体制的角度出发、在经济学框架内研究财政问题的“公共财政论”视为“旧市场财政学”；而将我所创立的、同时从市场经济体制（经济学）和市场经济价值观（哲学）两个“维度”理解市场经济对财政活动的意义、以学科交叉融合的方法研究财政问题的财政理论体系称为“新市场财政学”。

“新市场财政学”正式作为论文的题目首次见诸于2017年。我曾经在《中央财经大学学报》2017年第5期发表了题为“新市场财政学：旨在增强财政学解释力的新范式”的论文中向学术界正式全面介绍和阐述了新市场财政学的理论框架体系建设的设想。在论文中，我运用规范研究方法，以政府和市场之间的关系作为切入点，剖析了当代主流财政理论存在的缺陷，通过重新定义市场模型，重新解释政府（以及以政府为代表的公共部门）、企业（以及以企业为代表的私人部门）和市场之间的关系，初步构建了一套新的财政学核心概念体系，并从核心概念体系、理论渊源以及理论与实践的关系等三个维度描述了新市场财政学范式的基本特征与理论体系构建的设想。

当代“公共财政论”是指美国财政学家马斯格雷夫（Richard Abel Musgrave，1910—2007）于 1959 年创建完成的财政理论体系，该理论体系是在经济学理论框架内、以市场经济体制（形式）为时代背景、以市场失灵理论作为财政学的理论基础、以解决市场失灵问题为主要财政政策目标而形成的政府三个主要财政职能[①]为线索构建而成，属于市场经济环境下“财政特殊”[②] 的理论体系。新市场财政学理论依然属于市场经济环境下“财政特殊”的理论体系，与“公共财政论”相比较，“新市场财政学”的“新”主要体现在以下几个方面：首先，新市场财政学不仅仅从形式的角度，即从市场经济体制的角度考察财政问题，同时也从哲学的角度，即从市场经济价值观的角度考察财政问题，新市场财政学对构成财政活动基础环境的市场的理解是二维的，而不是一维的；其次，新市场财政学将以满足社会共同需要目标作为财政学的核心概念，而不是把解决市场失灵目标作为财政学的核心概念。财政学需要探寻人类社会财政活动一般规律与市场经济背景下呈现的特殊规律[③]及其两者之间的关系问题，需要探寻人类社会通过财务收支活动满足社会共同需要

① 即财政的配置职能（The Allocation Function）、分配职能（The Distribution Function）和稳定职能（The Stabilization Function）。参见 Richard A. Musgrave 和 Peggy B. Musgrave，Public Finance in Theory and Practice，5th Edition，International Edition 1989，pp. 7－12. McGraw-Hill。在这部著作的第一章，Musgrave 教授夫妇实际上提出政府财政有四个职能，除了前面提到的三个财政职能以外，他们还提出财政具有第四个职能，即政府预算协调职能（Coordination of Budget Functions），意思是由于政府预算需要达成多种目标，而这些目标在实践中是相互重叠的，有些甚至是相互矛盾着的，从而使得政府预算方案复杂化，因此有效的预算设计方案应当整合协调不同的预算目标，使之公平高效——这就是关于财政的第四个职能的基本含义（参见该书第一章第五节 Coordination of Budget Functions）。估计是由于 Musgrave 全书的理论体系设计，实际上也是他们创建的公共财政学理论体系本身实际上是以前三个职能为逻辑起点设计而成的，加之第四个职能本身与前三个职能有高度的交叉重叠，所以 Musgrave 本人和学术界其他人后来也很少提及第四个职能。国内财政学界在引进马斯格雷夫的公共财政理论体系时也只是重点介绍前三个财政职能。

② 何振一教授在阐述“社会共同需要论”“公共财政论”和“国家分配论”之间的关系时提出了“财政一般”“财政特殊”和“财政管理理论和方法论”等三个层次财政理论构成体系的观点：“……一个完整的财政科学理论体系是由三个层面的理论构成的，财政一般理论体系是基础层次，它是鉴别和认识各个财政个别的个性及运行规律特殊性的尺度，又是财政学科建设的理论基石；第二个层次是各个财政特殊的理论体系，它是贴近财政现象形态，用来揭示各个财政个别的特殊属性和特殊运行规律的理论体系；第三个层次是最高的一个层次，是关于财政管理理论和方法论的学科体系，是揭示财政体制、财政制度和财政政策构造法则的理论体系。这三个层次缺一都不是完整的科学体系……”。参阅柳光强、尹情、杨卡：《经世治国济民心——访著名财政学家、中国社会科学院荣誉学部委员何振一教授》，《财政监督》2013 年第 7 期。

③ 何振一教授认为，“作为研究市场经济财政个别的‘公共财政论’忽略了中国社会主义市场经济财政特殊性及其特殊规律的理论研究，因此，没有真正构造其中国特色的公共财政理论体系……”。参阅柳光强、尹情、杨卡：《经世治国济民心——访著名财政学家、中国社会科学院荣誉学部委员何振一教授》，《财政监督》2013 年第 7 期。

的一般规律在市场经济条件下的特征与表现形式；再次，新市场财政学将财政定位于综合经济社会系统的“中枢”位置——即财政活动作为集经济、社会、政治和法律等属性于一身的、以公共机构的财务收入/支出活动为载体的“综合性的社会范畴”，而不是像“公共财政论”那样仅仅将财政作为政府解决“市场失灵”问题的财政政策工具。财政学必须破除经济学的理论羁绊，以多学科交叉融合的方法构建财政学自身的、综合性社会科学的分析范式和理论体系。

财政学为什么必须从“二维”的角度理解当代市场经济对财政活动的意义？我理解，当代市场经济实际上是人类社会历史发展进程中的一种综合性的社会现象，“经济体制”只是市场经济在经济领域的一种表象，除了经济领域之外，市场经济在人类社会的道德领域、政治领域、社会关系领域、法律制度领域等方面都存在相应的表现形式，其中，哲学领域的市场经济“价值观”是所有这些领域的最高表现形式，因此，我用“价值观”代表市场经济的一个特殊“维度”，而用“经济体制”代表市场经济在经济领域的表象，以此来强调市场经济在“经济领域”的特殊性。运用上述“二维”方法观察中国财政问题，我们会发现：所谓中国特色市场经济财政的独特性主要并不体现在市场经济形式本身上，而是体现在制度性特征和影响财政行为的制度环境上。中国政府（以及所有公共部门）的财务收入/支出活动既要受制于中国特殊的政治制度、法律体系和社会环境，又要遵从市场经济的基本规律，两者之间既有一致性、又有矛盾性。这表明，中国的财政问题比英美等西方市场经济发达国家的财政问题要复杂得多；与此同时，当代世界的主流财政理论“公共财政论”主要是基于英美等西方国家的政治制度、法律体系和社会环境实践形成的，我国学术界如果机械地套用这种理论研究中国的财政问题肯定会遇到“水土不服”的问题。因此，中国的财政学者在财政科学研究的过程中必须深入研究中国财政实践，深入研究在中国特殊的政治制度、行政体制和社会环境下财政收支的决策过程、行为效果，深入探索体制、价值观与市场经济规律之间的关系——这一方面意味着中国的财政科学研究必须立足于本国的财政实践，同时也意味着中国财政科学的发展不应该、也无法与全球财政科学研究割裂开来。中国财政运行在受制于中国特殊的政治制度、法律体系和社会环境的同时，依然以市场经济作为财政行为的基础，中国的财政依然属于“市场经济”背景下的“财政个别”的范畴。

以“二维”的方式理解市场经济及其对财政活动的意义并在此基础上构建新的财政理论，不仅在财政领域确定了市场经济的客观存在[①]性，而且还可以从人类社会历史发展的角度客观地考察市场经济的实质及其对财政活动的内生性的影响力所在。首先，从经济形式（市场经济体制）的“维度”考察财政现象，可以探索财政活动规律在市场经济体制下的特征、表现方式等；可以探索以货币形式表现的财务收入/支出财政活动及其背后的人与人之间的社会关系；探索财政收入结构、财政支出结构及其社会、政治、文化效应等；可以探索市场经济体制下财政融资的方式、规则、规律及其与一个国家或者地区的中央银行的关系、财政与金融体系之间的关系以及财政政策与货币政策之间的关系，等等。其次，从哲学意义的价值观的维度[②]考察财政现象，可以探索和发现：当代世界市场经济之所以会成为全人类共有的经济形式，其本身必然会蕴含着全人类共同持有的思想与普遍认同的价值观，而这种思想和价值观往往在其成为被普遍采用的经济形式之前，作为其萌芽和内在的灵魂而先于形式本身而存在；正是由于有了这种普适性的价值观，市场经济形式才得以存在、普及和发展。

在我国，市场经济作为一种经济体制，通常被认为是“舶来品”，是我国改革开放之初从西方国家引入的；但是在市场经济中通行的“公平交易”原则及其所蕴含的“交易双方都有追求自身利益的天然的平等权利”的价值观，特别是构成这种价值观的思想，在我国古代社会知识界则早已有之，因此，我国实际上也具备了实施市场经济的思想条件和价值观基础，尽管这种思想并没有

---

① 也有学者“担心”由于我国财政学术界没有“没有真正弄懂”“市场失效论”和“公共产品论”而忘掉了市场经济在我国的客观存在。请参阅张馨教授的《“市场失效论”和“公共产品论”不成立吗——论市场经济下财政学的理论基础》,《财贸经济》2021 年第 1 期。

② 从哲学的角度理解，“价值观”有广义价值观和狭义价值观之分，其中，广义的价值观包含道德哲学、社会哲学、政治哲学、美学、女权主义和宗教（moral philosophy，social and political philosophy，aesthetics，and sometimes feminist philosophy and the philosophy of religion）等哲学领域的价值观；而狭义的价值观则主要是从伦理价值（axiology）的角度形成的道德价值标准（normative ethical theory），即事务或者人的行为是“好”还是“坏”以及“好”或者“坏”的程度如何。参见斯坦福百科全书价值观词条，Value Theory，Center for the Study of Language and Information（CSLI），Stanford University，Library of Congress Catalog Data：ISSN 1095 - 5054. First published Tue Feb 5，2008；substantive revision Thu Jul 28，2016. 笔者在这里主要是从广义的角度理解市场经济的价值观问题，相应地，基于财政科学的交叉科学属性，社会哲学和政治哲学等多视角研究方法也为本文所采纳。

成为我国古代社会的主流价值观①。

总之，仅仅从市场经济体制这样“一维”的角度理解当代社会的财政现象和财政规律是不够的，而应该从经济体制和价值观这样“二维”的角度去理解现代社会的财政现象和财政运行规律，因为只有如此，才能构建一个能够全面揭示财政运行一般规律的、具有强大解释力的财政科学；只有如此，才能从更深层次的价值观角度来理解我国为什么可以实施市场经济，并在市场经济的环境下建立现代财政制度和体制，这是因为我国实际上早已具有了实行市场经济的“基因”；也只有如此，才能理解我国财政体制与制度建设过程中为什么会有可能出现财政体制、财政制度与《宪法》《预算法》等法律规定不能完全匹配等问题，从而为我国财政体制改革与发展留下了特殊的空间②。

以市场经济形式和价值观“二维”的方法理解财政，可以证明中国的财政活动是全球财政活动的一个有机组成部分，世界各国财政都是以“市场经济”为“锚地”、具有多边关系，相互之间的经验和做法可以借鉴；可以理解财政科学为什么必须对包括我国在内的全球财政现象都具有解释力，而不应该仅仅以某一具体的国家财政实践为基础和解释对象——“公共财政论”实质上就是局限在以英美等国家的市场经济体制为基础的、仅仅从市场经济形式的角度解释财政现象的一种财政理论，这种财政理论的局限性是不言而喻的。我国改革开放四十年的财政实践证明，如果财政理论无视中国的本土财政实践经验，无视市场经济“基因”——即市场经济价值观在中国的本土的客观存在及其表现方式，该财政理论对中国的财政实践就没有任何解释力。因此，“公共财政论”在我国的适用性是有限的，我国和全球需要一个科学的、普适性的财政科学理论。

① 例如，我国战国时期的思想家韩非（又称韩非子，生卒约公元前280年—公元前233年）曾经提出：“法不阿贵，绳不绕曲。法之所加，智者弗能辞，勇者弗敢争，刑过不避大臣，赏善不遗匹夫”（《韩子·有度》），这里实际蕴含着人人平等的思想，这与现代市场经济社会通行的价值观有异曲同工之妙，同时与儒家的“礼不下庶人，刑不上大夫”思想主张之间形成了鲜明的对照，这也说明了构成市场经济核心价值观的思想在中国古已有之；同时，由于这种思想在我国古代并不构成社会的主流价值观，说明了为什么在我国时至今日，尽管构成市场经济价值观的思想古已有之，但是市场经济作为一种体制却不是产生于中国，而是舶来品的原因所在。

② 李俊生，侯可峰．“乡财县管”导致乡镇财政能力弱化的机理与改革建议——基于田野调查和面板数据分析的结果［J］．预算管理与会计，2015（06）：18－22，17.

四、期待与建议

作为从事财政学教育与科学研究 30 余年的财政学人，我深感我们这一代人既幸运、又责任重大。非常幸运的是：迄今为止，我和我的同代人即经历了自 1978 年以来我国财政改革开放的全过程，目睹了我国财政改革历程的成功与艰辛，又先后受到了包括来自苏联的“苏联财政理论”、产生于我国本土的“国家分配论”财政理论和来自英美国家的“公共财政论”理论的教育，体验了三种不同的财政理论对我国财政改革与发展的解释力和预测力；难以释怀的是：作为一名财政学人，40 年来，虽然每天都在目睹我国财政改革与发展的进步与出现的问题，但是却无法用所学的任何理论去解释这些进步，去解决这些问题，更不用说为决策者提供有效的财政改革与发展建议，遑论为学生提供理解和解决未来财政发展的理论和钥匙。因此，作为财政学人，深感我国财政理论基础薄弱，我国财政基础理论建设任重道远——这也是我萌发创办一个财政基础理论学术交流平台的深层次的原因所在，借此机会，也向财政学术界同仁提出如下倡议：

1. 建议财政学界同仁以市场经济作为全球通行的社会经济形态和普适性全球价值观为基本的社会背景来研究财政基础理论问题。

2. 希望财政学界同仁共同努力，通过探索构建有机融合经济学、政治学、社会学和法学等科学理论与方法于一体的、新的财政科学理论体系。

3. 期待财政学界同仁通过对当代财政学中的重要理论、核心概念等进行批判性地审视、剖析，逐一突破，构建一套新的、具有解释力和预测力的核心概念体系，通过《新市场财政学研究》杂志这个学术交流平台，就上述目标达成共识，共同推进财政科学理论体系的建设。

Paradigm and Idea: The Establishment of the Basic Theory of Fiscal Science under the Market Economy Environment

Li Junsheng

Abstract: This paper introduces the aim and scope of *the Journal of Neo-Public Finance* by reflecting on the scientific nature of public finance theory and identifying the scope of neo-public finance theory. Firstly, due to the complexity and interdisciplinary nature of fiscal phenomenon, the dominance of economic paradigm on public finance research limits the explanatory and predictive power of public finance theory. Therefore, it is helpful to develop a new paradigm that is of interdisciplinary perspective and can be used to study the financial problems emerging from the market economy of China and the world in general. Secondly, public finance and political economy are two similar yet different subjects. This paper demonstrates the similarities and differences between public finance and political economy from the perspective of the history of economic ideas, pointing out that researchers should focus on the financial activities of "public institutions" and their political, economic and social motives and impacts. Thirdly, the similarity between neo-public finance and traditional public finance lies in that both of them treat market economy as the theoretical background, whereas the neo-public finance features two basic ideas: (1) Replacing "market failure" with "social common needs" to rebuild the core concept of public finance; (2) Highlighting not only the "economic system" but also the "values" underpinning the market economy. In particular, the market values have historical roots in Chinese society, which makes neo-public finance, a market-background public finance theory, plausible. Finally, the author puts forward three points of suggestion to readers and contributors on constructing the basic theory of public finance in China.

Keywords: Fundamental theory of public finance　Neo-public finance　Discipline attribution

CLC number: F810　Document code: J

On November 12, 2016, the China Academy of Public Finance and Public Policy and the Center for China Fiscal Development (CCFD) of the Central University of Finance and Economics (CUFE) jointly held "the Conference for the Theoretical Innovation of Neo-Public Finance and the Ceremony for the Founding of the Institute for Neo-Public Finance Study (INPFS)." At this meeting, I introduced the conceptual framework of "neo-public finance" to colleagues from research institutes, such as the National Academy of Economic Strategy and the Chinese Academy of Fiscal Sciences, institutions of higher learning such as Peking University, the Renmin University of China, and Georgia State University, and representatives from academic journals. Their enthusiastic reception of this idea prompted me to establish a journal to discuss fundamental fiscal theories. After four years of support from my academic colleagues, the CCFD, and the INPFS, the *Journal of Neo-Public Finance* is finally ready to meet its first readers. As the journal's founder and chief editor, I would like to take a moment here to reflect on the journal's origins and purpose, discuss the relationship between fiscal science and other disciplines, and discuss my views on research and research methodologies related to the study of fundamental fiscal theories.

I. The journal's origins: Breaking up economics' monopoly on fiscal science and establishing a scientific paradigm of fiscal theory

The Journal of Neo-Public Finance primarily publishes research on fundamental fiscal theories. It seeks to provide a platform for critical discussion and exchange among researchers working in this field. Its long-term goal is to encourage the development of an interdisciplinary research methodology or paradigm that conducts scientific studies of domestic and foreign fiscal problems in the market economy. In this way, it hopes to expand upon and improve contemporary public finance theory,① which is dominated by economics, and develop a new and more scientific paradigm. ② The development of a new, interdisciplinary paradigm would improve fiscal theoretical research by providing new and robust analytical tools. In this section, I will briefly describe two reasons why the research community must break economics' monopoly on fiscal theoretical research.

The first reason why the economics paradigm must be broken is that fiscal phenomena are not purely economic in scope—they are complex mosaics of economic, political, social, cultural, and moral factors. These factors in the market economy are mainly reflected in the financial activities of public institutions (governments, quasi-governmental organizations, and other public fi-

---

① I use the term "public finance theory" to refer to British and American fiscal theory, which constitutes the essential background of contemporary mainstream Chinese fiscal theory. China's academic community published a large volume of teaching materials and academic works that comprehensively introduced and elaborated upon British and American fiscal theories in the 1940s and have reintroduced Keynesian ideas into China from Western countries since the mid-1990s.

② My use of the term "scientific paradigm" is inspired by the American philosopher and historian Thomas Samuel Kuhn (1922—1996), who defined such a paradigm as "universally recognized scientific achievements that, for a time, provide model problems and solutions for a community of practitioners." See Kuhn, T. S. *The Structure of Scientific Revolutions* (3rd edition). Chicago: University of Chicago Press, 1996, pp. 10. In my view, public finance theory relies too heavily on economics and has become an inadequate tool for researching fiscal theory and practice in ways that contribute to the development of a scientific paradigm.

nance actors). The fiscal activities of these institutions create complexity as they are not necessarily for-profit schemes but instead are aimed at meeting certain society's common needs studies of fiscal activity which take economics as their theoretical base, namely, by only analyzing profit-seeking economic phenomena, can only obtain lopsided conclusions. Such an approach would, for example, assess a government's budget as a corporate accounting ledger; however, in reality, such budgets are legal documents that are composed of various political, economic, social, cultural, and moral factors and whose legitimacy is derived from a kind of societal "game" played by the executive and the legislative branches of government. Such game-playing is ubiquitous in budgeting, from initial discussion to draft submission (to the legislature), public consultation, debates among elected representatives, then completing legislative procedures to produce legislative documents, and finally submitting them to the administrative agency (government) for budget execution. Various interest groups, cultural groups, and administrative agencies make game plans to better compete over the allocation of fiscal resources. In short, if we restrict our studies of public institutions' financial activities to research methodologies and paradigms derived from economics, we cannot adequately explain or explore fiscal activity in a scientific way. To fully account for and explore such a complex and multi-layered process as budgeting, we must adopt a composite methodological approach appropriate to a kind of social science that specializes in fiscal issues. It cannot reveal the internal law of fiscal activities in meeting society's common needs only with the economic paradigm.

Second, economics' monopoly over fiscal theory must be broken because this monopoly has severely weakened the explanatory power and predictive power of fiscal science, largely by absorbing fiscal science into the study of economics. As such, fiscal science's explanations are restricted to economic characteristics and phenomena and focus on the degree to which fiscal activities satisfy economic goals. Such an approach fails to provide a comprehensive picture of fiscal activities or explore how fiscal activities seek to satisfy society's common needs.

In a market economy, fiscal activities first appear to behave as financial activities, for example, the incomes, expenditures, and management of public institutions. Therefore, fiscal activities seem to be general microeconomic activities and are often studied as such. ① By doing so, we turn fiscal science into a component of microeconomics. However, microeconomic research mainly studies the allocation of scarce resources among individuals or individual enterprises and economic relations among them. Thus, applying this paradigm to the study of government's fiscal activities emphasizes institutions and enterprises' individual competition with one another rather than public finance's essential characteristic of meeting society's common needs.

Economists, especially since the birth of Keynesian economics in the 1930s, have also depicted governments' fiscal activities as the domain of macroeconomics, which primarily studies the economic operation, structure, and policies on various macro-levels (e. g. , the regional, national, or international level). For example, such research has examined how governments and large institutions such as central banks use various monetary, fiscal, and industrial policies to regulate the economy. Such research is generally concerned with studying the national economy and people's livelihoods, for example, the gross domestic product (GDP), unemployment, national income, price indexing, inflation, the macro-investment environment, energy issues, international trade, and national and regional finance. Contemporary public finance theory takes a macroeconomics-inspired approach by taking "market failure" as its starting point and studying fiscal policy (taxation policy, budgeting, government debt, etc.) to settle economic issues. This oversight runs

---

① For example, the American public finance researcher Harvey Rosen frames government's fiscal activities in precisely this way: "Our focus is on the microeconomic functions of government, the way government affects the allocation of resources and the distribution of income." See Rosen, H. and Gayer, T. *Public Finance* (10th edition). ISBN10: 0078021685, ISBN13: 9780078021688, 2014, pp. 4.

rampant throughout the field. For instance, Joseph Stiglitz's four core issues of public finance are macroeconomic, not fiscal issues.① Answering these four so-called "core questions" in public finance is essentially addressing the timing (when), methods (how), reasons for intervention (why), and effects (impact) of government macroeconomic regulation and control in terms of macroeconomics. However, the issue of fiscal methods, decision-making rules, and satisfaction of society's common needs prevails when evaluating the fiscal activities of public institutions.

In summary, the economic paradigm monopolizes the fiscal science paradigm, dwarfing it into a branch of economics. The so-called "explanatory power" and the "predictive power" in the Anglo-American fiscal theory represented by contemporary "public finance theory" only meet human society's needs to explore fiscal laws partially from an economic perspective. However, it cannot fully interpret the law of fiscal operations and predict fiscal development trends based on economic, social, political, and ethical aspects. Simultaneously, the economic paradigm's monopoly over the fiscal science paradigm has also caused chaos in the fiscal science system. For instance, in the contemporary "Public Finance Theory" textbook, the author has never clearly justified whether public finance belongs to "macroeconomics" or "microeconomics."

II. The journal's role in fostering academic exchange on the relationship between public finance and political economy

In recent years, students have often asked me about the relationship between public finance and political economy—whether public finance is the po-

① The four core questions are: (1) When is the right time for the government to intervene in the market? (2) How should the government intervene in the market? (3) What is the impact of government intervention in the market? (4) Why does the government use fiscal means to intervene in the market? See Stiglitz, Joseph E. *Economics of The Public Sector* (3rd edition). New York: W. W. Norton & Company, 2000.

litical economy of economics, for example. I suppose that many scholars are concerned about this issue as well. Indeed, there is a very close relationship between public finance and political economy. Public finance and political economy researchers take rather interdisciplinary approaches, and both rely on research methods derived from economics, political science, and sociology. However, these two domains of scholarship have different research objects, purposes, research paradigms, and theoretical bases. Therefore, although public finance and political economy share interdisciplinary characteristics and even historical origins, they are distinct disciplines with different goals, methods, and natures. In this section, I will briefly describe the historical trajectory of these disciplines and then discuss how and why the *Journal of Neo-Public Finance* seeks to build discussion and understanding of the relationship between them among scholars.

The historical origin of the two social science disciplines suggests that the theories of public finance and political economy seem to have developed from the same origin and together constitute the source of contemporary economics. Political economy studies the connections between people, society, governments, and the market. Like many other scholarly disciplines which originated within Europe, the founding concepts of political economy mainly stem from a few ancient Greek thinkers, such as Plato (ca. 428/42 – 348/347 BC) and Aristotle (384 – 322 BC). Even the term "political economy" is rooted in the Greek *polis* (city/state) and *oikonomos* ("family or governor of the country"). These thinkers studied state affairs from both political and economic perspectives; thus, it appears as though these early political economists and today's scholars of public finance both study the administration of the state. Such a high-level resemblance may even lead people to think that the issues studied by public finance are a component of the state administration discussed by the political economy. In this sense, we suggest that the two disciplines share the same historical origin. However, in Plato's and Aristotle's ages, systematic political economy theories were not established, nor were those of public finance. Hence, we can only conclude that political economy and public finance, as social sciences of that period, discussed adjacent topics because ancient Greek thinkers cared more about the administration of city-states or countries. Therefore, we consider the ancient Greek thinkers' theories, such as those of Plato and Aristotle, as pioneers of public finance and political economy. In this sense, public finance and the political economy are social sciences of a shared origin.

However, the common origin of these disciplines should not fool us into thinking that they are the same. Today, political economy and public finance have different foci. The former studies economic issues (the economic behavior of the state or its government, the impacts of this behavior on the economy, relations of production, and so on). The latter primarily studies the financial activities of public institutions and the various economic, social, and ethical motivations and impacts behind these activities. The former is primarily economic in scope, and the latter aims to be more comprehensive and interdisciplinary, comprising political, economic, social, and moral ethics. Public finance focuses on the comprehensive impact of "state" or "government" financial behaviors on society, economy, and politics.

The history of the European political economy proves that political economy and public finance are indeed different disciplines. Between the sixteenth and eighteenth centuries, the European political economy was dominated by mercantilists such as Sir James Steuart (1712—1780), who advocated strong governmental control of the economy. In 1767, Steuart published *Inquiry into the Principles of Political Economy*, which is widely considered to be the first English book that elaborates a systematic theory of political economy—nine years before Adam Smith's (1723 - 90) much more famous *An Inquiry into the Nature and Causes of the Wealth of Nations*. Steuart believed that human beings' self-interested behavior prevents society from reaching its common goal (which he defined as the public good), and he advocated for the government's role in economic life for this reason—again, a radical departure from Smith's idea of the "invisible hand," which guides the free market. However, scholars date modern political economy to Smith, David Hume (1711 – 76), and François Quesnay's (1694 – 1774) systematic critiques of the mercantilist school and their secular approach to the study of the dynamic political, economic, technological, natural, and social factors, which contribute to the formation and distribution of wealth. Smith, in particular, first comprehensively described the theory of political economy in his epic book *An Inquiry into the Nature and Causes of the Wealth of Nations* and saw the government's role as that of a "watchman" – retreated and distant from public life. Subsequently, we can see that political economy and public finance part ways.

From the eighteenth century on, public finance and political economy adopted different methodological perspectives. For example, German public finance researchers began to adopt cameralism in this period.① Cameralism took the acquisition of the "common good" as its research object; it saw government budgets as a pool of capital, which transformed private property into public property in the market economy and provided funds for public services.② In short, cameralism's research paradigm shifted toward core concepts such as the fiscal commons and public choice. It pushed researchers to go beyond mere economic considerations of public finance and to include the maintenance of social security and social order within the scope of public finance. These problems essentially belong to the field of contemporary fiscal activities. The history of fiscal theory is the treasure house of fiscal science and theoretical and ideological sources for exploring and constructing a scientific fiscal theoretical system. The historical maxim of "boldly explore and carefully seek" is also of significance for the fiscal science community to

---

① See Backhaus, J. G. and Wagner, R. E. "Society, State, and Public Finance: Setting the Analytical Stage." In: Backhaus, J. G. and Wagner, R. E. (eds.) *Handbook of Public Finance*. Springer, Boston, 2005.

② See Cunhal, Alexandre Mendes. "Polizei and the system of public finance: tracing the impact of Cameralism in eighteenth-century Portuga." In Kurz, H., Nishizawa, T., and Tribe, K. (eds.) *The dissemination of economic ideas*. Cheltenham: Edward Elgar, 2011, pp. 65 – 83.

study the history of fiscal theories and summarize the paradigm of fiscal science from the perspective of the core concept system. Therefore, I suggest that academic colleagues of fiscal history (including the history of fiscal doctrine and fiscal theory) pay attention to this journal and submit manuscripts.

III. The novelty of neo-public finance in two dimensions: understanding the significance of market economy for fiscal activities from the "economic system" and "values" dimensions

Readers of this journal might also seek to understand the term neo-public finance and why it is modified by the term "new market." This section will assess my previous research, which sparked the establishment of this journal, and discuss these terms in some detail. In short, I regard public finance theory as "old market" public finance because it studies fiscal issues from the perspective of the market economic system and within the framework of economics. By contrast, neo-public finance recognizes two dimensions of the market economy's significance for fiscal activities—one economic system (economics) in scope and one value-driven (philosophy) in scope.

I first introduced the term neo-public finance in a paper published in 2017. ① That paper used the normative research method and formally and comprehensively introduced and elaborated my vision of neo-public finance as a novel theoretical framework, one that takes the relationship between the government and the market as an entry point to analyze the defects of mainstream fiscal theories. This paper redefined the market model, explained the relationships among the public sector, private sector, and the market, and established a set of new core concepts for the future scientific study of fiscal activity and theory. It identified the neo-public finance paradigm's core concepts,

① Li, J. "Neo-Public Finance: A Paradigm for Enhancing Explanatory and Predictive Power." *Central University Journal of Finance and Economics* 5 (2017).

theoretical origins, and how the paradigm views the relationship between theory and practice.

Neo-public finance is in opposition to contemporary public finance theory, which assumes the background of the market economic system, is inspired by market failure theory. It takes the failure of governments' fiscal policies to perform essential functions (e. g., allocation, distribution, and stabilization) in light of market failure as its major object of study. ① Thus, it is a form of special public finance theory. ②By contrast, neo-public finance theory considers both the market economic system and the values of the market economy when studying fiscal issues. Thus, it interprets the market two-dimensionally rather than one-dimensionally. Furthermore, it assumes that public institutions' fiscal activities fundamentally aim to fulfill society's common needs rather than resolve problems caused by market failure. In so doing, it

① For more, see Musgrave, R. A. and Musgrave, P. B. *Public finance in theory and practice* (5th international edition). New York: McGraw-Hill, 1989, p. 7 – 12. In the first chapter of this book, the Musgraves proposed four functions. In addition to the three mentioned above, they also proposed a fourth function, namely coordination of budget functions, which means that the government budget needs to achieve various objectives. These objectives are overlapped or even contradictory in practice, making the government budget program complicated. Therefore, an effective budgeting program should integrate and coordinate different budget objectives for fairness and efficiency. The meaning of the fourth function is in Chapter 1, Section E. It is estimated that the logical design of Musgraves' book and their theoretical system of public finance started from the previous three functions, together with the highly overlapping feature of the fourth function with the first three functions, so the Musgraves and others in the academic community rarely mentioned the fourth function. When introducing Musgrave's theoretical system of public finance, the Chinese scholars only focus on the first three functions.

② When expounding the relationship among " society's common needs theory," " public finance theory," and " national distribution theory," Professor He Zhenyi put forward the view that " general public finance," " special public finance," and " public finance management theory and methodology" constitute a system of three levels of public finance theory. He suggested that a complete theoretical system of fiscal science is composed of three levels. The theoretical system of general public finance is the basic level. It is not only the yardstick to identify and recognize the individual characteristics and operation patterns of each special public finance but also the theoretical cornerstone for constructing the fiscal science discipline. The second level is the theoretical system of each special public finance, which is close to the form of fiscal phenomena and is used to reveal the unique attributes and operation patterns of each special public finance. The third level is the highest. It is the disciplinary system of public finance management theory and methodology and is the theoretical system that reveals the structural rules of the fiscal system, institution, and policy. See Liu G., Yin Q., and Yang, K. "Managing the world, governing the country and benefiting the people: an interview with Professor He Zhenyi, a famous financial scientist and an honorary fellow Chinese Academy of Social Sciences." *Caizheng Jiandu* 5 (2013).

can better explore special patterns in the market economy, the means by which fiscal activities fulfill society's common needs, and the relationships among them. Finally, it positions public finance at the center of a country's socio-economic system.

This approach allows scholars to discuss fiscal activities as a "comprehensive social realm" with dynamic economic, social, political, and legal attributes in which public institutions perform financial revenue and expenditure activities. Neo-public finance is unlike "public finance theory," which treats public finance simply as fiscal policy tools for the government to solve market failure. Public finance must untangle its theoretical fetters of economics and construct its analytical paradigm and comprehensive theoretical social sciences system through interdisciplinary integration. It is important to provide this kind of two-dimensional picture of the modern market economy's significance for fiscal activities because it is an all-encompassing phenomenon, which has corresponding forms in all areas of social life, including morality, politics, social relations, and legal system. The value of the market economy in the field of philosophy is the highest form among all. Therefore, I use the term "values" to refer to a special dimension of the market economy and the term "economic system" to denote the appearance of the market economy in the economic field to emphasize the particularity of the latter field. In doing so, we can better observe how China's fiscal activities blend a form of a market economy with China's various unique political, legal, and social systems and values to produce a "market economy with Chinese characteristics." The unique features of this system create fiscal problems for China, which are much more complicated than those in the West.

Furthermore, because this approach is developed in a Chinese context, it can provide an effective counter to mainstream public finance theory and assist scholars who study China's fiscal activities. Mainstream theory is primarily based on the historical development, political system, and social norms of the United States and the United Kingdom. Therefore, it is often confounded in its attempts to understand China's fiscal practices, decision-making processes, and the behavioral effects of public revenue and expenditure in the context of China's unique historical development, political system, and social norms. By contrast, neo-public finance theory can better explore the various relationships between the market economy and values. This would allow researchers in various global contexts to conduct research that addresses both the market economy's role in fiscal behavior and the unique historical, political, and social characteristics of countries worldwide.

Interpreting the market economy and its significance to fiscal activities two-dimensionally and hence constructing a new fiscal theory not only determines the existence of the market economy in the fiscal field but also investigates the essence of the market economy beyond economics and reveals its endogenous influence on fiscal activities. ① This theory will allow scholars to explore the characteristics and manifestations of the law of fiscal activities in the market economic system, including the social relationships between the people behind public finances, the structure of public revenue and expenditure, and the social, political, and cultural effects of both; the means, rules, and patterns of fiscal activity under a market economic system and the relationships among these means, rules, patterns, and the specific institutions concerned; the relationship between the financial and fiscal system; and the relationship between fiscal and monetary policy. It will also allow a detailed examination of why the contemporary world market economy has become the common economic form of humanity because it inevitably contains universally recognized thoughts and values. These thoughts and values are often regarded as sprouted and exist as an inner soul before becoming a widely adopted economic form. This is due to the universal values that the market e-

① Some scholars worry that because Chinese researchers do not necessarily understand market failure theory or the theory of public goods, they may forget that China has a market economy. See, for example, Zhang, X. "Market failure theory and public goods theory: on the theoretical basis of finance under the market economy." *Finance and Trade Economy* 1 (2021).

conomy can exist, prevail, and develop.

This emphasis on values can help us understand the historical trajectory of the market economy in China. Many scholars suggest that the market economy was imported to China from Western countries at the end of the last century. However, the basic principles of the market economy, such as fair trade and the idea that all actors within the market pursue their self-interest (as is their right), among ancient Chinese intellectuals. ① Therefore, a value-oriented approach, such as neo-public finance theory, can reveal how China has the historical and social basis for implementing the market economy by examining this system beyond its merely economic characteristics.

In summary, neo-public finance theory attempts to interpret fiscal phenomena by considering the influence of both the systems and the values of the market economy, rather than to interpret one-dimensionally from the perspective of the market economic system. Such an approach can better reveal and explain the general patterns of fiscal activities and, importantly, better explain how China can both participate in the global market economy and establish its own unique system based on deeper values. Such an approach can help researchers better understand that some of the problems which are unique to the Chinese context, including the incompatibility between this fiscal system and various legal provisions. ② Such an approach has applications beyond the Chinese context; it will allow scholars to understand better the mul-

---

① For example, Han Fei, a thinker in the Warring States period of China (aka Hanfeizi, ca. 280 – 233 BC), once proposed that "Law is not biased towards the noble just as the carpenter's line marker does not bend on rugged surfaces. When laws are imposed, the wise dare not to quibble, the strong dare not to fight. Law does not pardon a minister when punishing evil, and it does not neglect any ordinary man when rewarding kindness." (*Hanzi Youdu*). This quote reflects the idea of equality among all people—a common value of the modern market economy and society. This idea exists in sharp contrast with the Confucian idea that "rites are allowed for the ordinary people and punishment is not imposed on the nobleman." The *Hanzi* demonstrates how the core values of the market economy in ancient China and can help explain why these values are still considered a foreign product, because they were not mainstream.

② Li, J. S. and Hou, K. F. "Mechanism and Suggestions on the Weakening of Township Financial Capacity Caused by the Village-finance-supervised-by-county Reform Based on the Field Study and Panel Data Analysis." *Budget Management & Accounting* 6 (2015): 17 – 22.

tilateral relationships among countries' public finances, the global market economy. Thus, it is why fiscal science must have explanatory power for the global fiscal phenomena.

The limitations of the public finance theory are self-evident. It is limited to the market economic system based on countries such as the UK and the US and explains fiscal phenomena only from the form of the market economy. The forty-year fiscal practice following China's reform and opening-up has proved that the public finance theory has no explanatory power on China's fiscal practice if it ignores China's practice and the gene of market economy (i. e. , the existence and manifestation of market economic values in China). Therefore, the applicability of public finance theory in China is limited, and we need a scientific and universal fiscal science theory for not only China but also the world.

IV. Expectations and hopes for the journal

As a fiscal science scholar with more than 30 years of teaching and research experience, I sincerely feel that our generation is lucky while shouldering a great responsibility for the future. We have witnessed the success and hardships of China's late-century fiscal reforms. We have learned from Soviet fiscal theory, Chinese state distribution theory, and Anglo-American public finance theory. However, hard as we try, we cannot use these theories to adequately explain and predict China's fiscal reforms and development, equip our students to study the modern world and deal with future fiscal development, or provide policymakers with effective fiscal reform strategies and suggestions. I sincerely feel that Chinese scholars stand upon a weak theoretical foundation in this field, and have established this journal to meet the challenge of building a new, more robust one. I would like to close my remarks with three proposals to my colleagues:

1. I recommend that we treat the market economy as a universal global

socio-economic form and value as the essential social background for studying fundamental theoretical fiscal issues.

2. I hope that we can work together to explore and build a new fiscal science theoretical system that integrates economics, political science, sociology, law, and other scientific theories and methods.

3. I propose that we critically examine and analyze the core concepts in contemporary public finance and build a new set of core concepts and the theoretical system of fiscal science through this journal.

财政演化与人的发展*

乔宝云　刘乐峥

摘　要：财政制度演化具有自身的内在规律。政府、市场和社会结合形成的治理形态在各自领域围绕降低参与主体的交易成本互相竞争，政府财政活动在这个过程中自我演进形成财政规律。如果把交易成本看成一个变量，那么主流的财政学理论，特别是市场失灵理论是这个一般框架下交易成本为零的极端和特殊的情形。交易成本取决于人，例如人的禀赋特质、人群结构，如种族、宗教、贫富差距等，交易成本随着人的发展变化而不断变化，进而引起市场、政府和社会的演化，以及市场、政府和社会之间关系的调整。不同环境下，财政可能体现为交换关系，也可能体现为分配关系，以自愿交换为特征的财政关系能以帕累托改进的方式，保证社会福利改进与经济发展同时实现，而实现交换关系的基础是人的平等与发展。

关键词：财政演化　交易成本　帕累托改进　人的发展

［中图分类号］ F810.2　**［文献标识码］** A

一、引言

如果观察现代社会的运行，可以发现市场规律逐渐得到尊重，而财政规律却常常被忽略。在现代市场经济社会，让市场发挥资源配置的决定性作用已经成为常态。从亚当·斯密提出“看不见的手”的观点后，关于市场规律的理论逐步清晰。市场规律的成功运用，在于价格调节机制撮合参与主体自愿产生利

* 基金项目：本研究得到中央财经大学“中国现代财政制度建设研究”项目（批准号：02379416002）和国家自然科学基金项目“财政政策的收入分配属性研究”（批准号：71373292）资助。

［作者简介］：乔宝云，中央财经大学中国公共财政与政策研究院院长，教授；刘乐峥，中央财经大学中国公共财政与政策研究院副院长，副教授。

益交换，实现帕累托改进。反之，从另一方面看，违背财政规律的政治诉求和行动时有发生。例如，欧盟在统一货币与各国独立财政体系同时存在的环境下，容易衍生高福利政策和政府债务持续扩张，违背财政规律注定让这种难以持续的政策设计付出巨大的代价；再如，美国奥巴马政府和特朗普政府摇摆的财政政策主张也都说明无论左或者右的政策设计都会为财政规律所左右。

从运行机制特征看，与市场不同，财政并没有价格这一明显的信号，它带有强制性特征的交易具有不确定性，没有保证社会福利改进与经济发展同时实现的机制。同时，作为一种治理体系，财政的发展不是随机无序的，而是有其自身演化的规律。财政规律之所以被忽略，原因在于财政容易被看成政治斗争和妥协的结果。然而事实上，规律是不以人的意志为转移的客观存在，财政制度作为结果只是财政规律的表现方式。财政内在的机理运行在特定的环境下产生了特定的财政制度，制度之间的差异性恰恰说明了财政规律演化的客观性。

中国共产党第十九次全国代表大会报告指出，中国特色社会主义进入了新时代，我国主要矛盾已转变为人民日益增长的美好生活需要与不平衡、不充分的发展之间的矛盾，并提出要加快建设现代财政制度、建设创新型的国家和打造共建共治共享的社会治理格局。从国家治理的高度来看，主流经济学对财政规律的理解存在不足，新时代呼唤财政研究创新的基础理论。值得注意的是，李俊生教授[1][2]率先质疑了基于市场失灵的财政学基础理论，提出了更有解释力的市场平台与参与型政府①的新市场财政学基础理论，引起了理论和实践界的广泛重视。实际上，“国家分配论”、基于市场失灵的“公共财政论”[3]、基于“政府失灵”的“公共选择论”[4]、提倡创新社会组织的“社会财政论”[5]、强调民主制度的“制度决定论”[6][7]等都是在分别假定政府、市场、社会②等治理体系为最优（即交易成本为零）的条件下推理出的财政诉求，是财政规律在极端假设下的表现。自中共十八届三中全会、四中全会后，国内学者从国家治理体系现代化的角度论述了现代财政制度的意义和法治特征[8][9]。尽管广泛讨论了财政的公共服务属性、民生财政等内容，但从文献来看，学者们对法治

① 新市场财政学认为，市场是资源配置的平台，政府、个人、企业都是在这个平台内的交易参与者，财政体现了政府与个人、企业交易的状况，而不是如基于市场失灵理论所述的体现了政府通过行使职能弥补市场失灵。

② 本文中，当社会与政府或市场作为一组相对的概念同时出现时，社会指的是除政府、市场外的资源配置组织形态与关系，例如，宗教组织、婚姻关系等。

及现代财政制度的认识都同样存在静态化的理解，例如，不能解释我国过去基本有效的财政制度为什么现在需要改革。

新时代多元社会里，现代财政制度如何在法治治理体系下，为市场、社会和政府提供平等沟通的渠道，促进不同主体互动、实现人的发展[10]，是时代的挑战，也是财政基础理论发展的机遇。本研究提出了一个财政基础理论框架，其中交易成本是一个变量。在这个广义的框架下，主流的财政学理论，特别是市场失灵理论是交易成本为零的极端和特殊情形。交易成本取决于人的特征，例如人的禀赋特质、人群结构等，随着人的发展变化不断变化，进而引起市场、政府和社会的演化，以及市场、政府和社会之间关系的调整。不同环境下，财政可能体现为交换关系，也可能体现为分配关系，以自愿交换为特征的财政关系能以帕累托改进的方式，保证社会福利改进和经济发展同时实现。要实现交换关系，基础是人的平等和发展。

本文的阐述按如下顺序展开：第二部分评述财政理论文献，说明财政理论研究的路径和方法；第三部分以一个简单的理论模型分析财政的性质；第四部分解释理论模型；第五部分给出总结性结论。

二、财政理论文献评述

财政与政府的关系非常矛盾。财政既体现政府收支活动，又约束政府收支。这个矛盾运动过程本身就是财政发展变化的历史。可以说，财政的演进映射了政府职能演变和发展的历史。不同时期社会发展的特点产生了不同的财政学说，这些学说不仅满足当时的理论需求，同时也影响财政实践。实际上，这些影响有时还非常巨大，如亚当・斯密的政府功能界定和财政理论奠定了延续几个世纪的、市场经济环境下的财政实践基础。

财政研究的重点往往与国家治理体系的变化有关。在相对稳定的国家治理体系下，财政基础理论往往容易形成共识，研究重点从注重基础理论的思想层面逐渐转向注重基础理论应用的技术层面，因为这时技术层面研究的边际效果更大。但是，若国家治理体系不够稳定，就显现出财政基础理论研究的重要性。一方面，技术层面研究的实效依赖于思想层面的研究；另一方面，每个国家当面临自身差异化的问题时，如果不能从基础理论层面对财政问题做出符合实际的回答，或者简单地全盘接受发达国家的实践经验，就很难形成合理的发展路径。

国内外学术界对财政基础理论从不同方面做了广泛的探索，下面我们试图对此进行简单归纳和评述。

（一）观念 vs. 规律

财政基础理论文献展现了两种不同的研究思路。一种思路研究的问题是：财政是什么？遵循什么样的规律？另一种思路研究的问题是：财政应该是什么？或者准确地说我们希望财政是什么？前一种思路着重研究财政的内在规律，后者着重研究财政观念或伦理，常带有强烈的价值诉求。然而，很多文献研究并没有很好地区分两种思路，导致双方讨论往往不在同一个频道上。

如果定义“财政是政府的收支活动”，那么，在这个收支活动中，政府、市场和社会及其相关的利益者实际上都在试图表达什么是合理的财政行为，或者财政应该是什么的概念。从政府角度看，财政是政府独立的收支活动；从市场角度看，财政是政府服务于市场的收支行为；从社会角度看，财政是政府服务于社会的收支行为。逻辑上三种表达都是“财政是政府的收支活动”的子集，是一种约束性表达。这三种表达（或者说治理体系）谁占优，就会产生相应的财政“应该是什么”的判断性理论。

如果国家是全能的（如全面计划经济），财政就是国家（政府）的收支行为，“国家分配论”是财政发展方向的自然判断。批判借鉴苏联理论形成的“国家分配论”是中国传统财政理论的主要流派之一，强调财政作为政府工具、为政府服务的性质。“国家分配论”以财政活动满足国家职能的需要作为理论研究起点，强调国家的意志，实际上排斥其他主体的意志。基于国家是全能的假设，“国家分配论”强调财政以政府为目的，是从政府到个人的单向管理工具，逻辑上倾向于财政“量能原则”。“国家分配论”在“政府全能”的假设下可能是合适的选择，但随着市场经济的发展，“政府全能”的假设不复存在，“国家分配论”与发挥市场资源配置中的基础性作用在逻辑上必然产生本质冲突。

当认识到“政府全能”的假设不符合市场经济的实际时，政府职能就不再由政府本身决定。引入的市场成为最重要的政府职能决定要素，是决定财政性质的根本制约因素。亚当·斯密谈及“看不见的手”时指出，分散决策的经济人互动和竞争产生有效市场。但即使在最有效的市场，君主或国家的义务也应包括：保护本国社会的安全、设立严正司法行政机构保护人民不受他人的欺侮或压迫和建立维持某些公共机关与工程。市场强调价格机制调节供需，对应的财政理论是“市场论”。从维护市场出发，“市场（财政）论”逻辑上倾向于政府、市场双向互动的“受益原则”。

我国学术讨论中，较有代表性的市场财政理论是公共财政论。尽管相关讨论至今分歧仍存，但作为在发展市场经济这个特定历史背景下提出的理论，“公共财政实质是市场经济财政”[11]。“公共财政论”基本沿袭了西方主流市场失灵财政理论，公共财政被视为市场经济体制下弥补市场缺陷的手段和发展方向。

除市场外，另一个政府职能决定要素是社会。在不否定政府和市场的同时，奥斯特罗姆[5]等学者创新性地提出新的集体行动和自主组织方案处理公共事务，在“市场失灵”和“政府失灵”的情况下把社会作为另一个选择。“社会（财政）论”框架改变了公共事务处理上政府与市场之间“非此即彼”的理念，提出公共事务管理可以通过多种组织和多种机制（多中心主义）完成，发展社会能够提高人民福利。“社会财政论”明确以社会为目的，强调多数人利益，从逻辑上倾向于财政“正义原则”。

中共十八届四中全会公报明确提出要全面推进依法治国，建设社会主义法治国家，促进国家治理体系和治理能力现代化。国家治理体系与法治体系存在一体两面的关系[12]。国家治理体系里，财政制度涉及中央、地方、市场、社会等各方面的利益关系。中共十八届三中全会定位“财政是国家治理的基础和重要支柱”，提出建设现代财政制度的目标。建立现代财政制度，核心是“建立与国家治理能力与治理体系现代化相适应”的财政制度[13]。

从国家财政到公共财政再到现代财政，文献试图回答的问题是财政应该是什么，衍生的量能、受益和正义等财政原则是不同价值观念的体现。“国家分配论”强调国家利益，“市场论”强调市场功能，实际体现资本或者偏好市场机制的利益诉求，“社会论”强调财政服务于社会和社会工具的性质，把财政延伸到多数人的利益，或者用多数人的利益代表全部人的利益。

财政活动有其自身的规律，这个规律是不以人们意志为转移的客观存在。规律可以服务于不同的观念，同时，任何观念的实现都离不开对规律的认识、把握和运用。从国家财政到公共财政再到现代财政，体现了财政观念的变化，这个过程是观念发展的过程，同时也说明观念具有多样性。当然，观念与规律有重合的部分，但观念毕竟不是规律，不同国家、不同历史时期、不同人群有不同诉求，体现为不同的观念。财政实践就是不断认识、运用财政规律，服务于特定观念的活动，但是，我们需要清楚财政的规律是什么，才能有效运用它。

毫无疑问，“财政应该是什么”是研究财政理论的重要问题，但也不是财政问题的全部。我们只有把不同价值观念从分析中剥离，或者说把不同价值观念作为外生变量，才可能发现内在财政规律，回答“财政是什么”的问题。

（二）失灵 vs. 演化

财政有没有自身演化的规律？当我们试图回答“财政是什么”的问题，或者探讨财政规律问题时，不同的方法论会产生不同的结论。“财政演化”与“市场失灵”是在不同思维架构下形成的对规律认识的方式。“演化”与“失灵”都可以理解为不同的观念，但是，如果从规律范畴来认识，“演化”假设财政有其自身演化的规律，而“市场失灵”则假设财政是市场的附属，其存在与变化是市场这一外生属性推动的。“演化”与“失灵”可以视为需要检验的假设。“失灵”理论的假设本质上独立于时间、空间存在，所产生的结论是唯一的、静止的、已经认知的最优状态，而“演化”理论的最优状态是与时间、空间相联系的，所以最优状态是多样的、动态的和不完全认知的。相应地，解决失灵需要借助于外力，相反，演化源于内在能力。正如后文所述，二者的不同在于是否考虑机制运行中推动财政演进的内在交易成本。

亚当·斯密以后，许多经济学家通过一系列假设严格证明竞争市场的有效性。反过来看，这些假设不满足导致“市场失灵”，从而以此界定政府活动的最大空间。“市场（财政）论”的产生是历史的必然，它强调财政作为市场工具服务于市场的性质，假设的是政府、市场“二元环境”。在这一理论中，市场经济是市场在资源配置上起基础性作用的经济组织形式，充分竞争的市场是一种有效率的运行机制。市场存在失灵、收入分配不公及经济波动等缺陷，为政府介入或干预提供了必要性和合理性的依据，但政府职能只限于解决市场做不好的事，起弥补作用，同时保护和影响市场。因此，符合市场经济要求的公共财政模式是一种弥补缺陷财政。

20 世纪美国经济大萧条以后，一些经济学家忙于指责“市场失灵”，另一些则指向“政府失灵”。布坎南[14]认为，在民主社会中政府的许多决定并不真正反映公民的意愿，且政府的缺陷至少和市场一样严重。他提出作为公共利益代理人的政府的作用是弥补市场经济的不足，并使各经济人决策的社会效应比政府进行干预之前更高，否则政府的存在就无任何经济意义。“政府失灵”理论是引发 20 世纪 80 年代世界范围内声势浩大的新公共管理运动的重要理论基础，这一运动视政府为“经济人”，以企业方式“再造”“重塑”政府，弥补政府管理中的缺陷和不足。

公共选择理论解决“政府失灵”的基本假设为市场是有效的，意图在政府中引入市场竞争机制解决问题。但这个假设存在根本的缺陷，因为政府与市场的目标不可能完全重合。而在奥斯特罗姆的框架中，在“市场失灵”和“政府失灵”的情况下，社会可作为另一个选择。当然这是一个非常有创造性的思路，但是如果沿着“失灵”而不是“演化”的方法论，也有可能得出“社会失灵”的结论。在国内财政基础理论研究领域，李俊生教授[1][15]强烈意识到市场失灵理论解释现实世界的不足，率先挑战了市场失灵理论的逻辑，认为市场是交易的平台，政府、企业、其他个人或社会都是其中的参与者。

特别重要的是，“市场失灵”理论基于“竞争市场有效”，隐含假设交易成本为零，而且市场是静止的。如果交易成本大于零，用动态的、演化的方法看待经济发展过程和技术变迁会有不同的发现。科斯[16][17]认为，只要财产权是明确的且交易成本为零或者很小，那么，无论在开始时将财产权赋予谁，市场均衡的最终结果都是有效的，能够实现资源配置的帕累托最优。因此，市场的有效性实质上依赖于交易成本为零的假定。然而，在现实世界中，权利的明确是很困难的，交易成本也不可能为零，甚至很高。如果实际上交易成本永不为零，那么合法权利的初始界定会对经济制度运行的效率产生影响，市场的有效性及推演出的财政弥补市场失灵的理论基础将被动摇。

交易成本如何促使市场演化呢？科斯的工作可理解为展现了基于明确权利下经济与社会演化的一个途径。市场交易产生契约交易成本，契约交易成本由市场成本与其他可替代选项的成本之间的均衡决定，市场自动实现优化；社会成本与市场交易成本不同，社会成本经常属于非契约交易成本。非契约交易成本不一定能够通过市场实现优化。对交易成本进一步的研究集中在不完全契约理论。这些理论都在一定程度上描述了市场、社会、政府在产权基础上围绕降低交易成本竞争的演化机制。

交易成本经济学指出，人类社会活动里，相对其他形态能适应新环境并降低交易成本，促进人的发展的组织形态将能够生存，变化过程就是制度的演变[18]。这一思想体现在国家治理里，就是政府、社会、市场所具有的治理体系围绕降低交易成本在互相竞争演化。实质上，市场有效及相应衍生出的主流财政理论的最优性质源自交易成本为零，这是围绕交易成本竞争演化的特例或者极端情况。例如，公司的出现用层级和行政化的生产组织治理形式代替了雇主劳工间的大量谈判，降低了交易成本，所以现代生产组织中公司非常常见，而如果交易成本一直为零，那么市场里应该每个人都是个体户。经典的污染外部性问题中，双方通过市场方式商讨的成本可能远远高于成立政府机构监管的成本，因此，这一领域成为政府（财政）的职能很常见，而不是交易成本为零时双方互相洽谈。

总体来看，社会、市场和政府各自独立运行和决策是演化的基础，外部环境的变化是演化的条件。对于市场，政府、社会等都是外部条件，政府、社会的变化都可能引起市场适应新环境，产生新变化，但这种变化是市场机制本身内在力量产生的自我纠正、自我发展。同理，政府其实也在自我演化。从历史的角度看，很容易得出政府存在的独立性而非市场的依附性。政府从一开始就不是因为纠正“市场失灵”而产生，甚至在市场出现之前就已经存在了，因此，它的演化有其内在必然性。当然，社会、市场和政府可以不断进化，也可能不断退化。对文献的研究表明，明确的权利是进化的基础。如果破坏了这个基础，那么就有可能退化，这也是为什么我们强调法治的原因，因为法治是界定并保护权利的基础。

回到财政的一个基本属性问题。财政是政府强制的收支行为，这种强制有存在的必要性，但能不能创造新的价值并且自我进化呢？回答这一问题需要考虑财政属性是分配还是交换。

（三）分配 vs. 交换

财政能不能创造新的价值？这个问题的答案界定了财政的基本属性。因为交换关系能创造新的价值但分配关系却不一定能这样，所以研究财政规律需要回答的核心问题是财政究竟是分配关系还是交换关系。亚当·斯密强调分工产生供给和需求，交换不断地促进分工，推动经济发展，这个专业化过程创造了新的价值。然而，在供给和需求的互动中，交换并不是唯一的方式。政府同样是分工的产物，虽然从公共财政的角度理解这也是一种公共服务的供需关系，但是由于政府行为本身具有强制性，且往往缺乏价格机制调节，这与市场交换不同。进一步讲，政府的行为可能是交换，也可能是分配。

财政究竟属于分配还是属于交换关系？其中根本差别在于个体利益变化状况。在交换关系下，不同利益方双向平等互动，各自福利都没有减少，即帕累托改进，否则一方不会选择交换。帕累托改进意味着社会总价值的提高，隐含的意义是财政作为交换关系能够创造新的价值。分配关系则不尽然，它是利益主导方的单向行为，不以平等互动为基础，而是价值从一部分人的手里转移到另外一部分人的手里，过程本身并没有创造新价值的要求。在阶级斗争的观念下，财政很容易理解为一种分配关系，为特定的阶级服务。从社会福利的角度看，交换关系由参与主体自愿达成，一定是帕累托改进和提高福利的，但分配关系蕴含财富转移，是否能最终提高福利具有不确定性。从这个意义来看，推动财政更多地形成交换关系是财政改革的一个重要任务。

无论我们期望财政是什么，也无论我们认为财政应该是什么，实际上，财政可能是分配关系或交换关系，也可能同时具有分配关系和交换关系。我们需要理解这种关系内在的、不以我们价值观念的变化而转移的客观性。要理解这种客观性，就要研究它的内在规律。

如果在规律范畴研究，“失灵”理论本身假定政府以服务市场为目的，以“市场有效”为基础，而市场机制体现的就是交换性质。遵循这个逻辑，财政应该完全是交换关系。但是，这个结论与历史和现实恰恰不能完全重合，因此把它作为一种财政规律是不太合适的。所以，我们在这里把“失灵”视为属于观念范畴而不是规律范畴似乎更加合适。

剥离价值判断，财政是政府强制的收支行为。这种政府强制的收支行为在一种环境下表现为分配关系，在另一种环境下表现为交换关系，因此我们有必要对环境进行界定，研究财政在环境变化过程中的演化。我们通过下面的一个简单模型来说明这个问题。

三、理论模型

任何交换关系只有在各方共同同意的情况下才有可能形成自愿交易。当然交换关系可以是契约交易，也可以是非契约交易，依据的是正式或者非正式的契约。要注意的是，任何一种交换关系的自愿性都必须以有退出选择作为保证。然而，退出存在成本，人在市场、政府和社会活动中的不同策略正是来自于考量这种成本不同产生的结果，财政是交换还是分配也是受此驱动的。

（一）基本模型

财政关系如果是一种交换关系，其交换的结果必然要求符合帕累托改进。实现帕累托改进要求以下几个条件：其一，存在初始设置。初始设置表明了参与各方的利益基础。没有初始设置，就没有基准，也就无所谓作为比较概念的帕累托改进，这是讨论任何财政问题的基础。其二，个体通过自我发展改进各自福利已经实现自我平衡。这个假设是要分清政府与市场的关系。政府与市场在各自领域里运行，通过自身的内在机制实现平衡。当政府插入市场（或反过来），市场机制运行的外部环境或约束条件改变，新的均衡产生。其三，退出成本大于0。这个假设是要分清政府与社会的关系。对自然人而言，政府与社会最大的不同在于退出强制性的政府活动往往具有比退出社会活动更大的成本，此时交易成本的最重要部分是退出成本。

我们建立一个简单的模型来说明退出成本如何影响公共资源的配置。假设一个社会存在 A 和 B 两个不同类型的人在完全信息下就一个项目进行纳什谈判，$a \geqslant 0$ 和 $b \geqslant 0$ 分别表达 A 与 B 的退出成本。项目可能的净收益（扣除其他交易成本）是 T。决策过程设定为 A 先提出方案，之后 A 和 B 谈判。

用后向归纳法解这个问题：

$$\max w = (x + a)(T - x + b)$$

其中：x 是 A 的净收益，$T - x$ 是 B 的净收益。

均衡状态：

$$x = \frac{T - (a - b)}{2}$$

$$T - x = \frac{T + (a - b)}{2}$$

这是经典的纳什谈判解，即双方均分退出成本调整后的收益。

由 A 提出方案，意味着解需满足以下参与条件：

$$x = \frac{T - (a - b)}{2} \geqslant 0$$

即

$$T \geqslant a - b$$

定理 1：如果 $a \geqslant b$，则 $T^* \geqslant 0$，$T^* \in T$，即均衡点社会净收益增加，而且能够实现帕累托改进。

证明：我们知道

$$x = \frac{T - (a - b)}{2} \geqslant 0$$

如果 $a \geqslant b$，则对于任何 $T^* \in T$

且

$$T^* - x = \frac{T^* + (a - b)}{2} \geqslant 0$$

$$T^* \in T$$

显然，与不发生该项目相比，这一结果产生了新的收益，而由于交易发生的基础是每个人各自得到相应的收益，所以每个人都存在收益增加，即实现了帕累托改进。

定理 2：如果 $a < b$，则存在 $T^* < 0$，$T^* \in T$，即社会净收益减少，而且存在 $T^* - x < 0$，或者说均衡点不能保证帕累托改进。

证明：

对于 $a < b$，存在 $0 > T^* \geqslant (a - b)$，且

$$T^* - x = \frac{T^* + (a - b)}{2} < 0$$

结果表明，退出成本差异形成了纳什谈判中的优势和劣势。退出成本低的一方可能利用这种优势去降低退出成本高的一方的收益，导致最终均衡不是帕累托改进。在没有退出交易成本的情况下，交易不会达成，但是由于决定交易威胁点的退出成本过高，劣势一方只能接受这样的交易。

值得注意的是，上述博弈中有权力提出方案的一方在提出方案时一定先保障自身至少获得正的净收益，这是一种优势，那么退出成本高的一方可以通过获得这种优势而被弥补。由此可以推出以下定理 3。

定理 3：如果只有退出成本高的代表才有权力提出方案，那么社会净收益增加，交易能够自动实现帕累托改进。

证明非常直接，$a \geqslant b$ 且只有 A 才有权力提出方案，那么均衡状态必然是帕累托改进。

这是一个非常有意思的结论。考虑世界分为两类人：一类是数量占多的多数人，另一类是剩余的少数人，两类人具有互为竞争性的利益诉求。如果多数人的退出成本高于少数人的退出成本，那么社会可以自动实现帕累托改进。而在多数人的退出成本低于少数人的退出成本的情况下，如果附加少数人才有权力提出方案的条件，那么均衡状态自动实现帕累托改进。

在现实世界中，通常多数人才有权力提出方案，结果是不是帕累托改进，取决于多数人与少数人退出成本的大小。如果我们理解财政活动的形成为参与的利益双方（在我们假定的世界中即多数人与少数人）的一种谈判结果，在多数人的退出成本高于少数人的退出成本的情况下，财政形成的是交换关系，即形成的均衡一定是帕累托改进。在多数人的退出成本低于少数人的退出成本的情况下，财政形成的实际上是分配关系，即收益由一方转向另外一方，但这种分配关系是否是帕累托改进具有不确定性。

（二）一个特例

定理 4：如果 $a=b$，无论 A 代表多数人还是少数人，则 $T^* \geqslant 0$，$T^* \in T$，即社会净收益增加，而且均衡点都能够自动实现帕累托改进。

证明：我们知道

$$x = \frac{T-(a-b)}{2} \geqslant 0$$

如果 $a=b$，那么则对于任何 $T^* \in T$

$$x = \frac{T^* - (a-b)}{2} = \frac{T^*}{2} \geqslant 0$$

即

$$T^* \geqslant 0,\ T^* \in T$$

而且

$$T - x = \frac{T^* + (a - b)}{2} = \frac{T^*}{2} \geqslant 0$$

一个社会，究竟是多数人还是少数人有权力提出方案？在情况不确定的情况下，只要退出成本相等，那么均衡点社会净收益必然提高，而且自动实现帕累托改进。显然，在退出成本 a 与 b 存在差异的情况下，无论多数人决策还是少数人决策，都存在社会净收益减少且其中还有一部分人受到伤害的可能性。

四、模型的解释

上述简单模型可以引申出退出成本在推动财政演进中的重要作用。现实生活中，政府与社会经常在互动：一些领域社会发挥了重要的作用，一些领域政府起到了主导作用。从模型来理解，这是退出成本影响的结果。社会与政府之间的互动会发生职能转变的情况，我们称为社会功能政府化或政府功能社会化。与之相对应，财政的职能也就发生了相应的演化。

演化的动力来自何处？实质上，政府、社会、市场属于不同领域的治理形态，各自都可能在相应的领域具有优势。交易成本的不同以及变化，会造成某种治理形态在某些领域因为交易成本过高而不具优势，或者本来具有优势的治理形态随着退出成本的变化而不再具有优势。因此，能产生更低交易成本的其他治理形态会逐步占据优势，取代原有的治理形态。这种进程是以财政的方式来体现的，所以表现为财政的演进①。作为交易成本的一种，模型中专门模拟的退出成本在这一演进过程中起到了重要的驱动作用。退出成本在模型中决定了纳什谈判威胁点的位置，当退出成本高时，即使某个领域一个治理形态在削减其他交易成本上具有优势，也可能无法取代原有的治理形态。

我们使用农村社保体系演变作为一个简单的例子说明退出成本的重要作用。以往中国的农村，农民长期自己负责医疗和养老，很多时候依赖于家庭或宗族形成社会化的保障体系，这是社会化的职能。但是，随着市场经济的发展，户籍限制逐步放松，人口流动逐步增强，这一体系逐步演变成为如今的

① 应该注意到这种演进不一定代表财政或政府的扩张，也可能是政府化的组织形态因为在某些领域与社会相比具有更高的交易成本而退出，导致政府的职能社会化，从而体现为财政规模缩小。

"新农合"等带有政府职能性质的保障体系，实际上是社会职能政府化的体现。从模型理解，受计划经济体系影响，我国过去长期实施户籍管制，人口不能自由流动，城市生产率相对农村不算突出，导致农民必须依赖于土地。在这种情况下，如果模型中的双方是农民和城市居民，农民的退出成本很高。上述模型中的交易体现为财政不进入这一领域，农民也在贡献财政收入。这实际上形成了一种潜在的财政分配而非交换关系。双方都是同一家庭农民时，退出成本一致，并且，就其他交易成本看，家庭式的保险机制在处理信任产生的交易成本上可能很低，当政府以财政形式进入这一领域时，形成的社会保险机制需要处理陌生人之间的信任机制问题，是否能够显著地降低交易成本是不确定的①。因此，对农民的社保治理形态体现为家庭式而不是政府主导的方式并不奇怪。这种家庭式保障体系的合作交换关系在社会领域内部自身演进，对于农民来说相对于完全没有保障是一种帕累托改进。

随着社会经济的发展，中国的城镇化和工业化过程显著地降低了退出成本。户籍制度不再像以前那样严苛，大量农民工进入城市并逐步市民化，流动性的增加导致退出成本显著降低，城市居民与农民的交易退出成本逐步趋向一致。当退出成本趋向一致的时候，达成的交易不再是分配关系而是交换关系。具体体现在财政上，这意味着政府必须把一部分社会保障项目净收益分配给农村，形成新的均衡，这就形成了政府化的社会保障体系，也就是社会职能向政府转移了。这一过程对城市居民也是帕累托改进，这是因为社会保障项目覆盖农村带来更多的劳动力和生产力，使项目净收益扩张了，而且扩张后分配给城市居民的部分比原来也扩大了。

应该注意的是，退出成本的最主要来源实际上是流动性成本。从全社会角度来看，降低整体的流动性成本能够增加社会净收益，就更容易形成合作的交换关系，创造新的价值。流动性成本降低，实质上是以人为本的发展，它可能来自人本身素质的提高，例如，高知识素质的居民有更大的职业选择自由度；也可能来自制度环境给予的收益，例如，户籍制度放宽给予居民更多的选择。因此，财政体系增加公共服务（包括养老体系）的可携带性，能够进一步降低退出成本，更加促进帕累托改进的交易达成，财政也就更容易体现为交换

① 注意，总的交易成本是退出成本与其他交易成本之和。当退出成本很高，占据绝大部分交易成本时，降低其他交易成本并不能有效降低总交易成本。这样，决定性的因素是双方退出成本的差异。

关系。

为了解释财政的演化，我们基于前面的模型考察不同情形下社会功能政府化和政府功能社会化的动态过程实现帕累托改进。在简单交换的情况下，达成交易帕累托改进就能够自动实现，这往往是在市场领域内最常见的情况。在合作情况下，帕累托改进可能有不同的路径。从前面的模型可以看出，存在两种情形，$a=b>0$ 和 $a=b=0$。如果要满足 $a=b>0$，往往需要 A 和 B 的共同努力才能实现帕累托改进，而 $a=b=0$ 时，A 和 B 通过各自努力可以实现帕累托改进。在治理形态和财政的作用上，这两种情形体现为不同的社会进步路径。

可以通过欧洲国家和美国的政府治理及财政差异来理解交易成本差异导致的财政演化路径差异。简单比较欧洲国家（尤其是大陆国家）与美国的财政规模，可以发现欧洲国家的财政收支占国民收入的比重远超美国，政府财政职能更加宽泛。受历史、宗教、文化、政治、经济等方面的影响，欧洲居民的退出成本比属纯移民国家的美国居民更高。从政府治理结构看，以分封制为基础演化而来的欧洲政府体系通常都由一般型的政府构成，即一个封邑政府提供所有的公共服务，居民退出意味着失去该政府提供的全部公共服务；美国大量采用功能型的政府模式，一项公共服务（如学区或警察政府）对应一个政府，居民退出一项公共服务对应的政府不代表失去所有的公共服务。所以，欧洲居民的退出成本更高，美国居民流动性更高。这种差异，用模型的语言，导致欧洲更接近 $a=b>0$ 的情况，美国更接近 $a=b=0$ 的情况。现假定有一项社会交易磋商，如果交易双方退出成本不同且都大于 0，交易可能不是帕累托改进。要促进交易达成并实现帕累托改进，在退出成本较高的情况下可采用的做法是尽量使双方的交易成本一致，在欧洲体现为大量以平等为目的的财政手段。如果谈判是在美国，由于退出成本更接近 0，可以通过流动让具有相似交易成本的双方居民发生交易，只要交易达成就是帕累托改进，并不必然要均等化的财政手段介入，双方各自谈判即可，财政这时更应该保障流动性，更好地让相似交易成本的居民成为交易双方。因此，实践中美国具有更加发达的社会组织（如各种行业的自发式协会），即一些在欧洲国家本属于政府职能范围的项目是社会组织在运行，这是政府职能社会化的体现。这一简单的比较说明，不同的财政制度选择实际上是交易成本，尤其是退出成本不同所导致的，其中居民流动性的不同会起到重要的作用。这一点实质上与蒂布特[19]模型的思想具有一致性。

上述模型和后续分析中，我们主要基于简单的二元模型，但在多元社会环境里，人们偏好差异化增加了合作的复杂性，因此，以平等化为手段的财政体系受到的挑战更大①。然而，分析的核心是帕累托改进实际上引领了制度的演化：各种政治经济社会环境下退出成本的差异可能让财政制度千差万别，但财政制度演变都是为了更好地降低交易成本，形成帕累托改进的交易。

不同条件下财政演化路径的共同目的都是为了实现人的发展，降低交易成本，这一认识对推进中国现代财政制度建设，实现国家治理体系和治理能力现代化具有重要意义。在不同的路径下，政府与社会都通过基于适应并降低交易及退出成本的竞争在互动，实现人的基本权力平等和提高要素的流动性，让人能够充分发展。多元社会下现代财政的演化发展让人民具有更加公平的权利，让交易成本更低。一方面，现代财政要求法治体系。法治界定和保护了人民的权利，这是交换的基础。另一方面，平等的权利和降低的交易成本促进人的创新和发展，激发社会自身发展的动力，更有利于实现帕累托改进。当前，进入“新常态”的中国，主要矛盾已转变为人民日益增长的美好生活需要与不平衡、不充分的发展之间的矛盾，面临中等收入陷阱和阶层固化带来的要素流动性问题的挑战。在这一时代背景下，现代财政制度建设的一个鲜明意义是要平等社会的交易成本，更要降低退出成本，强化要素的流动性，促进人乃至社会的发展。

五、结论

市场失灵与市场有效理论一样，都是遵循交易成本为零的逻辑假设。在交易成本为零的条件下，社会存在两个子集合：一个是市场有效子集，另一个是市场失灵子集。这个逻辑框架有很强的分析优势，提供了有力的静态分析工具，特别是政府与市场关系的基本框架。但它也存在严重的缺陷。它无法与现实世界相吻合，因为交易成本不可能为零；它也无法说明社会经济的动态变化，因为它提供的是静态均衡。

在一个更一般的框架中，如果把交易成本看成一个变量，那么市场有效和

① 可以理解为政府需要参与的领域越多，职能越多，所需要平等化的地方其实也就越多。

失灵理论就是这个一般框架下的极端和特殊的情形。更重要的是，我们可以从交易成本的变化中探索制度演化的规律。交易成本不仅仅是市场交换特有的概念，而是市场、政府和社会共有的概念。政府的强制合作、社会的自愿合作都会产生交易成本。正是交易成本的存在，使市场、政府和社会不断演化，相互之间竞争发展。

交易成本是人的函数。交易成本随着人的发展变化不断变化，进而引起市场、政府和社会的演化，以及市场、政府和社会之间关系的调整。财政演化是以财政内因为根据，以各种外因如市场、社会为条件的能动活动。这个财政内因就是人民需求，其基础是人民权利的界定，这个基础是起点，也是一个标尺，没有这个基础，就无从衡量发展，当然也就无所谓进步。其动力是人民权利的发展。实现权利发展的途径可能是分配甚至暴力方式，也可能是合作交换方式，不同实现途径之间存在围绕交易成本的竞争关系。同时，不同实现途径产生不同的社会福利和经济发展状态。社会福利改进与经济发展之间的矛盾冲突在交换状态下通过帕累托改进可以实现统一。因此，帕累托改进不仅是一种状态，也可以理解为一种自动和自发的力量。

中国自改革开放以来，经济取得了巨大的成就，从不发达国家进入中等以上收入国家的行列。中国的发展，一方面充分发挥了市场的作用，另一方面也充分体现了政府和社会的功能，发挥制度优势，在市场、政府、社会的共同作用中优化了交易成本。中国特色的发展道路是对人类发展的独特贡献。同时，也应该注意到，发展过程中的不足也不断显现，制度交易成本上升，社会阶层固化，可能面临着中等收入陷阱的挑战。如何应对挑战，实现可持续发展，关键在于释放新动能，而新动能的基础就是人的发展。人的发展和进步不仅仅是一种道德诉求和财政伦理，更是财政演化的规律。实现社会福利与经济发展的统一，既要不断强化法治，保证人民的权利，也要通过提高人民素质发展人民能力。这也是新时代财政的使命。

参考文献

［1］李俊生．盎格鲁-撒克逊学派财政理论的破产与科学财政理论的重建——反思当代“主流”财政理论［J］．经济学动态，2014（04）：117－130.

［2］李俊生．新市场财政学：旨在增强财政学解释力的新范［J］．中央财经大学学报，2017（05）：3－11.

［3］ Musgrave R A. The theory of public finance: a study in public economy ［J］. Journal of Political Economy, 1959, 99 (1): 213 – 213.

［4］ Buchanan J M, Tullock G. The Calculus of Consent ［M］. University of Michigan Press, 1962.

［5］ 埃莉诺·奥斯特罗姆．公共事物的治理之道：集体行动制度的演进［M］．余逊达，陈旭东，译．上海：上海译文出版社，2012.

［6］ 青木昌彦．比较制度分析［M］．周黎安，译．上海：上海远东出版社，2001.

［7］ Besley T, Persson T. The origins of state capacity: Property rights, taxation, and politics ［J］. American Economic Review, 2009, 99 (4): 1218 – 1244.

［8］ 高培勇．论国家治理现代化框架下的财政基础理论建设［J］．中国社会科学，2014（12）：102—122，207.

［9］ 刘剑文，侯卓．现代财政制度的法学审思［J］．政法论丛，2014（02）：13 – 21.

［10］ 乔宝云，刘乐峥，吴卓瑾．建立现代财政制度：从政府工具到法治平台［A］．“新市场财政学”理论创新学术研讨会论文集［C］．北京，2016：46 – 68.

［11］ 安体富．论我国公共财政的构建［J］．财政研究，1999（06）：1 – 6.

［12］ 喻中．作为国家治理体系的法治体系［J］．法学论坛，2014，29（02）：5 – 12.

［13］ 楼继伟．深化财税体制改革建立现代财政制度［J］．求是，2014（20）：24 – 27.

［14］ 詹姆斯·M. 布坎南．自由、市场和国家［M］．吴良健，桑任，译．北京：北京经济学院出版社，1988.

［15］ 李俊生，姚东旻．互联网搜索服务的性质与其市场供给方式初探——基于新市场财政学的分析［J］．管理世界，2016（08）：1 – 15.

［16］ Coase R H. The nature of the firm ［J］. Economica, 1937, 4 (16): 386 – 405.

［17］ Coase R H. The Problem of Social Cost ［J］. Journal of Law & Economics, 1960, 3 (4): 1 – 44.

［18］ Tadelis S, Williamson O E. Transaction cost economics ［M］. The Handbook of Organizational Economics. Princeton University Press, 2012.

［19］ Tiebout C M. A Pure Theory of Local Expenditures ［J］. Journal of Political Economy, 1956, 64 (5): 416 – 424.

The Evolution of Government Finance and the Development of Human Being

Qiao Baoyun　Liu Lezheng

Abstract： The evolution of a fiscal institution is governed by its own rules. Governance structures in various fields, formed by interactions of government, market, and society, compete with respect to reducing transaction cost. In this process, a fiscal system evolves itself, which embodies the law of government finance evolution. If we view the transaction cost as a variable in the general framework, mainstream schools of public finance theory, the "market failure" theory in particular, only show extreme cases where transaction cost is zero. The transaction cost depends on the characteristics of human beings such as endowments, as well as, demographic structures such as race, religion, and income distribution, etc. The development of human beings leads to changing transaction costs that result in the evolution of government, market and society, as well as, their relationships. Under different circumstances, government finance could be presented as the exchange relationship or the redistribution relationship. However, a fiscal system characterized by voluntary transactions is able, in a manner of pareto improvement, to achieve social welfare improvement and economic development simultaneously. To establish exchange relationships, the fundamental requirements are equality and development of the human being.

Keywords： The evolution of government finance　Transaction cost　Pareto improvement　Human development

CLC number：F810. 2　Document code：A

I. Introduction

In terms of the functioning of modern society, it can be seen that the law of market is gaining greater respect while the law of public finance is often overlooked. In the modern market economy, it has become a norm to have the market play the decisive role of resource allocation. Since Adam Smith elaborated on functions of the "invisible hand", greater clarity has been added to theories regarding the law of market. The successful application of the law of market can be attributed to the matching of participants in their voluntary exchange of interests through the price adjustment mechanism, thus achieving Pareto Improvement. On the other hand, political demands and actions that violate the law of public finance continue to occur. For example, with the presence of unified currency in the EU and the separate fiscal system of each country at the same time, there is a high possibility of high welfare policies financed by expanding government debt constantly. However, the law of public finance is bound to cost such policy design very much and renders it unsustainable. Also, the swinging policies of the Obama and Trump Administrations indicate that the policy design, be it to the left or right, hinges upon the law of public finance.

In terms of the functioning feature, fiscal transactions operate in a mandatory way with some uncertainty, which differentiates it from market trades that are guided by the clear signal of price. And it does not have a mechanism to ensure the simultaneous achievement of social well-being improvement and economic development. Meanwhile, as a governance system, fiscal system does not develop in a random or out-of-order way, but in conformity with its law of evolution. The reason why the law of public finance is neglected lies in that the fiscal system tends to be regarded as a result of political conflicts and compromises. But as a matter of fact, law is an objective reality independent of human's will and fiscal system as the outcome is simply an embodiment of the law of public finance. The internal mechanism of government finance gives rise to the particular systems in a given environment, the differences among which proves the objectivity for the evolution of the public finance law.

The report of the 19th Session of National Congress of CPC points out that socialism with Chinese characteristics has crossed the threshold into a new era and the principal contradiction facing Chinese society has evolved to that between unbalanced and inadequate development and the people's ever-growing need for a better life. And it proposes to step up efforts to build an innovative country and create a social governance landscape featuring co-construction, co-governance and sharing. From the perspective of state governance, mainstream economics leaves much to be desired in the understanding of the law of public finance. The new era prompts the need of innovative research on the fundamental theory on public finance. It is noteworthy that Professor Li Junsheng[1][2] first questioned the public finance theory that is based on market failures and proposed a new market public finance rationale boasting more explanatory power i. e. the theory of market platform-participatory government①, which aroused substantial attention and interest in the academia, as well as, the practitioners' society. Actually, the State Allocation Theory, the Theory of Public Finance based on market failures[3], the Theory of Public Choice based on "government failures"[4], the Theory of Social Finance that advocates innovating social organizations[5], and Institutional Determinism that highlights the democratic system [6][7], etc. are the appeals or judgment derived from the premise that a governance structure-government, market, or society②-is optimal (i. e. zero transaction cost), a reflection of the law of public finance under extreme conditions. After the Third Plenary Session of the 18th CPC Central Committee and the Fourth Plenary Session, domestic

① The new public finance theory treats market as a platform for resource allocation, and government, individuals and firms are transaction parties in this platform. Therefore, public finance reflects the transactions between government and individuals or firms. In contrast, in the traditional theory of market failure, government functions to fix the deficiencies of market.

② In this paper, when emerging with government or market as a group of concepts in comparison, society is referred to as an organization or governance structure allocating resources, in addition to government and market; for instance, religion or marital relationships.

scholars are expounding the significance and feature of rule of law with regard to modern fiscal systems from the perspective of modernizing the state governance system[8][9]. Although the service and welfare properties of public finance have been discussed extensively, there is still a static understanding of the rule of law and the modern finance system, e. g. it is difficult to explain the necessity of reform to the basically effective fiscal system of our country in the past.

In the diversified society of the new era, how to provide an equal platform for market, society and government to communicate, how to improve the interaction among different main bodies and achieve human development with modern fiscal system under the system of rule of law[10], are the challenges faced to, and also an opportunity for, the development of fundamental theory of public finance. We propose a generalized framework of fundermental theory of public finance, in which transaction cost is treated as a variable. Under this general framework, mainstream fiscal theories, especially the theory of market failure, is an extreme and special case with zero transaction cost. The transaction cost depends on human characteristics, such as endowment and demographic structures. The cost varies with human development, leading to the governance evolution of market, government and society, and also the adjustment of relationships among the three. Fiscal activities can be embodied as an exchange relation or distribution relation under different contexts. In the sense of Pareto Improvement, simultaneous enhancement of social welfare and economic development can be achieved under fiscal relations featured by voluntary exchanges, whose realization requires human equality and development.

What follows in this paper are: section 2 is a literature review on fiscal theories and corresponding research approaches, section 3 provides a simple model to analyze the properties of fiscal activities, further interpretations to the model are given in section 4, and section 5 concludes the paper.

II. A Literature Review on Fiscal Theories

The relationship between public finance and government is quite contradictory. A fiscal system is a reflection as well as constrain to revenue and expenditure activities of government. The whole dynamic process of this contradiction itself is the history of fiscal development. So to speak, the evolution of public finance is a mapping of the evolution and development history of government functions. Different fiscal theories emerged characterizing the salient features of social development in different periods, which not only meet current demand for theory, but also influence fiscal practices. In fact, such influence can be enormous. For example, the definition of government functions and fiscal theory proposed by Adam Smith laid a solid foundation for fiscal practices that last for centuries under the market economy environment.

The focus of fiscal research is always related to changes in the state governing system. The fiscal theories can establish consensus, with a relatively stable governing system. Under such circumstance, the research emphasizes more on technique level focusing on the application of theories rather than ideology that concentrates on developing the fundamental theory, as at the time technical improvement is able to exert more marginal effects. However, an unstable governing system demonstrates the importance of research on fundamental fiscal theories. On one hand, the effectiveness of research on technique level relies on research on ideology. On the other hand, every country faces its own differentiated problems. It will be hard to form a reasonable development path if we can't answer fundamental problems of fiscal theory in a way consistent with practices, or simply accept the practical experience of developed countries.

Voluminous research studies have been conducted on fundamental theories of public finance by academics home and abroad. The following provides a review on these theories.

a. Concepts vs. Laws

There are two strands of research approaches in the literature regarding fundamental fiscal theories. One focuses on what public finance is and what kind of law it follows. And the other one studies what public finance should be, or to be more specific, what we want it to be. The former approach emphasizes on inner law of public finance, while the latter one has an emphasis on the concept or ethnics with a strong value judgment. However, these two approaches aren't clearly distinguished in the literature, which may lead to divergent discussions.

If we define public finance as revenue and expenditure activities of government, then in this activity, government, market, society and other stakeholders are all trying to specify what a reasonable fiscal activity is, or what the definition of public finance is. For government, public finance is government revenue and spending activities of independency. For market, public finance is revenue and spending activities by government while serving the market. For society, it is revenue and spending activities by government that serves the society. Logically, the above three are all binding expressions as subsets of "public finance being revenue and expenditure activities of government". Either one of them (or governing systems) being dominant will lead to corresponding judgmental theories of what public finance is.

If a state is almighty (e. g. All-round planned economy), government finance will be the revenue and expenditure activities of the state (government). "State Allocation Theory" is a naturally derived judgment on the development direction of public finance. The State Allocation Theory, as one of the main schools of China's traditional fiscal theories, which is derived with critiques from the theory in Soviet Union, stresses public finance as a governmental instrument that serves the government. The logic starting point for the research on the "State Allocation Theory" is to meet the needs of government/state functions through fiscal activities, which puts emphasis on state's will while in effect rejecting the will of other participants in society. Based on such a presumption that the state is almighty, "State Allocation Theory" underlines that public finance, for the purpose of government, is a unidirectional management tool from government to individuals. Logically, it's inclined to the "ability-to-pay principle" of public finance. "State Allocation Theory" might be an appropriate option under the assumption of an "almighty government". However, with the development of market economy, such an assumption does not exist anymore, which causes essential conflicts between "State Allocation Theory" and playing the fundamental role of market in allocating resources.

If there's no such assumption of an "almighty government", government functions will no longer be decided by the government itself. The market becomes the decisive factor of government functions, as well as, a constraint that determines the nature of public finance. When talking about the "invisible hand", Adam Smith points out that interactions and competitions among rational humans with a decentralized decision making process generate efficient markets. However, even for an efficient market, the obligation of the monarch or state should include the safeguarding of national security, founding of judicial administration to protect its people from bullying and suppression, as well as, the establishment and maintenance of certain public organizations and projects. The market emphasizes on adjusting supply and demand by price. In such case the corresponding fiscal theory is "Market-oriented Theory". From the perspective of maintaining the market, the "Market-oriented (fiscal) Theory" is logically inclined to the "benefit principle" of bidirectional interactions between government and market.

Among China's academic discussions, the most representative fiscal theory is the theory of "public finance". As a theory being put forward under the specific background of developing market economy from the previous planned economy in which fiscal activities play an all-all-round role, "'the theory of public finance' is in essence the government finance theory serving for market economy"[11], even though there's still divergence among the discussion to this day. "The theory of public finance" basically follows the mainstream fiscal theories of market failure in western countries, which is regarded as a method and development direction for remedying market failure under the market economy. So it is actually a "Market-oriented theory".

Except the market, another decisive factor for government functions is society. While admitting the role of government and market at the same time, Elinor Ostrom[5], with other scholars, creatively puts forward new theories of collective action and self-organization to deal with public affairs, and takes society as another option under the circumstance of "market failure" and "government failure". The framework of "Society (fiscal) Theory" has changed the either-or thinking between government and market when dealing with public affairs. It also points out that the management of public affairs can be completed through various organizations and mechanisms (polycentrism), and people's welfare can be improved by social development. The "Social Public Finance Theory" targets society, putting an emphasis on the interest of the majority and logically being inclined to the "justice principle" of public finance.

The document of the fourth plenary session of the 18th Communist Party of China Central Committee states to improve a socialist system of laws, build a country under the socialist rule of law, and push on with modernization of the country's governing system and capabilities. A country's governing system and the system of the rule of law are like two sides of an organic entity[12]. In the state's governing system, the public finance system involves interest relationships among the central government, subnational government, market and society. The third plenary session of the 18th Communist Party of China Central Committee defined public finance as the foundation and one fundamental pillars of state governance. It also put forward the key objective of establishing modern fiscal system that adapts to the country's governing system and capabilities[13].

From state public finance to market-oriented public finance and modern public finance, literature tries to explain what finance should be, and the derived fiscal principles represent different values, such as ability-to-pay principle, benefit principle and justice principle. "State Allocation Theory" emphasizes on national interest, while "Market-oriented Theory" focuses on market functions, which reflects the interest appeal of capital market or prioritizing market mechanisms. "Social (Fiscal) Theory" stresses that public finance is used to serve society and social instrument, which extends public finance as the interest of the majority or represents the interest of all people with interest of the majority.

The fiscal activity has its own law, which is objective and beyond the will of human beings. Laws can serve different concepts. Meanwhile, the accomplishment of any concepts needs recognition, understanding and application of laws. From state allocation public finance to market-oriented public finance, and modern public finance, the variation shows the changes in fiscal concepts. This process is a development process of concept and it also manifests that concepts are diversified. For certain, there's an overlap between concepts and laws, but concepts are not laws. Concepts differ because in different nations and historic periods, appeals of different groups of people emerge. The practices of public finance are to recognize and apply the law of it so as to serve specific concepts. Nonetheless, we need to figure out what the law of public finance is so as to effectively apply it.

There is no doubt that an important normative question of researching fiscal theories is "what public finance should be", but it's not the whole picture of fiscal research. We can find the inner positive law of public finance and answer "What public finance is" only if we separate variant values from analysis or consider different values as exogenous variables.

b. Failure vs. evolution

Does public finance have its own evolution law? When we answer what public finance is or discuss the law of it, different conclusions come with different methods. "Fiscal evolution" and "market failure" are different ways of law cognition formed under different thinking frameworks. "Evolution" and "failure" can be interpreted as different concepts in a sense. However, from the perspective of finding rules or laws, one should note that "evolution" assumes that public finance has its own endogenous law of evolution, while "market failure" assumes public finance, whose existence and changes are pushed forward by the market, is an affiliation of the market, which is an exogenous factor. "Evolution" or "failure" can be regarded as an assumption that can be tested. The assumption of "failure" theory is independent of time and space, and the conclusion derived is an exclusive, static and cognitive optimal status. In contrast, "evolution" is connected with time and space with optimal statuses being diversified, dynamic, and incompletely cognitive. Correspondingly, we need an external force to solve failure. On the contrary, evolution is driven by inner capability. As described below, the difference between evolution and failure lies in whether we consider the inner transaction cost for improving fiscal evolution in the operation of mechanism.

Many economists have made assumptions to prove the effectiveness of a competitive market after Adam Smith put forward the market theory. Alternatively, failing to meet these assumptions induces "market failure", which defines the maximum space of government activities. From historical development point of view, the emergence of "Market-oriented (fiscal) Theory" may be inevitable. It emphasizes the nature of public finance as a market-oriented tool that serves the market with the assumption of binary context of either government or market. According to this theory, market economy is a form of organizing economy with the market playing the fundamental role in allocating resources. A competitive market is an efficient operation mechanism. Due to market defects such as the failure of market, maldistribution of income and economic fluctuations, it provides the basis for the necessity and justification of government interventions. However, the government functions are only limited to resolve problems as a remedy measure, and also to protect and influence the market. Therefore, the public finance mode that meets the demands of market economy is best described as remedy public finance.

After the Great Depression, some economists were busy at blaming the "market failure", while the others were criticizing the "government failure". James Buchanan believes that many decisions made by government cannot reflect the will of citizens in a democratic society and the defects of government are as severe as market's. He proposes that government, as a representative for public interest, should remedy deficiencies of market economy and provide services such that a better social effects is generated by the general public through rational decisions than what would have been the social welfare without government intervention. Otherwise, the existence of government will make no economic sense. The theory of "government failure" is the important fundamental theory that caused the New Public Management Movement in the 1980s. This movement regarded government as an "economic organization", and advocates "reforging" and "reshaping" the government with an approach of enterprises, so as to remedy the defects and shortcomings in government management.

The basic assumption of the Theory of Public Choice for solving "government failure" is that the market is effective. It intends to introduce the competition system of market into government organization. However, this assumption is flawed because the target of government is different from the target of market. In Ostrom's framework, society can be considered as another option under the circumstance of "market failure" and "government failure". This is very creative. But if we take the methodology of "failure" rather than "evolution", it may lead to a conclusion of "social failure". While looking back to basic fiscal theory and practices studies in China, Professor Li Junsheng[1][15] realized the inadequacy of market failure theory in explaining phenomena in the real world and took the lead in questioning the logic of market failure theory. He believes that market is a platform for transactions, which involves government, enterprises, individuals or society.

What's more important is that the "market failure" theory is based on "effective competitive market", implying an assumption that the transaction cost is zero and also the market is static. Given that the transaction cost is never zero, different conclusion will be drawn if one views the process of economic development and technological changes with a dynamic and evolutive method. Ronald Coase [16][17] believes, as long as the property rights are specific and transaction cost is zero or very low, the final outcome of market equilibrium will be effective and a Pareto Optimality of resource allocation can be achieved no matter whom the initial property rights are endowed with. Therefore, the effectiveness of market relies on the assumption of zero transaction cost for a matter of fact. However in the real world, defining the right is difficult and the transaction cost can't be zero or maybe even considerablely high. Once one considers non-zero transaction cost, the initial distribution of property right will exert influence on the operation of the economic system, thereby causing the market effectiveness and theoretical basis of public finance remedying market failure to be shaky.

How then can market evolution be promoted with transaction costs? Coase's idea shows a way of economic and social evolution based on defining the right. In market, transactions generate contract transaction costs. That cost is determined by equilibrium between market costs and costs of other alternative options, which may be optimized automatically through market. Social cost differs from market transaction costs in that it belongs to non-contract transaction costs that can't be optimized automatically through market. Further research on transaction costs mainly centers on incomplete contracting theory. To some extent, these theories describe an evolution mechanism of competition centering on lowering transaction cost within market, society and government on the basis of property right distribution.

Transaction Cost Economics points out that in human activities, the organizational form that is capable of adapting to new environments and lowering the transaction cost when compared with other forms, and thereby improving human development, will survive. The process of this change is the evolution of institutions [18]. The illustration of this idea within the context of state governance, is that governance structures of government, society and market compete and evolve on lowering the transaction cost. Substantially, zero transaction cost is the reason of market's effectiveness and derived optimality of mainstream fiscal theories, which is a special or extreme case of competition and evolution centering on transaction cost. For example, the emergence of firm replaces a mass of negotiations between employers and employees with a hierarchical and administrative governance form of production, organization and management. It lowers the transaction cost, which makes firm a commonly used form of organizing production. If the transaction cost were zero, every individual in the market would be self-employed. In the classic problem of pollution externality, the cost of negotiation through the market is much higher than the cost of setting up a government regulator. Therefore, it's much more common to let the government take charge of this problem as its function, rather than negotiation between participants involved as zero transaction cost theory would predict.

In general, the basis of evolution is independent operation and decision-making of the society, market and government. The changes of external environment are conditions inducing evolution. To market, government, society, etc., are external factors that may lead to new environments and new changes in market. However, such changes are self-correction and self-development generated from inner strength of the market mechanism. In the same way, government is also on its path of evolution. From the perspective of history, we can tell that the existence of government is of market-independent rather than market-dependent. The emergence of government is not a result of a remedy for "market failure", and it even comes into being before the existence of market. Thus government evolution is deemed to be inevitable. For certain, society, market and government can evolve forward constantly, but they may also degenerate. Research in literature indicates that right specification is the basis of evolution. Society, market and government may degenerate once the basis is undermined. This is why we emphasize on the rule of law for it being the basis of defining and protecting rights.

Now let's go back to the fundamental question of public finance. Supposedly public finance is a mandatory revenue and expenditure activity of government, and being mandatory may well be justified. But is it possible that public finance can create new values and evolve by itself? We need to think over the fundamental attribute of public finance to answer this question, i.e., distribution or exchange.

c. Distribution vs. Exchange

Can public finance create new values? The answer to this question defines the basic attribute of public finance. As an exchange relationship definitely creates new values and a distribution relationship might not be able to do so, the core question of studies on fiscal laws is to define public finance as a distribution relationship or an exchange relationship. Adam Smith stresses that supply and demand are generated from specialization of labor. Exchanges can constantly improve specialization of labor and promote economic development, while new values are also created in this process. However, exchange is not the only way of interaction between supply and demand. Government is also the result of labor specialization. From the perspective of public finance, though it's a supply and demand relationship of public services, it lacks adjustment of price mechanism and the government behaviors in general are mandatory, which makes it different from market exchanges. Furthermore, the government behavior can be exchange or distribution.

What relationship does public finance belong to? Distribution relationship or exchange relationship? The fundamental difference lies in individual interests. In an exchange relationship, interactions among different stakeholders are equal, with no reduction of interest for either one of them, i. e. , Pareto Improvement. Otherwise, they can stop exchanges. Pareto Improvement means an increase of total value of society, which points to an implicit meaning that public finance activities can create new values as an exchange relationship. In contrast, distribution relationship is totally different. It's a unidirectional behavior of stakeholders that's not based on equal interactions. The values are transferred from a part of people to the others with no imperative demands for creating new values. With the concept of class struggle, public finance can be easily defined as a distribution relationship that serves a particular class. From the perspective of social welfare, an exchange relationship is achieved by participants voluntarily. It must be Pareto Improvement and can definitely improve welfare. Distribution relationship contains transfer of wealth, but with the uncertainty of welfare improvement. In this sense, it's an important task for fiscal reform to make public finance an exchange relationship.

No matter what we expect public finance to be, or what we think it should be, public finance can be a distribution relationship or an exchange relationship, or it can be both. We need to understand with objectivity that such a relationship is inner and independent of our values. To understand this objectivity, we need to study its inner laws.

If we study from the perspective of laws, "market failure" theory assumes that government's target is serving market and takes "market efficiency" as a foundation, while the market mechanism essentially embodies the nature of exchange. With this logic, government finance behavior should ALL be exchange relationships. But this conclusion is not consistent with history and reality, which makes it inappropriate to consider the market failure theory as a fiscal law. Therefore, it's more appropriate to consider "market failure" as a concept rather than a law.

Putting value judgments aside, public finance is a mandatory revenue and expenditure activity of government, which can be manifested as a distribution relationship in one context and an exchange relationship in another. Therefore, it's necessary to define contexts and study the evolution of public finance in the course of context changes. We' ll explain this point through a simple theoretical model.

III. Theoretical Model

A voluntary transaction cannot be achieved without consent. Based on whether the contract is formal or informal, an exchange relationship can be either a contract or non-contract transaction. It should be noted that the voluntariness of any kind of exchange relationship should be guaranteed with options to withdraw. However, there are exit costs. Such costs need to be considered within market, government and social activities to make different strategies. The exit cost is also a decisive factor for determining whether public finance is of exchange or distributional nature.

a. Basic model

If we regard fiscal relationship as an exchange relationship, the result of exchanges must accord with Pareto Improvement. The following conditions need to be considered to realize Pareto Improvement. First, there's initial setting. The initial setting indicates an interest basis of participants. Without initial setting, there is no benchmark to refer to and it will be meaningless to consider Pareto Improvement, a concept of comparison. This is the basis of studying any fiscal questions. Second, individuals improve their own welfare by self-development and have achieved self-balance. This assumption is meant to distinguish the relationship between government and market. Government and market operates in their own fields and achieve equilibrium through inner mechanisms. When government interferes with market (or vice versa), the external environment or binding conditions of market mechanism will change, which eventually generates a new equilibrium. Third, the exit cost is above zero. This assumption is meant to distinguish the relationship between government and society. For natural person, the biggest difference between government and society is that the exit cost from mandatory government activities is much higher than it is from social activities. At this point, the most important part of transaction cost is the exit cost.

We built a simple model to explain how the exit cost influences the allocation of public resources. We assume there are 2 types of people, A and B. They adopt Nash bargaining on one project with complete information and the exit costs of A and B are denoted as $a \geqslant 0$ and $b \geqslant 0$, respectively. The net profit or gain (deducting transaction cost) is T. The decision-making process will ask A to put forward the plan, and then to negotiate with B.

We solve the problem with backward induction:

$$\max w = (x + a)(T - x + b)$$

where x is A's net gain and $T - x$ is B's net gain.

The equilibrium turns out to be:

$$x = \frac{T - (a - b)}{2}$$

$$T - x = \frac{T + (a - b)}{2}$$

This is a classic Nash Bargaining Solution, i. e. , both sides get equipartition of gains after adjustment of the exit costs.

Putting forward the plan by A means the following conditions need to be met:

$$x = \frac{T - (a - b)}{2} \geqslant 0$$

i. e. :

$$T \geqslant a - b$$

Proposition 1: If $a \geqslant b$, then$T^* \geqslant 0$, $T^* \in T$, and the equilibrium net social gains increase and Pareto Improvement can be realized.

Proof: We know

$$x = \frac{T - (a - b)}{2} \geqslant 0$$

If $a \geqslant b$, then for any $T^* \in T$

$$T^* \in T$$

and

$$T^* - x = \frac{T^* + (a - b)}{2} \geqslant 0$$

Obviously, new gains are generated from this result if compared with the case that this project isn't started. Owing to the basis of this transaction is that every individual gets new gains accordingly, everyone gets an increase in gains, i. e. , a realization of Pareto Improvement.

Proposition 2: If $a < b$, then there exists $T^* < 0$, $T^* \in T$, i. e. , a reduction of net social gains. Moreover, there exists $T^* - x < 0$, or the equilibrium cannot guarantee the realization of Pareto Improvement.

Proof: For $a < b$, there exists $0 > T^* \geqslant (a - b)$, and we have

$$T^* - x = \frac{T^* + (a - b)}{2} < 0$$

The result indicates that the difference of exit costs causes the advantage and disadvantage in the Nash Bargaining game. The side with low exit cost may use it as an advantage to cut down the gain of the other side with high exit cost, which leads to a result that final equilibrium is not a Pareto Improvement. Such transaction won't be concluded under the condition of no exit cost. There is a realization of such transition is because the exit cost that determines the threat point of the game is so high such that the underdog side may have no choice but to accept the transaction.

It should be noted that the side with the right to put forward plans will surely guarantee its own net gains when proposing. This is an advantage. The side with a high exit cost can be made up by gaining this advantage. This leads to the following proposition 3.

Proposition 3: If only the side with a high exit cost is entitled to put forward plans, then social net profits increase and Pareto Improvement can be realized by the transaction itself.

The proof is straightforward. $a \geqslant b$ and only A is entitled to put forward plans. Then the equilibrium must be Pareto Improvement.

This is a very interesting conclusion. Consider a world consisting of two types of individuals: the majority and the minority. Suppose the majority outnumbers the minority and the two groups hold competing interests. If the exit cost of the majority is higher than it is for the minority, then the society can realize Pareto Improvement automatically. If the majority has lower exist cost than that of the minority and the minority is entitled to put forward plans, then the equilibrium will realize Pareto Improvement automatically.

In reality, only the majority generally has the right to put forward plans. Whether the result is a Pareto Improvement is contingent on the exit cost of the majority and the minority. If we consider the formation of fiscal activities as a negotiation outcome of all participants (i. e., the majority and the minority in our model), and if the exit cost of the majority is higher than the exit cost of the minority, the formation will be an exchange relationship, i. e., the equilibrium must be Pareto Improvement. On the contrary, it will be distribution relationship, i. e., the profit will transfer from one to another. However, it's uncertain whether the distribution relationship is a Pareto Improvement.

b. A special case

Proposition 4: If $a = b$, no matter A represents the majority or the minority, then $T^* \geqslant 0$, $T^* \in T$, i. e., net social gains increase and equilibrium can realize Pareto Improvement automatically.

Proof: We know

$$x = \frac{T - (a - b)}{2} \geqslant 0$$

If $a = b$ then for any $T^* \in T$,

$$x = \frac{T^* - (a - b)}{2} = \frac{T^*}{2} \geqslant 0$$

i. e.

$$T^* \geqslant 0, T^* \in T$$

And

$$T - x = \frac{T^* + (a - b)}{2} = \frac{T^*}{2} \geqslant 0$$

In society, should it be the majority or the minority that is entitled to put forward plans? Under the uncertain circumstance, as long as exit costs are equal, the net social gains in equilibrium will increase for certain and automatically realize a Pareto Improvement. When there's a difference in exit costs between a and b, it's possible that net social gains will decrease and part of the people will be affected no matter who is the decision maker, the majority or the minority.

IV. Further interpretation

The above simple model can be extended to deduce the important role of exit cost in promoting fiscal evolution. In real life, government and society always interact with each other. Society plays an important role in some fields while government takes leads in others. In terms of the model, this is a result of influence caused by the exit cost. Interactions between government and society may cause changes of functions. We call this governmentalization of social functions or socialization of government functions. Correspondingly, the fiscal function evolves.

Where does the drive of evolution come from? Substantially, government, society and market are different forms of governance in different fields with advantages in relevant fields. The differences and changes in transaction cost may make certain existing governance forms less attractive because of its higher transaction costs. Therefore, other forms with low transaction costs will gradually become dominant and replace the original governance form. Such a course is reflected in the form of public finance, which is manifested as a fiscal evolution①. As one type of transaction cost, the purposefully modeled exit cost plays an important role in the course of evolution, which determines the threat point of Nash Bargaining. When the exit cost is high, a governance form won't be able to replace the original form even it has advantages in cutting down other transaction costs.

We will take the evolution of China's social security system in rural areas as an example to explain the importance of the exit cost. In the past, under the influence of planned economy, rural residents had to pay for medical treatment and old age support by themselves. But more often, they relied on their family or clan for a socialized security system. This is a socialized function. However, with the development of market economy, the restriction on household registers loosens, and population mobility is increasingly frequent. This system gradually evolves into a security system by government function, such as the new rural cooperative medical insurance. In fact, it's a typical embodiment of governmentalization of social functions. From the perspective of the model, with the system of planned economy, the government carried out restrictions on household registration for a long time, and free mobility of population was not allowed. The productivity of urban areas was not prominent compared with rural areas,

① It should be noted that evolution doesn't mean the expansion of fiscal system or government. It might be withdrawing of governmentalized organization form from certain fields because of its higher transaction cost and this is a shrink of government size.

which resulted in rural residents having to cling to lands. Under this circumstance, if two sides of the model are correspondingly rural residents and urban residents, the exit cost for rural residents will be very high. On one hand, the transaction in the above model is conducted without specific involvement of government; on the other hand rural residents also contribute to fiscal revenue at the same time, which implies an underlying distribution relationship of public finance rather than exchange relationship. When both sides are rural residents from the same family, exit costs are almost identical. And from the perspective of other transaction costs, the transaction costs generated from the addressing of mutual trust issues within a family insurance mechanism might be very low. In this case, when government were involved as a fiscal form, the social insurance mechanism would need to address trust issues among strangers, which makes it uncertain whether it will lower the transaction cost①. Therefore, it's normal that the governance form of social security is family-centered rather than government-dominated. The cooperation and exchange of such family-centered security system evolves inside of society, which is a Pareto Improvement for rural residents if compared with no security.

With social and economic development, the course of China's urbanization and industrialization lowers the exit cost remarkably. Household registration is not as strict as before. A lot of migrant workers work in urban areas and gradually become urban residents. Such increase of mobility lowers the exit cost, which makes exit costs for urban residents and rural residents convergent. When exit costs are converging, the transaction will be embodied as an exchange relationship rather than a distribution relationship. Reflected on public finance, it means government must distribute a part of net benefits of social security projects to rural areas to form a new equilibrium, which leads to the formation of a governmentalized social security system, i. e., the transfer of social function to government. For ur-

① Note: The gross transaction cost equals the sum of exit cost and other forms of transaction costs. When the exit cost is high, that accounts for a big part of transaction costs. Lowering costs of other transactions won't lower the gross transaction costs effectively. So the decisive factor is the difference of exit costs between two sides.

ban residents, this course is also a Pareto Improvement, because it will bring more labor forces and productivity when the government social security system covers rural areas. It will also bring more net profits with more gains being distributed to urban residents.

It should be noted that the main source of exit cost is mobility cost. From the perspective of the entire society, lowering the whole mobility cost will increase net social benefits, which makes it easier to form cooperative exchange relationships and create new values. The lowering of mobility cost is actually a development that puts people first. It might be a result of improvement of population quality. For example, residents with high skills and higher education have more options to choose their careers. Or it might be a result of gains from the institutional environment. For example, the relaxing of controls over household registration may offer more choices to residents. Therefore, if the fiscal system increases portability of public services (including pension system), it will lower the exit cost and promote the realization of Pareto Improvement. Consequently, public finance tends to be embodied as an exchange relationship.

To further explain the evolution of public finance, we study the realization of Pareto Improvement for dynamic processes of governmentalization of social functions and socialization of government functions based on the above model under various circumstances. Pareto Improvement can be realized automatically when it's just simple exchange, which is the most common circumstance in market. When it becomes cooperative relationship, there are different ways for Pareto Improvement. From the above model, we can tell there are two cases: $a = b > 0$, and $a = b = 0$. To meet the need of $a = b > 0$, it requires joint efforts of A and B to realize Pareto Improvement. When it's the case of $a = b = 0$, then A and B can realize Pareto Improvement separately by their own efforts. These two cases are different ways of social progress when we talk about governance and public finance.

We can understand the impact of differentiated transaction costs on differences in paths of fiscal evolution by comparing differences in governance and public finance between European countries and America. By comparing the government size between European countries (mainly continental countries) and America, we find that fiscal revenue accounts a bigger part of national income in European countries than it does in America. And the fiscal function of government is broader for European countries. Influenced by factors such as history, religion, culture, politics and economy, the exit cost of European residents is higher than it is for American residents since America is a country of immigrants. From the perspective of governance structure of government, the European government system, evolved from the historical system of enfeoffment, is constituted by general purpose governments, i. e. , the fief government (in history) provides all public services. If a resident quits from her current location, it means she will lose all public services provided by the government. For America, they adopt the model of a specific function government. One government is responsible for one specific public service (such as school districts or police agency) . Withdrawing from one public service doesn't mean the loss of all public services. So the exit cost of European residents is much higher, and consequently the resident mobility is higher in America. Such differences, in terms of the language adopted in the above model, make Europe more likely to be the case of $a = b > 0$ and America to be the case of $a = b = 0$. Now suppose that there's a negotiation on a social issue. If exit costs of both sides are different and above zero, the transaction might not be a Pareto Improvement. To promote the establishment of the transaction and realize Pareto Improvement, we can try to equal the transaction cost of both sides when the exit cost is high. This is the case in Europe where its fiscal practices emphasizing on bringing equality. If it's in America, because the exit cost is much lower, even nearly zero, transaction can be conducted between residents with similar transaction cost through mobility. It remains Pareto Improvement as long as the transaction is concluded. The intervention of fiscal means on the purpose of equality is not always necessary, and the two sides just need to negotiate with each other. At this point, public finance should play the role of guaranteeing the mobility to make sure that residents with similar transaction cost become transaction parties. Therefore, social organizations are well developed in America (such as self-initiated associations in various industries), i. e. , some projects that should be run by government in European countries are run by social organizations, which is an example of socialization of government function. This comparison indicates that differences in fiscal systems actually depend on transaction cost, especially the difference in exit costs, in which resident mobility plays an important role. This is essentially consistent with the idea of the Tiebout model[19].

The above model and following analysis are all based on a simple binary model. While in a pluralistic society, the heterogeneity of people's preference increases complexity of cooperation. Therefore, a fiscal system with equalization as its main objective is more challenged①. The core of analysis is that Pareto Improvement actually leads the evolution of systems: the fiscal systems vary because of differences of exit costs in the political, economic and social environment, but the evolution of fiscal systems serves to lower the transaction cost and form transactions of Pareto Improvement.

The way of fiscal evolution under different conditions share the same purpose, i. e. , to achieve human development and lower transaction costs. It's of great importance for promoting the development of China's modern fiscal system and realizing the modernization of national governance system and capabilities. Even with different ways, government and society interacts with each other through competition in adapting to and lowering transaction costs and exit costs, so as to realize the equality of basic human rights, improve factor mobility and achieve full development of human beings. The evolution of public finance in a pluralistic society enable people more equality of rights, which further lowers the transaction cost. On one hand, modern public finance requires the rule of law system that defines and protects human rights. This is the foundation of voluntary

① It means that government needs to be involved in more fields with more functions, which introduces more fields to be equalized.

exchanges. On the other hand, equal rights and lowering of transaction costs promote innovation, and stimulate social development, which are favorable to realize Pareto Improvement. At present, China has entered into the new era. What we face now is the contradiction between unbalanced and inadequate development and the people's ever-growing need for a better life, as well as the challenge of constrained factor mobility brought by the middle income trap and class solidification. In this new era, a vital role of the modern fiscal system is to equal social transaction costs, more importantly, to lower exit costs, to strengthen factor mobility, and to promote human and social development.

V. Conclusion

The theory of market failure is same as the theory of market efficiency. They all follow the logical presumption of zero transaction costs. When the transaction cost is zero, there are two subsets: market efficiency and market failure. This logical framework has the great advantage of analysis. It provides a strong static analysis tool, especially the basic framework of relationship between government and market. However, this framework is inherently defective. It doesn't tally with the real world because the transaction cost can't be zero. It also can't explain the dynamic changes of social economy because what it provides is static equilibrium.

In a general framework, if we consider the transaction cost as a variable, then market efficiency and market failure will be the extreme and special case of this framework. What's more important, we can explore the evolution laws of systems through changes of transaction costs. The transaction cost isn't just a specific concept of market exchanges, but a common concept for market, government and society. Transaction cost can be generated from mandatory cooperation of government or voluntary cooperation of society. It is the existence of transaction costs that causes the constant evolution of market, government and society, as well as encourages competition and development among them.

Transaction cost is essentially a function of human beings. It changes with human development, which leads to the evolution of market, government and society and also the adjustment of their relations. Fiscal evolution is a dynamic activity with the internal cause of public finance as its basis and the external causes such as market and society as its condition. The internal cause is driven by people's needs, whose basis is the definition of people's rights. This basis is not only a starting point, but also a measurement. It will be hard to measure development without this basis, not to mention progress. It's motivated by people's rights. The development of rights can be realized through distribution, violence, cooperation or exchange. Different ways are competing with each other centering on transaction costs. At the same time, they also generate different social welfare and economic development. The contradiction between improvement of social welfare and economic development can be unified through Pareto Improvement by making exchanges. Therefore, Pareto Improvement is not only a status, but also an automatic and self-generated force.

Since reform and opening up, China's economy has achieved great progress. China has grown from an underdeveloped country into an upper middle-income country. On one hand, China's development gives full play to the market. On the other hand, it fully embodies the function of government and society and takes advantage of institutions, which optimizes transaction costs with combined efforts from market, government and society. The development path with China's characteristics contributes to human development. Meanwhile, it should be noted that there's defectiveness accumulating, such as raising transaction costs of systems, social class solidification and the challenge of the middle income trap. The key to coping with these challenges and achieving sustainable development is to release new driving forces that are based on human development. The development and progress of human beings are not only a moral appeal or fiscal ethnics, but also an application of the law of fiscal evolution. To realize the unification of social welfare and economic development, we must strengthen the rule of law, guarantee people's rights, improve the skill of people, and develop people's productivity. These are also the missions of fiscal system in the new era.

References

[1] Li J. The Failure of "Anglo-Saxon" Theory and Reconstruction of Scientific Fiscal Theory—A Reflection on "Mainstream" Modern Fiscal Theory [J]. Economic Information, 2014 (4): 117-130.

[2] Li J. New Public Finance: A Paradigm for Enhancing Explanatory and Predictive Power [J]. Journal of Central University of Finance & Economics, 2017 (5): 3-11.

[3] Musgrave R A. The theory of public finance: a study in public economy [J]. Journal of Political Economy, 1959, 99 (1): 213-213.

[4] Buchanan J M, Tullock G. The Calculus of Consent [M]. University of Michigan Press, 1962.

[5] Ostrom E. Governing The Commons: The Evolution Of Institutions For Collective Action [M]. Cambridge University, 2012.

[6] Aoki M. Toward A Comparative Institutional Analysis [M]. MIT press, 2001.

[7] Besley T, Persson T. The origins of state capacity: Property rights, taxation, and politics [J]. American Economic Review, 2009, 99 (4): 1218-1244.

[8] Gao P. Theoretical Construction of Fundamental Fiscal Theory under the Framework of Governance Modernization [J]. Social Sciences in China, 2014 (12): 102-122+207.

[9] Liu J, Hou Z. Thoughts on Modern Fiscal System [J]. Journal of Political Science and Law, 2014 (2): 13-21.

[10] Qiao B, Liu L, Wu Z. Establishment of Modern Fiscal System: From Government Tools to Rule of Law Platform [A]. Essay Collection of Theoretical Innovation Seminar on "New Public Finance" Theory [C]. Beijing, 2016: 46-48.

[11] An T. Establishment of China's Public Finance [J]. Finance Research, 1999 (6): 1-6.

[12] Yu Z. Rule of Law System, China's Governance System [J]. Legal Forum, 2014, 29 (2): 5-12.

[13] Lou J. Deepening of Reform on Fiscal Taxation System and Establishment of Modern Fiscal System [J]. Qiushi Journal, 2014 (20): 24-27.

[14] James M. Buchanan. Li berty, markets and the State [M]. Harvester Press, 1988.

[15] Li J, Yao D. Exploration on The Nature and Supply Modes of Internet Search—An Analysis Based on New Public Finance [J]. Management World, 2016 (8): 1-15.

[16] Coase R H. The nature of the firm [J]. Economica, 1937, 4 (16): 386-405.

[17] Coase R H. The Problem of Social Cost [J]. Journal of Law & Economics, 1960, 3 (4): 1-44.

[18] Tadelis S, Williamson O E. Transaction cost economics [M]. The Handbook of Organizational Economics. Princeton University Press, 2012.

[19] Tiebout C M. A Pure Theory of Local Expenditures [J]. Journal of Political Economy, 1956, 64 (5): 416-424.

当代财政学理论创新：必要性及其方向*

马 珺

摘　要： 本文以“财政是国家治理的基础和重要支柱”这一理论命题的提出为背景，探讨了当代财政学理论创新的必要性、可资借鉴的思想资源，就实现理论创新的方向和研究工作提出建议。文章还简单论述了财政学理论创新对中国财政制度改革的含义。

关键词： 财政学　思想资源　理论创新

［**中图分类号**］F810　［**文献标识码**］A

寻求一个好的国家治理模式，是人类社会面临的基本问题，《中共中央关于全面深化改革若干重大问题的决定》（以下简称《决定》）提出“财政是国家治理的基础和重要支柱”这一理论命题，为中国财政学基础理论建设提供了新的机遇、注入了新的活力。如何全面、历史地理解“财政是国家治理的基础和重要支柱”，并确立一个能够胜任“国家治理的基础和重要支柱”的现代财政制度，作为一个重大的理论和实践问题，被推到财政理论界的面前。本文拟就新的时代背景下当代财政学理论创新的必要性和方向做一论述。

* 基金项目：2014年度国家社会科学基金重大项目（第二批）“公共经济学理论体系创新研究”（14ZDB121）；中国社会科学院基础研究学者资助项目（2014—2018）“财政学：历史、发展及在中国的传播”。

［作者简介］：马珺，中国社会科学院财经战略研究院研究员，博士生导师；主要研究方向：财政思想史、财政税收理论与政策。

一、实现理论创新是当代财政学人的历史使命

习近平在2016年5月召开的哲学社会科学工作座谈会上的讲话中，向广大哲学社会科学工作者提出了以马克思主义为指导，开拓创新，加快构建中国特色哲学社会科学体系的历史任务。他指出，“当代中国正经历着我国历史上最为广泛而深刻的社会变革，也正在进行着人类历史上最为宏大而独特的实践创新”，哲学社会科学工作者应该“立时代之潮头、通古今之变化、发思想之先声，积极为党和人民述学立论、建言献策，担负历史赋予的光荣使命”①。

在众多哲学社会科学门类中，财政学理论创新的任务尤为迫切。自改革开放以来，财税体制改革一直扮演着改革先行者的角色，或通过国家财政的“放权让利”，积极为其他领域改革创造条件；或通过政府角色的规范与归位，引领整个中国经济体制改革进程。同期财政理论关于政府职能定位及其与市场关系的深入研究，发挥了“知识变革和思想先导”的作用，为我国经济体制改革的顺利推进提供了有力的理论支撑。然而，最近十余年以来，主流财政理论囿于单一的经济学视角和对资源配置问题的过度关注，导致其对变化环境中各项具体改革及国家制度变革的理论支持相对走弱，在某些方面的影响力已明显落后于法学、社会学等邻近学科。这一现象背后的主要原因在于，迄今为止中国财政学界在“财政学应当研究什么”，以及如何进行研究等事关学科发展的基本问题上，未能与时俱进、推陈出新，导致理论研究在很多方面不仅未能起到引领和推动作用，甚至跟不上财政改革实践的进展，很多财政学研究限于单纯地跟随和阐释现行政策。

当前中国的改革进程已进入依靠经济体制改革单兵突进难以奏效的阶段，必须走全面深化改革之路，才能实现国家治理体系和治理能力现代化的改革总目标。《决定》提出的“财政是国家治理的基础和重要支柱”这一命题，放弃了此前将财政视为单纯资源配置手段的主流观念，将财政与国家治理相联系，这一源于中国改革实践的理论洞察，明显超越了此前主流理论对财政学学科属性的认知，是对过去千百年来人类思想史上国家理论与财政思想的高度提炼与

① 参见2016年5月17日习近平《在哲学社会科学工作座谈会上的讲话》，http://politics.people.com.cn/n1/2016/0518/c1024-28361421-2.html。

精确概括，不仅对全面深化改革的各项实践起到政策纲领的作用，更具有高度的理论创新性。广大财政理论工作者应当以此为契机，反思过去在教学、研究范式方面的不足，坚持问题导向、立足中国实际，融合人类历史上一切先进的思想文化成果，致力于推进财政学研究的理论创新[1]。

二、财政学理论创新可以借鉴的思想资源

财政学界究竟能否很好地回答这个问题，首先要看我们拥有哪些可资借鉴的思想资源。概括而言，现有的思想资源大致可划分为以下几类。

一是源自苏联的“苏式财政学”。苏式财政学看重对“国家本质”与“财政本质”问题的追问，强调财政作为阶级斗争工具及其在国家政权建设与维护上的作用，其教学内容则注重为计划经济下的财政实务部门培养技术人才。苏式财政学虽然触及了财政在国家治理中的作用及如何发挥作用的问题，但其提供的答案被实践证明不能令人满意。改革开放以后，中国国家建设的思路从以阶级斗争为纲，转向以经济建设为中心，经济发展模式从社会主义计划经济向有中国特色的社会主义市场经济转型。与此同时，与计划经济体制相适应的“苏式财政学”式微，而与社会主义市场经济体制相适应的“公共财政学”兴起。财政理论的转型有其经济和政治基础，但是这一转型的一个负面效果却为当时几乎所有的理论家所忽略，即，随着苏式财政学的退出，其所内涵的对“财政与国家治理”问题的关注也遭到忽略，此后的中国财政学研究基本上都围绕如何应对资源配置的市场失灵问题而展开。

二是经典意义上的“马克思主义”财政学以及各种西方马克思主义。马克思本人在其政治经济学著作中阐述了国家、税收、公债等财政问题，为建立马克思主义财政学奠定了基础，马克思生前也曾拟将国家（财政）理论作为资本主义经济制度研究的组成部分，但在其有生之年并未达成此愿。其后继者以及各种西方马克思主义者也同样地没有建立完整的财政学说。对苏式财政学的反思与抛弃，产生了一个未被充分预见的副产品，经典意义上“马克思主义”财政学研究因此被蒙上了阴影，导致这一研究方向也随之淡出主流财政学者的视线，从而使今天的财政学研究失去了一个借以从事比较与批判分析的对比视角。

三是中国文化及历史传统中的财政思想。中国历史上有丰富的财政思想，

诸如“量入以为出”“量出以计入”“使民以时”“寓禁于征”“善政得民财，善教得民心”“藏富于民”“休养生息”等；更有大量的治国之术，如“治大国若烹小鲜”“为政以德，譬如北辰，居其所而众星拱之”“政之所兴，在顺民心；政之所废，在逆民心”“民惟邦本，本固邦宁”等，不一而足。这些优秀的思想遗产虽然寓意隽永、源远流长，却因有失现代科学研究所要求的逻辑性与系统性，从而与系统的、学科意义上的财政学研究无缘。与之对应的数千年的王朝财政实践，虽可为现代国家治理下的财政运行提供借鉴，却不足以为现代国家所效法实践。

四是交易范式财政学。该范式源于欧洲大陆财政思想，20 世纪中期以来，经诺贝尔经济学奖得主詹姆斯·布坎南等人之手得以整合、复兴。在这一研究范式中，国家不是仁慈的、全知全能的抽象集体利益的代表，而被理解为社会成员交易互动的总合结果，它既非行动主体，也非特定组织，而是内生于经济社会秩序之中的交易“过程”，它一旦形成，则又构成社会成员交往互动的规则和平台[2][3]。个人作为活跃在社会生活舞台上的主角，他们为自身及其团体的利益而行动，探求使双方或各方都能从中受益的公共问题解决原则与方案，从而使“治理”一词又回到了经济学和财政学的中心。正因为如此，作为一个过程、平台、规则框架，对国家行为的评价只能以是否“公平正义”为最终标准，而不是“社会福利最大化”[4]。后者注重的是结果是否有效率，前者则强调过程是否公正，原因在于，如果失去了社会互动过程中的公平正义，所谓的社会福利最大化往往化为一些人侵犯其他人利益的借口。然而，当代交易范式财政学在 20 世纪 60 年代之后，并未对财政学主流理论产生应有的影响，特别是其所主张的主观自我和个体主义方法论，并未能根本性地影响主流财政学的发展方向。

五是英美主流财政学。当代英美主流财政学确立于第二次世界大战结束之后，它强调国家的非生产性，以及有机主义国家观念，又被称为“配置范式的财政学”。它接纳了经济学研究向科学化、形式化和实证主义的转变，从而落实了财政学作为新古典经济学应用分支的学科定位。作为新古典经济学在财政领域的应用，它关注政府的微观功能，即个体如何对政府干预做出反应[5][6]。经济学家依据对个体反应的科学研究和特定的规范标准，提出政府影响资源配置和收入分配的政策建议，历史上曾经主导财政学研究的国家和社会治理问题，就此退出了财政学研究的视域。

上述各类财政学思想源流中，当前在中国唯一彰显的是英美主流财政学传统。英美主流财政学的引入与普及，使中国财政学研究整体性地向科学化、技术化和形式化方向深入。20 世纪 70 年代以来，英美财政学研究的实证和应用取向明显，也带动了“财政与国家治理”关系问题，以及国家治理问题本身从中国财政学者研究视域内消失。

然而，将“治理”这一关键词搁置一旁，则无以理解财政作为一种制度体系应当如何发挥其作为国家治理的基础和重要支柱的作用，仅仅依靠这一传统所提供的学术资源，显然无以回应上述重大理论命题。对于那些进入稳态社会的发达国家而言，其财政学者遵循配置范式、埋首于既定制度框架下的技术配置细节尚可以理解，而中国仍处于转型阶段，重要领域的制度建设尚未完成，中国的财政学要对未来国家制度建设做出贡献，研究者有必要认识到并注意克服上述缺陷。

遗憾的是，财政学在中国的发展虽历经百余年，却仍在“财政学应当研究什么”以及如何研究等事关学科发展的基本问题上无法达成共识，甚至已经不自觉地产生了观点和立场分化。财政学者相互间各言其是、缺乏对话的现状，成为未来财政学理论创新的最大现实障碍。这一背景足以引起我们思考，我们应当以一种怎样的态度来面对中西方历史上以及当下的全部思想资源，以便既能够确立中国财政学术研究的主体性和独立性，又能包容和涵盖古今中外的学术智慧，以利未来开拓创新？针对这一问题所能给出的答案，不仅事关财政学科的未来，亦与当下国家治理的各项制度建设息息相关，亟待财政学者搁置己见并相互倾听，以在财政学的创新方向和创新之路上达成必要的共识。

三、财政学研究如何实现理论创新：建议及方向

（一）几点建议

近年来，随着对英美主流财政学研究范式学习和应用的不断深入，也产生了对其展开反思的内在需求。推动财政学界系统性地对此展开研究的事件，正是《决定》对财政作为国家治理的基础和重要支柱的官方定位。这一定位促使财政学者整体性地重新审视主流研究范式中的财政学研究对象和研究方法，以及财政学在中国近百年来的发展。本文认为，只有立足中国历史与现实，并融

会中西方的相关思想资源，方能避免以偏概全，并对这一论题给出中肯而系统的回应。为此，本文提出如下建议。

1. 认真研究西方财政理论，指出其合理成分及适用条件，以为我所用。

财政学首先是一种社会理论。它与其他社会科学，如政治学、法学、社会学一样，分享着一个共同的研究主题，即社会是如何可能的。具体地说，彼此分立着的个体如何以各方均能认可的方式组成社会，并以公平的方式分享合作收益和分担合作成本，这是全部社会科学（也包含财政学）所要处理的主题。因而，财政学的研究对象，既应包含对物的研究，即对稀缺条件下社会资源有效配置的研究；也应包含对人的行动及人际互动关系的研究，即人们以怎样的方式来面对和解决稀缺性和社会秩序问题。当代西方主流财政理论专注于前者（配置问题），而极大地忽略了后者（治理问题）。在采纳其科学研究方法的同时，我们要认识到财政学还应当扩展研究的视野，关注更广义的“治理”问题，此其一。其二，在引入西方财政学教学与研究资源的过程中，我们应当全面、客观、公正地对待西方财政理论成就，避免以偏概全。在学习和应用配置范式财政学的基础上，也应深入研究吸收交易范式财政学的合理成分，使之互相补充，为国家治理背景下的财政理论与实践服务。

2. 对苏式财政学系统纠正。

苏式财政学对国家治理问题的关注有其合理成分，然而，其所主张的治理模式却不能适应现代国家治理的需要，特别是其政治上讲阶级对立与专政、经济上讲统制与计划的立场，在阶级矛盾已经不再是社会主要矛盾的今天，已经不宜继续用作指导国家财政实践的理论基础。当前，我国社会主要矛盾已转化为人民日益增长的美好生活需要和不平衡不充分发展之间的矛盾，在这一新的时代背景下，社会主义和谐社会和现代国家的建立，客观上需要一种基于道德上平等的社会成员之间的合法互动、交易、共享的合作型财政理论，应警惕主张斗争、强制、剥夺的苏式财政学借弘扬马克思主义经济学之名起死回生。习近平《在哲学社会科学工作座谈会上的讲话》中提到，马克思主义最可贵的精神品质就是要有批判精神，对于被证明为错误了的历史实践，财政学者应敢于真实面对、客观承认，对相关理论上的错误应进行系统纠偏，以正视听。

3. 对改革开放以来的财政学术实践认真总结，立足国情，拿出创新成果。

改革开放以后，中国财政学者在放弃苏式财政学的基础上，一度热心于创建具有中国本土特色的财政学理论体系。随着老一代本土学人逐渐退出，新一代具有海外教育背景的学者加入，自20世纪90年代中后期以来，创建具有中国本土特色财政学理论体系的理论热情已日趋低落。由于这一波留学归国学者的教育背景几乎清一色师承英美主流经济学传统，大规模引入西方主流财政学教育资源一时间蔚为风尚，进入21世纪之后，财政学在中国出现了配置范式一统天下的格局。

向西方主流财政学研究范式靠拢，加速了中国财政学研究国际化的进程，促使中国财政学教学在短短十余年中，迅速拉近了与英美主流财政学教学、研究模式的距离，无论是课程设置、教材选用、研究主题选择，还是研究的科学化、实证化、应用化方面，都取得了前所未有的进步。但不可否认的是，西学引进的过程中出现了偏向英美传统而忽视欧陆传统的倾向，学术引进的片面性也造就了今日中国财政学主流的单一性。同时，来自发达国家学术示范的压力，进一步导致了对中国既有学术传统、学术资源以及学术努力的漠视。其后果是，财政学界多注重拿来主义，忽视为我所用，注重模仿与学习，忽视比较与批判，以至于多年来少有针对西方财政传统的分梳、鉴别，更少有兼顾中国学术传统和中国国情的创新性成果。

习近平在讲话中强调中国哲学社会科学研究要有主体性和原创性。他强调，对于哲学社会科学我们的正确态度应当是，“批判地接受我们自己的历史遗产和外国的思想”“既反对盲目接受任何思想也反对盲目抵制任何思想”，强调“我们中国人必须用我们自己的头脑进行思考，并决定什么东西能在我们自己的土壤里生长起来。”财政实践事关社会与国家治理，社会和国家都不是机器，财政学除了在数目字管理方面要强调技术性和科学性，它更是一门有关社会公务事务如何处理的学问，而社会不是一部可以任意调试的机器，每个社会成员的选择都会对最终结果产生影响。接地气的财政学需要对人、人的行动以及人类行动所遵循的制度、历史和文化进行研究，在这个意义上，财政学的研究既有其一般性、科学性的一面，也有其特殊性、历史性的一面。

（二）财政学理论创新的方向

相对于其他经济学科，财政学在国内的发展是滞后的，不仅滞后于国际学术发展的步伐，也同样滞后于财政改革实践的步伐。改革开放以来，财政学研究虽有重大进展，但是跟随和模仿国外的研究较多，创新和发展包含中国经验的研究较少；研究工具方面取得的进步较大，而思想、思维创新的进步较小；财政学研究取得的进步大，而财政学教学，特别是本科教学取得的进步小。将财政定位于国家治理的基础和重要支柱，抓住了财政活动的本质，超越了主流财政学界对于财政学学科性质的认识。财政学界应抓住这一契机，推动新的历史条件下财政学基础理论的创新。

第一，研究对象的转向。财政学在本质上是一门关于社会如何构成和国家如何治理的学问，它研究社会成员在特定的历史、政治、经济、文化等环境下，如何通过交往互动而实现有序、正义的公共治理[7]，因此财政学研究不应自设边界，将研究对象定位于收入、支出、平衡、管理等狭义财政问题。我们主张放大财政学研究的视界，由以单纯的资源配置问题为中心，转向以广义治理问题为中心，由于后者的研究范围足以囊括前者，因此这一转向并不意味着放弃配置范式。财政学者应该建立起自己的专业自信，坚持问题导向的研究，避免把财政学矮化为英美新古典主流经济理论的应用分支，不要把财政系办成一个个的“小经济系”。

财政学研究对象的转向，有助于推动探索公平、有效的公共事务治理机制。自 20 世纪 70 年代以来，世界各国涌现了各种有关公共事务治理机制的创新尝试，探索市场和社会机制在公共治理中的作用与限度，最近若干年来，中国财政政策实践正逐步尝试引入相关理念。研究对象的转向，也有利于吸收和借鉴国际经验，探索政府、市场和社会三种治理机制间的合理关系，实现政治秩序、市场活动和社会机制的平衡，为“加强和创新社会治理，推进社会治理精细化，构建全民共建共享的社会治理格局”服务。

第二，研究范式的多元化。在主流研究范式之外，被财政理论界长期忽视的“交易范式”值得认真总结借鉴。这一研究范式将每个社会成员作为社会舞台上的主角，研究社会成员为自身及其团体的利益而采取行动、通过商谈、妥协与合作，探求使各方均可从中受益的公共问题解决原则与方案，从而将“治理”一词重新置于财政学研究的中心。在这一研究范式下，财政活动不再被看作是政府对社会经济的外部干预，而被看作为内生于社会成员自主实施的交易过程。政府在其中的职责，将由直接推动结果公正，转向致力于打造公正的交易规则与平台，并以程序公正推动结果公正。

研究范式的转型，有利于推动形成多中心的治理结构。传统财政理论以单一行政中心的层级结构作为隐含的制度背景，政策上注重寻求在决策者看来唯一的最优模式，忽略了社会成员个体的主动性、积极性和参与性。而现实生活中的公共治理问题，绝大多数都是地区性和群体性而非全国性的，它们要求一种扁平化的、多中心的治理结构与之匹配。财政学研究的交易范式为此提供了另一种理论选择，它假定社会成员在既定的法律规则下，通过自主商谈和契约，决定公共事务的具体处理办法。财政学研究从最优化的配置范式向交易范式的转型，既体现了公共经济的受益原则，也反映了公共治理“人人参与、人人尽力、人人享有”的内在要求，有利于在比较制度分析的基础上发现行之有效的制度安排。

第三，研究视角和方法的多样性。英美主流财政学中科学主义和形式主义的盛行，从一个侧面反映了其对财政学学科属性的认识偏误，即将财政学等同于自然科学。假如社会是一部机器，假如财政学是自然科学，那么采取拿来主义，从科学主义、形式主义盛行的西方主流财政学界引进新的研究方法和研究技术，未必不是正确的选择。然而，财政实践事关社会与国家治理，事关人类如何在真实社会中处理好相互间的关系，如何化解冲突、实现合作，在有序的社会结构中达成各自的目标，并围绕这一目标规划财务安排。主流财政学虽然形式规范，但研究主题狭窄，研究对象单一，研究方法不足以适应人类财政行为的复杂性。

面对现代社会越来越分立的知识体系，财政学研究者应始终保持谦逊之心，认识到财政学研究必须能够包容不同的研究视角、研究方法和研究工具。有学者因此主张恢复财政学的跨学科研究传统，反对因追求科学化和形式化而损害对人类复杂财政行为的实际认知[8][9][10][11][12]，主张从对科学主义的依赖，走向包含制度和历史分析的多元方法论。未来财政学要在构建全民共建共享的社会治理格局方面发挥作用，财政学研究应更多地面对人本身，加强对人、人的行动以及人类行动所遵循的制度、历史和文化的研究，通过更好地理解人类及其行为，构建具有激励相容特征、符合长期效率要求的、正义的财政制度。

第四，坚持中国财政学研究的主体性。中国财政学研究的主体性，要求我们面对形形色色的研究传统和研究方法，既要做到不迷失自己，还要力争有所创新。作为一种外来的学科体系，在学术研究国际化已成潮流的今天，如何平衡本土问题意识与学术研究国际化之间的张力，始终是财政学研究必须面对的抉择。在今天的国际经济学界，国际化几乎就是科学化和形式化的代名词。此种形势下，中国的财政学研究如何做到既能融入国际学术界，同时又保有对自身问题及解决方式的独立判断，塑造和维护学术主体意识，在很大程度上取决于财政学者自己的选择，取决于我们如何面对已有的思想资源，进而做出取舍。这一选择既事关财政学学科的发展，也必然对当下国家治理的各项制度建设产生影响。它决定了未来中国财政学研究能否承担起为新的治理理论和治理战略提供有用的知识资源，并启发民智和增进社会共识。

财政学研究主体性要求保持学术研究从实践中来而又要高于实践，切实起到厘清和引领先进的公共治理理念的作用，而不是止于对财政实践和政策的简单追随与解读。当代财政学者应立足中国历史与现实，并融会中西方的相关思想资源，辨析其各自的合理成分及适用条件，在不断推进理论创新的基础上，推动财政税收制度创新，为建立健全现代财政税收制度、实现全面深化改革的总目标贡献智慧。

参考文献

［1］马珺．以理论创新推动财政体制改革［N］．经济日报，2016-10-28（14）．

［2］BUCHANAN J. M. What Should Economists Do?［J］Southern Economic Journal，Vol. 30，No. 3，Jan. 1964，213-222.

［3］WAGNER R. E. Fiscal Sociology and the Theory of Public Finance：An Exploratory Essay［M］. Cheltenham，UK：Edward Elgar Publishing，2007.

［4］曾军平．财政理论的重构：以公平规则的探索为主题［A］．马珺，高培勇．国家治理与财政学基础理论创新［C］．北京：中国社会科学出版社，2017.

［5］ROSEN H. S. Public Finance：Essay for the Encyclopedia of Public Choice［D/OL］. Center for Economic Policy Studies Working Papers，No. 80，Princeton University，2002.

［6］FELDSTEIN M. The Transformation of Public Economics Research：1970—2000［J］. Journal of Public Economics，Vol. 86，No. 3，2002，319-326.

［7］马珺．布坎南财政思想中的国家治理理论［J］．财政研究，2016（12）：28-37.

［8］刘守刚，刘雪梅．财政研究的政治学路径探索［J］．江苏教育学院学报（社会科学），2010（03）：66-68.

［9］刘守刚．探索作为学科的“财政政治学”［A］．马珺，高培勇．国家治理与财政学基础理论创新［C］．北京：中国社会科学出版社，2017.

［10］刘志广．财政社会学与财政学基础理论创新框架［A］. 马珺，高培勇．国家治理与财政学基础理论创新［C］. 北京：中国社会科学出版社，2017.

［11］李炜光．财政何以为国家治理的基础和重要支柱［J］. 法学评论，2014（02）：54－60.

［12］高培勇．论中国财政基础理论的创新——由“基础和支柱说”说起［J］. 管理世界，2015（12）：4－11.

Theoretical Innovation of Modern Public Finance Researches: Its Necessity and Direction

Ma Jun

Abstract: This article discusses the necessities of the theoretical innovation of modern public finance against the setting that "public finance serves as the base and an important polar of state governance" as a theoretical proposition was put forward by the Central Committee of Chinese leading party. It also lists intellectual resources that can be used for references and gives suggestions on the directions in implementing such theoretical innovation. The implications of public finance theoretical innovation on fiscal reform are simply mentioned as well.

Keywords: Public finance Intellectual resources Theoretical innovation
CLC number: F810 Document code: A

Seeking a good governance model is the basic problem facing the human society. "the important decisions on major issues about comprehensively deepening the reform made by the central committee of the communist party of China" (hereinafter referred to as "decision") has put forward that "finance is the foundation and pillar of governance", which has provided basic theoretical foundation of China's public finance with a new opportunity and has injected new vitality in it. How to make a comprehensive and historical understanding of why "finance is the basis and pillar of governance" and establish a modern fiscal system qualified for "the basis and pillar of governance" has been pushed to the front of financial theory circle as an important theoretical and practical problem. This paper aims to elaborate the necessity and direction of public finance theory under the new era.

I. Theoretical innovation is the historical mission of contemporary public finance Scholars

In his speech at the symposium on philosophy and social science held in May 2016, Xi Jinping proposed to the general philosophical and social scientists the historical task of exploration and innovation under the guidance of Marxism and accelerating the construction of the philosophy and social science system with Chinese characteristics. He pointed out that "contemporary China is undergoing the most extensive and profound social transformation in the history of our country, and it is also carrying out the most ambitious and unique practical innovation in human history." The philosophical and social scientists should "stand in the forefront of the time, understand the changes through ancient and modern times, make first signs of thoughts, actively make new theories and offer advice and suggestions for the party and the people, and shoulder the glorious mission entrusted by history"①.

Among the various philosophical and social science, the task of innovation in fiscal theory is particularly urgent. Since the reform and opening up, the fiscal and taxation system reform has always played a pioneering role, either through the "decentralization and profit sharing" of the state finance and actively created conditions for other areas of reform, or through the standardization and the right positioning of the role of the government to lead the entire Chinese economic system reform process. During the same period, the in-depth study on the orientation of government functions and the relationship between the government and the market played a role of "knowledge change and ideological leadership", which provided a strong theoretical support for China's economic system

① Turn to Xi Jinping's Speech at the Symposium on Philosophical and Social Sciences on may 17, 2016, http: //politics. people. com. cn/121/2016/0518/C1024 - 28361421 - 2, html.

reform. However, over the past decade or so, the mainstream fiscal theory has been paralyzed by a single economic perspective, and excessive attention has been paid to the issue of resource allocation. As a result, its theoretical support for various specific reforms and national institutional reform in a changing environment has been relatively weakened, and its influence in some areas obviously lags behind the law and sociology. The main reason behind this phenomenon is that Chinese public financial academics has so far failed to keep up with the time and make innovations on basic issues related to the development of this discipline, such as "What should public finance study?" and how to do these research. Thus, the theoretical study has not only failed to play a leading role in many aspects, but have also failed to keep pace with the progress of fiscal reform. Many fiscal studies have been limited to simply follow and interpret existing policies.

At present, China's reform has entered a stage where relying on economic system reform alone can hardly be effective. It must take the road of comprehensively deepening reform in order to realize the overall goal of modernization of the state governance system and governance capacity. The "Decision" put forward the proposition that "public finance is the foundation and pillar of national governance." It gave up the prevailing notion that public finance is a simple way of resource allocation and linked public finance with national governance. This theoretical insight originated from China's reform practice has clearly surpassed the previous mainstream theory 's understanding of the nature of this discipline, and it is a highly refined and accurate summary of the national theory and fiscal thought in the history of human thought over the past thousand years. It acts as policy framework for all the practices of comprehensive and in-depth reform and has high degree of theoretical innovation. The financial theoreticians should take this as an opportunity to reflect on the deficiencies in the teaching and research paradigms in the past, persist in problem-based mind, base themselves upon China's reality, integrate all advanced ideological and cultural achievements through human history, and commit themselves to advancing theoretical innovation in fiscal research[1].

II. Ideological resources that can be borrowed for theoretical innovation of public finance

Whether the Chinese public financial academics can perfectly answer this question is based on which ideology resource can we borrow. Broadly speaking, the existing ideological resources can be categorized into the following types:

The first is Soviet-style public finance established in Soviet Union. The Soviet-style finance valued the questioning of the "essence of a state" and the "essence of public finance", and emphasized that public finance is a tool of class struggle and its function in the construction and maintenance of state power; its teaching content mainly focuses on training technical talents for fiscal department guided by planned economy. Although the Soviet-style finance has touched issues like the role of finance in national governance and how to play its role, the answers it provided have been proved by practice to be unsatisfactory. Since the reform and opening up, China's national construction has shifted from taking the class struggle as the guideline to focusing on economic construction, and the economic development model has shifted from a socialist planned economy to a socialist market economy with Chinese characteristics. At the same time, the "Soviet-style finance" that fit in with the planned economic system showed its weakness, and the "public finance" that adapts to the socialist market economic system rose. The transformation of fiscal theory has its economic and political foundation, but one negative effect of this transformation was ignored by almost all theorists at that time, that is, with the withdrawal of "Soviet-style finance", concerns about the issue of "public finance and national governance" was also ignored, and China's fiscal studies after that only focused on how to deal with the market failure in resource allocation.

The second is the classical "Marxist" public finance and various Western Marxism. Marx himself elaborated some fiscal issues such as the state, taxation, public debt, etc. in his political economic work, which laid the foundation for the establishment of Marxist finance. Marx had also planned to use the national (fiscal) theory as part of the study of the capitalist economic system before his death, but he did not achieve it during his lifetime. His successors and iwestern Marxists failed to establish a complete fiscal theory, either. The reflection and abandonment of the "Soviet-style finance" has produced an unforeseen by-product, and the study of classical Marxist finance has been overshadowed. Thus, this research direction faded from the sights of mainstream fiscal scholars and this caused a miss of comparative and critical perspective of today's fiscal studies.

The third is fiscal ideology in Chinese culture and historical tradition. There are abundant fiscal thoughts throughout Chinese history, such as "measure expenditure based on income" "make taxation according to expenditure" "make use of labor according to the farming season" "to prohibit some actions against social development by heavy tax" "good rules can bring people's wealth and good teaching can bring people's hearts" "leave the wealth among people" "to make a better life for people and accumulate wealth for the society" and so on; there are also numerous statecrafts, such as "govern a large nation is like cooking small fishes and the governor should do nothing that goes against the nature", "one should govern a nation by morality and people will respect and support the governor just like all the stars surround and protect the Polestar", "efficient political power comes from people's satisfaction while inefficient power is due to people's discontent", "People is the foundation of the country, and the country will be safe if the foundation is firmed" and so on and so forth. Although these excellent heritages of thoughts are meaningful and have a long history, they are not embraced by the systematic and disciplinary public finance for its lack of logicality and systematisms required by modern scientific research. Although the fiscal practice over thousands of years can provide reference for the fiscal operation under modern governance, it is not applicable enough for modern countries.

The fourth is trading paradigm public finance. This paradigm originated from European continent fiscal thinking and was integrated and rejuvenated by the Nobel Prize for economy winner, James Buchanan since 1950s. In this research paradigm, the state is not a representative of the benevolent, omniscient and omnipotent abstract collective interests, but the overall result of the trading and interaction of social members. It is neither an action subject nor a specific organization, but is a "process" endogenous to the economic social order. Once formed, it will then constitute the rules and platform of social interaction between members[2][3]. Individuals act as protagonists on the stage of social life. They act for the interests of themselves and their groups. They seek out principles and methods for solving public problems that can benefit each party, thus making the term "governance" back to the center of economics and public finance again. Because of this, as a process, a platform, and a framework of rules, its assessment of state behavior should only take "fairness and justice" as the final criterion, rather than "the maximization of social welfare"[4]. The latter focuses on whether the results are efficient, while the former emphasizes the fairness of the process. The reason is that if the fairness and justice in the process of social interaction are lost, the so-called maximization of social welfare often turns into an excuse for some people to infringe on the interests of others. However, the contemporary trading paradigm finance did not have influence on the mainstream theory of public finance after the 1960s. In particular, its advocate of the subjective and self-individualist methodology has not fundamentally affected the development direction of the mainstream theory.

The fifth is the Anglo-American mainstream public finance. The contemporary mainstream Anglo-American finance was established after the end of the Second World War. It emphasizes the non-productive nature of a country and the concept of organic country. It is also known as the "public finance of distributive paradigm." It accepts the shift of economics research to science, formalization, and positivism, thus deciding the orientation of finance as the applied branch of neoclassical economics. As the application of neo-classical economics in the financial field, it focuses on the micro-function of the government, which is how individuals respond to government intervention. [5][6] Economists proposed that government has influence on the allocation of resources and income distribution based on the scientific research on individual reactions and specific norms and standards. Historically, this suggestion played a leading role in the national and social governance issues of the fiscal studies, and then withdrew from the sight of the fiscal studies.

Of the various sources of fiscal ideology mentioned above, the only one currently highlighted in China is the Anglo-American mainstream finance. The introduction and popularization of it has collectively made the research of China's public finance into a scientific, technical, and formalized one. Since the 1970s, the fiscal studies in Britain and the United States has an obvious empirical and applicable orientation. It has also caused the issue of the relationship between "fiscal and national governance" and the issue of national governance itself to disappear from the sight of Chinese fiscal scholars.

However, if you leave the keyword "governance" aside, there will be no way to understand how finance should play its role of the foundation and pillar of national governance as an institutional system. It is obvious that relying solely on the academic resources provided by this tradition can't answer the above major theoretical propositions. For those developed countries that have entered steady societies, it will make mere sense that their fiscal scholars follow the allocation paradigm and focused on the technical configuration details under the established institutional framework. While China is still at a transitional stage, the institutional building in important areas has not yet been completed. China's public finance must make contribution to the future development of the national system. It is necessary for researchers to recognize and overcome the deficiencies mentioned above.

Regrettably, although the development of public finance in China took hundreds of years, scholars in this circle failed to reach a consensus on basic issues related to the development of this discipline, such as "what should public finance study" and how to study. What's worse, scholars have unconsciously generated different views and standpoints. Fiscal scholars' insistence on their own views and lack of dialogue have become the biggest practical obstacle to the innovation of fiscal theory in the future. This situation must arouse our thinking. Which attitude should we adopt to face the entire ideology resources of China and the West throughout the history and at this moment, so as to ensure the subjectivity and independence of China's fiscal academic research as well as to embrace and cover the academic wisdom at home and abroad of all times and thus helping to explore and innovate in the future? The answer to this question is not only important to the future of the public finance, but also closely related to the current construction of various systems of national governance. Now it's urgent for the fiscal scholars to hold their own opinions and listen to each other so as to reach necessary consensus on the innovation direction and the road to innovation of public finance.

III. How to realize theoretical innovation in public finance: suggestions and direction

a. Some suggestions

In recent years, with the continuous deepening of the study and application of the mainstream Anglo-American fiscal research paradigm, there has also been an intrinsic need to reflect on it. The event that promotes systematic research on this issue by the Chinese public financial academics is precisely the official positioning by the "Decision" of finance as the basis and pillar of national governance. This positioning made fiscal scholars reconsider the object and method of fiscal research within the mainstream research paradigm as well as the development of public finance in China during the past 100 years. The author of this thesis believes that only when we base ourselves on China's history and reality, and integrate and digest relevant ideological resources of China and the West, can we avoid over-generalization and give a balanced and systematic response to this topic. For this reason, the author proposes the following suggestions:

1. To make careful researches on western fiscal theories, point out the reasonable elements and their proper condition, so as to make use of them.

Finance is first and foremost a social theory. It shares with other social sciences, such as politics, law, and sociology, a common research topic, namely: how is society possible. Specifically, how separate individuals can form a society in a way that can be recognized by all parties and share the benefits and the cost of cooperation in a fair manner. This is the theme that all social sciences (including public finance) have to deal with. Therefore, the research object of public finance should not only include the study of objects, in other words, the study of the effective allocation of social resources in scarcity; but also include the study of human actions and interactions among people, in other words, how do people solve problems like scarcity and social order. Contemporary western mainstream fiscal theory focuses on the former (allocation issue) and ignores the latter (governance issue). Firstly, while adopting its scientific research methods, we must realize that public finance should also expand the horizon of research and focus on broader issues like "governance". Secondly, during the process of introducing western public finance teaching and research resources, we should take an comprehensive, objective and fair attitude and avoid committing overgeneralization. On the basis of studying and applying the allocation paradigm finance, it is also necessary to deeply study the rational content of the trading paradigm finance, so that they complement each other and serve the fiscal theory and practice under the context of national governance.

2. To systematically correct the "Soviet-style finance".

The Soviet-style finance's concern for the issue of state governance has its reasonable components. However, the governance model it advocates cannot adapt to the need of modern state governance. In particular, it politically advocated class opposition and dictatorship, economically advocated control and planning, which is no longer appropriate to serve as the theoretical basis of national fiscal practice when class conflict is no longer the main contradiction of the society. At present, the major contradiction in our society have been transformed into the contradiction between the people's ever-growing need for a better life and unbalanced and uneven development. In this new era, we need objectively establish a cooperative fiscal theory based on legal interactions, transactions and sharing among members of the society who are morally equal. We should be vigilant that the Soviet-style finance, which advocated struggle, compulsion and deprivation, is back to life in the name of carrying forward Marxist Economics. Xi Jinping has pointed out in his speech at the symposium on philosophy and social science that the most valuable quality of Marxism is to have a critical spirit. Fiscal scholars should dare to face and admit the historical practices that has been proved wrong. The theoretical errors should be systematically corrected so as to set the record straight.

3. To make careful summary of fiscal academic practice since the reform and opening-up and make new achievements based on the national reality.

Since the reform and opening up, Chinese financial scholars have once enthusiastically created a fiscal theory system with Chinese characteristics on the basis of abandoning Soviet-style finance. As the old generation of local scholars gradually withdrew, and the new generation of scholars with overseas educational background joined in, the theoretical enthusiasm for creating a fiscal theory system with Chinese characteristics has declined since the late 1990s. Because these scholars with an overseas educational background are almost all the followers of the mainstream economics of the United Kingdom and the United States, the large-scale introduction of western mainstream financial education resources has become fashionable for a time. After entering the 21st century, allocation paradigm finance has dominated the fiscal theories in China.

Moving closer to the mainstream western fiscal research paradigm has accelerated the process of the internationalization of China's fiscal studies, as well as prompted China's public finance teaching to rapidly narrow the distance from that of the UK and US in just 10 years. We have made unprecedented progress in curriculum setting, selection of teaching materials, selection of research topics, and scientific, empirical, and applied research. However, it is undeniable that in the process of the introduction of western thought, there has been a tendency to overemphasize the British and American traditions while ignore European continental traditions. The one-sidedness of academic introduction has also caused the monotony of Chinese mainstream public finance today. At the same time, pressure from academic achievements in developed countries has further led to disregard for China's existing academic tradition, resources and efforts. As a consequence, the Chinese public financial academics paid more attention to all-takenism and less to using is for our own purpose; they emphasized imitating and learning, while neglecting comparison and criticism. As a result, there have been few combing and identification of western fiscal tradition and less innovative achievements that integrated Chinese academic tradition and China's national conditions.

Xi Jinping emphasized in his speech that Chinese philosophy and social science research should be subjective and original. He emphasized that the correct attitude toward philosophy and social science should be, "Critically accept our own historical heritage and foreign thoughts." "Oppose blindly accepting any ideas and blindly resisting any thoughts." He emphasized that "We Chinese must use our own minds to think and decide what can grow in our own soil." Fiscal practice is concerned with social and national governance. Neither society nor the country is a machine. Public finance is not only a science that is technical and scientific in terms of mathematical management, but a science related to how to deal with public affairs. Given that the society is not a machine that can be debugged arbitrarily, personal choices of each member will have an impact on the final result. A down-to-earth type of public finance should make research on people and their actions, rules that people abide by, as well as history and culture. In this sense, the study of public finance has its general and scientific side as well as its specific and historic side.

b. Innovative direction of public finance theory

Compared with other economic disciplines, the development of public finance in China lags behind. It can neither keep with the pace of international academic development, nor the pace of fiscal reform practice. Although major achievements have been made in the study of public finance since the reform and opening up, studies that followed and imitated foreign ones were far more than those which contain innovative elements and Chinese experience; progress in research tools was greater than that in new thoughts and thinking patterns; progress in public finance research is greater than that in public finance teaching especially undergraduate education. To regard public finance as the foundation and pillar of national governance has seized the essence of fiscal activities and surpassed the knowledge of the nature of public finance in mainstream fiscal circle. The Chinese public financial academics should seize this opportunity to promote the innovation of the basic theory of finance under the new historical condition.

First, transfer of research object. Essentially, public finance is a subject on the constitution of the society and the governance of the country. It studies how members of society can achieve orderly and just public governance through interactions with others under specific historical, political, economic and cultural environment[7]. Therefore, the research of public finance should not set boundaries and regard such problems in narrow sense as income, expenditure, balance and management as its only objects. From our viewpoint, the research horizon of public finance shall be widened, transferring the focus from resource allocation issues to governance issues in broad sense. Since the research scope of the latter contains that of the former, this transfer does not mean giving up allocation paradigms. Public finance scholars should be more confident in their profession, stick to problem-oriented researches and avoid looking down upon public finance as a practical branch of Anglo-American Neoclassical mainstream economic theories and establishing departments of public finance as 'tiny departments of economics'.

The transfer of the research object propels the exploration of a fair and effective mechanism of public affairs governance. Since the 1970s, many countries have initiated plentiful innovative attempts relating to this mechanism to explore functions and boundaries of market and social mechanism in public governance. In recent years, China has been trying to introduce these concepts into its public finance policy practices. The transfer of research object can help absorb and learn from international experiences, explore reasonable relationship between government, market and society, realize the balance of political order, market activities and social mechanism and serve the aim of 'strengthening and innovating social governance, promoting refined social governance and establishing the social governance pattern constructed and enjoyed by the whole nation'.

Second, the diversification of research paradigms. Besides mainstream research paradigm, 'transaction paradigm' ignored by the world of public finance theories is worthy of careful summarization and absorption. Setting each individual as the protagonist of social stage, this paradigm studies that individuals take actions (e. g. negotiation, compromise and cooperation) out of the interest of their own and their community and seek principles and schemes on solving public issues to benefit all parties, thus resetting 'governance' as the research center of public finance. With this research paradigm, public financial activities would be regarded as a transaction process of independent enforcement developed inside individuals rather than government's interference in social economy. Instead of directly promoting result justice, the government should be committed to establishing fair transaction rules and platforms to promote result justice through procedure justice.

The transfer of research paradigm helps promote the establishment of polycentric governance structure. Traditional public finance theories regard the single hierarchical structure of administration center as the hidden system background, with policies' seeking the optimal pattern from the viewpoint of decision-makers, thus neglecting individuals' initiative, enthusiasm and participation. Nevertheless, in the real world, most public governance issues tend to be regional and colonial instead of national, thus requiring a correspondent flat and polycentric governance structure. Transaction paradigm studied by public finance provides another alternative theory for this, assuming that under fixed laws and regulations, individuals jointly decide specific solutions of public affairs through autonomous discussion and contracts. The transfer of public finance research from optimal allocation paradigm to transaction paradigm not only reflects benefit principle of public economy, but mirrors the internal requirement of public governance, i. e. 'everyone participates, everyone endeavors, everyone enjoys', which is conducive to find out effective institutional arrangement on the basis of comparing system analysis.

Third, the diversification of research perspectives and methods. The popularity of scientism and formalism in Anglo-American mainstream public finance reflects its misunderstanding toward the subject attribute of public finance from one side, i. e. equating public finance with natural science. Provided that society were a machine and public finance a natural science, it might be a wise choice to introduce new research methods and technologies from western mainstream public finance circle where scientism and formalism are popular. However, far from that, public finance relates closely to how to govern the society and the country, how people deal with each other in real life, and how they resolve conflicts, realize cooperation, achieve respective goals in an orderly society and make financial arrangements around this goal. Despite of the standard pattern, the mainstream public finance has narrow research subject and single research object, with research methods unable to adjust to complexity of mankind's public finance behavior.

Faced with more and more discrete knowledge system in modern society, researchers of public finance should always be modest, with the awareness that public finance researches must be capable to contain different research perspectives, methods and tools. Therefore, some scholars contend that we should revive the interdisciplinary research tradition of public finance, oppose harm to practical cognition on people's complex public finance behavior due to the pursuit of scientization and formalization, and transfer to multiple methodology containing system and history analysis from reliance on scientism[8][9][10][11][12]. In the future, public finance ought to play a role in establishing a social governance pattern with co-construction and sharing of all the people. Besides, public finance should focus more on the people and strengthen researches on people, people's behaviors and systems, history and culture that they ought to observe. Therefore, a public financial system can be established with incentive compatibility, long-term efficiency and justice through a better understanding of people and their behaviors.

Fourth, insist on the subjectivity of China's public finance research. The subjectivity of China's public finance research requires us to not only be clear-minded but also strive for innovation when faced with diverse research traditions and methods. As an introduced discipline system, faced with the trend of internationalization of academic research, the public finance has to deal with the tense between awareness in local issues and academic research internalization. In today's academic circle of international economy, internationalization is nearly synonymous with scientization and formalization. Under this situation, how China's public finance research can blend in international academic circle, possess independent judgment about self-owned problems and their solutions, and create and maintain academic subject consciousness, largely depends on scholars' choices and our attitudes toward existing thought resources and decisions we'll make. These choices and decisions not only relate closely to the development of the subject, public finance, but influence institutional construction of national governance. It decides whether China's public finance can provide remarkable knowledge resources for new governance theories and strategies and enlighten the people and promote social consensus in the future.

The subjectivity of financial research requires that academic research should learn from but overtop practices and practically clarify and lead advanced public governance theories, instead of only following and interpreting relevant practices and policies. Contemporary public finance scholars should be based on China's history and reality, absorb related Chinese and Western thought resources, discriminate their respective reasonable parts and applicable conditions and promote innovation of fiscal levy system on the basis of continual theory innovation, thus contributing intelligence to establishing sound modern fiscal levy system and realize the target of comprehensively deepening reform.

References

[1] Ma Jun. To promote fiscal system reform through theoretical innovation [N]. Economic Daily, 28th, Oct. 2016, 14th edition.

[2] BUCHANAN J. M. What Should Economists Do? [J]. Southern Economic Journal, Vol. 30, No. 3, Jan. 1964, 213 - 222.

[3] WAGNER R. E. Fiscal Sociology and the Theory of Public Finance: An Exploratory Essay [M]. Cheltenham, UK: Edward Elgar Publishing, 2007.

[4] Zeng Junping. Reconstitution of fiscal theories: taking the exploration of fair rules as theme [A]. Chief-edited by Ma Jun, Gao Peiyong, National governance and innovation of basic fiscal theories [C]. Beijing: China Social Sciences Press, 2017: 107 - 127.

[5] ROSEN H. S. Public Finance: Essay for the Encyclopedia of Public Choice [D/OL]. Center for Economic Policy Studies Working Papers, No. 80, Princeton University, 2002.

[6] FELDSTEIN M. The Transformation of Public Economics Research: 1970—2000 [J]. Journal of Public Economics, Vol. 86, No. 3, 2002, 319 - 326.

[7] Ma Jun. National governance theory in Buchanan's fiscal thought [J]. Fiscal research, 2016 (12): 28 - 37.

[8] Liu Shougang, Liu Xuemei. Political exploration of fiscal research [J]. Academic Journal of Jiangsu Second Normal University (social science), 2010 (3): 66 - 68.

[9] Liu Shougang. An exploration of the discipline "fiscal politics" [A]. Chief-edited by Ma Jun, Gao Peiyong, National governance and innovation of basic fiscal theories [C]. Beijing: China Social Sciences Press, 2017: 156 - 176.

[10] Liu Zhiguang. Framework of fiscal sociology and innovation of fundamental theories of public finance [A]. Chief-edited by Ma Jun, Gao Peiyong, National governance and innovation

of basic fiscal theories [C]. Beijing: China Social Sciences Press, 2017: 128 - 155.

[11] Li Weiguang. Why is public finance the basis and pillar of national governance [J]. Law Review, 2014 (2): 54 - 60.

[12] Gao Peiyong. On the innovation of China's basic fiscal theory—to begin with "the basis and pillar" [J]. Management World, 2015 (12): 4 - 11.

何以认识和改造世界：政治经济学的研究逻辑和方法*

朱富强

摘　要： 经济学探究的根本上是属于公共领域的社会事物，并承担认识和改造现实世界的任务。为此，经济学的理论研究就必须采取具有强烈现实性的四大方法：（1）实证分析和规范分析的契合，它强调将关注“是什么”的现象实证与探究“应该是什么”的本质规范相结合，从而能够涵盖工程学和伦理学两大内容；（2）遵循从本质到现象的研究路线，它强调要将基于内在结构的本体论和基于外在现象的解释论结合起来，从而能够深入到现象背后的本质问题；（3）设定可实现的理想状态为假设前提，它强调要将事物本质作为参照系来审视现实问题与引导未来发展，从而能够界分本体论和解释论这两大假设；（4）应用契合归纳和演绎的回溯法，它强调要充分利用人的知性思维将经验知识提升到超验体系而深化本体论认识，从而有效弥补了归纳实证和抽象演绎的缺陷。只有基于这四大研究方法，经济学才能成为“极高明而道中庸”的致用之学，才能实现认识和改造世界的双重目标。

关键词： 规范分析　引导假设　本体论　回溯法　经济方法

［中图分类号］ G633.23　**［文献标识码］** A

一、前言

无论从历史起源还是学科特性来看，经济学科的根本研究领域都在公共领

* 基金项目：广东省创新团队项目“社会主义市场经济理论基础与政策体系”（2016WCXTD001）。

［作者简介］：朱富强，江苏丹阳人，经济学博士，中山大学岭南学院/中央财经大学经济学院中国政治经济学研究中心。

域，这包括财富创造、劳动分工、收入分配、福利改进、社会规范等，因而“政治经济学”就是经济学科原初的也是恰当的名称[1]。同时，公共领域中的社会经济现象和现实问题都是一定社会关系下的个体行为及其社会互动产生的，需要关注影响个体偏好和行为的社会关系、制度变迁、集体行动等，需要引入伦理和公正的社会关怀，也需要嵌入法律、社会学、政治学、伦理学和哲学的分析，因而“政治经济学”名称又与社会经济学、公共经济学、制度经济学、集体经济学、人本主义经济学等名称具有共通性。不幸的是，边际革命以后，主流经济学将其研究重心转向了私人领域，集中探究既定制度下的资源配置和孤立环境下的个体行为；相应地，它一方面基于还原主义思维建立起了一个个精巧的数理模型；另一方面基于伦理自然主义，实证自然主义展开对现实的描述和解释。结果却是，现代经济学与管理学、伦理学、政治学等学科逐渐分离，越来越向数学和物理学等自然科学靠拢，乃至蜕变成为应用数学的一个分支；相应地，现代主流经济学变得越来越抽象，乃至蜕变成了数学逻辑和技巧人士偏爱者的智力游戏，而不再是发现和解决现实问题的学问。

其实，一门学科的研究思维、方法应该与其研究对象和内容相适应，正是着眼于私人领域的个体行为，产生了新古典经济学的形式逻辑和功能主义的分析路线。那么，着眼于公共领域的社会事物，经济学科的研究方法又应该有何特色呢？同时，尽管新古典经济学者基于对政治的嫌恶而将经济学科的名称由“政治经济学”改为“经济学”，并试图舍弃道德伦理因素而构建纯理论经济学，但它果真做到了吗？霍奇逊就指出，“新古典学派并没有割断与意识形态的连带关系。在他们对其价值判断保持沉默的同时，这些价值标准却在背后起着更为恶劣的作用……在政治实践方面，新古典学派实质上是主张在经济活动中免除政治和政府的干预。如果说斯密和李嘉图还曾力图使用理论工具来证明市场机制的所谓优越性，那么新古典学派则干脆要人们无条件接受这种优越性。他们在政治上保持沉默，但是在一片沉默之中却潜伏着对现状的煞费苦心的辩护。”[2]尤其是，作为一门致用之学，现代主流经济学承担起“认识和改造世界”这一任务了吗？霍奇逊继续写道：“尽管新古典正统派在经济学专业领域中占据统治地位，它却缺少马克思主义所具有的那种直接性、实质性和现实性。主流经济学倾向于在‘理论’方面蜕变为一种空洞的代数式的形式主义，而在‘应用’方面却蜕变为一种无生气的天真的经验主义。构造这样一种理论几乎成了一项单纯的逻辑游戏。[2]”为此，本文就政治经济学乃至经济学科应有的方法论做一系统的探索。

二、现象实证和本质规范的契合

作为以增进人类福利为根本目标的经济学，其研究内容包括工程学和伦理学两大方面：（1）工程学内容关注人与物之间的关系，包括资源的最优配置以及孤立的个体选择行为等；（2）伦理学内容关注人与人之间的关系，包括资源的社会分配以及人们之间的社会互动等。相应地，这两大内容也分别对应了不同的研究方法要求：（1）工程学内容的研究主要关涉人处理自然物的技术关系，显然与生产力水平以及工具理性有关，从而比较适合实证研究，也适合基于数学逻辑的抽象分析；（2）伦理学内容的研究主要关涉人与人互动的社会关系，显然嵌入了一定的社会需要和价值判断，从而更适用于规范分析，也适用于基于知识契合的综合分析。

一般地，涉及价值判断的资源分配等反映了社会发展的目的问题，而不涉及价值判断的资源配置则属于手段和工具范畴。同时，现代经济学在选择使用何种工具时，往往又依赖于对研究目的的设定。例如，现代主流经济学先验地认定企业的目标在于最大化股东价值，而且将之视为不言而喻的，但这一信条实际上却是一个规定企业如何活动和运营的规范性命题[3]。这意味着，尽管现代主流经济学将经济学规定为一门价值无关的纯技术性科学，并致力于发展分析方法和工具，乃至往往歧视目的的探讨；但显然，这种观点将非常复杂的社会事实过于简单化了，忽视了目的本身就嵌入在社会事物的产生和发展之中。事实上，即使现代主流经济学集中解决技术性问题，进而关注“实然”命题，但也会滑向“应然”命题。例如，最优化所涉及的各种边际替代率相等原理，其中就以社会效率为目标，而社会效率本身则隐含了一定的价值观[4]。

因此，尽管现代主流经济学极力主张舍弃有关立场和判断之类的伦理因素，积极倡导纯理论的发展，进而大肆宣扬经济学的实证性质，但这根本并不容易做到。究其原因，任何社会经济现象都是在一定的社会关系中发生的，都涉及人与人之间的利益关系。例如，哈丁就认为，伦理学本身就涉及资源分配问题[5]。如，现代主流经济学研究主要涉及“生产什么”“如何生产”“为谁生产”三大内容，而这明显涵盖了工程学和伦理学这两大方面：（1）如果说“生产什么”和“如何生产”主要关乎工程学问题的话，“为谁生产”就主要是伦理学问题，它涉及社会资源在人与人间的配置；（2）即使就“生产什么”而言，它也依赖于人际效用比较，涉及人际效用的取舍，从而必然涉及人与人间的关系；（3）即使就“如何生产”而言，技术也是特定强势者选择的，必然会体现特定个人或群体的利益，从而现有的生产组织也具有明显的社会性[6]。不幸的是，现代主流经济学却在一个封闭和静态框架下分析基于个人选择的资源配置，从而就抛开伦理关系而专注于所谓的“效率”问题。

同时，作为本质上的社会科学，经济学科具有双重特征：（1）在研究对象上，社会经济现象并不是像自然现象那样外在于人这一行为主体，而是为人类行为所衍生，进而，人对社会经济现象的认识和理解也根源于其经验和直觉。正是在这个意义上，经济学理论研究往往会嵌入深深的主观性。（2）在研究方式上，对社会经济现象的探究并不像自然科学那样仅仅是应用某些不可变更的原理，而是渗入了人类的理想和目的，进而，人类致力于改造不合理之处以期推进人类社会的健康发展。正是在这个意义上，经济学的研究又嵌入了强烈的规范性。即经济学理论充满了主观性和规范性：主观性主要体现在研究者的个人知识及其传承的社会认知；规范性则体现为研究者的社会关怀和立场视角[7]。

因此，尽管现代主流经济学赋予实证分析以客观性和科学性，乃至集中于对变量之间关系的计量实证，但这实际上根本无法做到。首先，任何社会制度设计以及政策主张都涉及了手段和目标的选择，都必然体现某种价值取向。显然，实证分析的主要目的往往也是为政策服务，因而往往也会嵌入强烈的主观性。例如，在实证分析过程中，无论是数据资料的选择还是分析工具的选择，无论是因变量还是自变量的选择，都充满了强烈的主观性。其次，经济学人在选择计量实证方法进行研究时，往往还嵌入一个基本目的：向读者宣传其观点。为此，他往往就会致力于以下两个方面的工作：（1）努力找出那些能够支撑自身观点的数据等证据；（2）使用具有明显感情色彩的措辞来向读者解释其发现[8]。再次，从学科性质来说，经济学根本达不到自然科学所展示的那种科学性，不能满足可检验性（实证论）和可重复性（还原论）这两大基本科学条件[9]，进而也就难以符合逻辑实证主义所设定的科学标准；相应地，经济学的理论发展主要不是基于可控实验的外部标准进行检验，而是依据内部标准的逻辑体系[10]。不幸的是，现代主流经济学人却热衷于在一个新古典宏观经济学和新凯恩斯主义宏观经济学框架下对现代经济理论的“证实”，并基于科学主义为这种“实证”分析提供辩护。

以上两个方面的分析都表明，经济计量分析的客观性只是一种虚构。相应地，经济学就绝不能仅仅被视为一门实证科学。究其原因，作为一门致用之学，经济学最根本的任务在于认识和解决具体的社会现实问题，而不能停留在对现象的描述和解释上。相应地，经济学理论体系也必然需要满足这样两大要求：一是理论需要源于生活经验和人伦；二是理论又不能停留在具体的经验层面，而应该上升到超验层次。基于这两者所构建的理论体系就是“极高明而道中庸”。同时，几乎所有的实证研究都是政策相关的，基本目的在于探究政策对某种价值目标的完成状况。由此，我们就可以看出其中的断层：一方面，纯粹实证独立于任何特定的伦理立场或价值判断，从而也就必然提不出任何政策；另一方面，任何政策主张必然以特定目的或立场为基础，以此为目的的实证分析必然会预设的某些价值立场。考虑这两者，经济学的理论研究必须把关注“实然”的实证分析和探究“应然”的规范分析结合起来：离开“应然”的“实证”分析没有多大价值，而不明白“实然”的“规范”争论也只能是纸上谈兵[11]。

就实证分析和规范分析的关系而言，这里继续做一具体说明。首先，实证分析必须以规范探究为前提。事实上，如果缺乏对社会事物的“应然”探究，即使严密的实证分析详细描述了“实然”状况，由此又何以提出改革社会制度的良好建议呢？毕竟从事实出发推出价值判断。正因如此，当前中国一些经济学人所撰写的实证文章往往是一种牵强附会的八股式文章。其次，规范探究也应该以实证分析为基础。事实上，如果缺乏对社会事物“实然”的充分认识，即使已经辨识出它“应然”的要求，由此又如何制定当下政策呢？毕竟理想往往并不能马上实现。正因如此，传统经济学人往往热衷于空泛的“主义”之争上。相反，将实证分析和规范分析统一起来就可以形成一条从本质到现象的完整研究路线：一方面借助规范分析来揭示社会事物的内在本质和发展要求；另一方面又借助实证分析来剖析现实对本质的偏离及其原因，由此也就可以为改进现实制度确立基本方向和途径。

纵观经济学说史，经济学科自诞生以及成为一门独立学科之初就包含了注重规范分析的伦理学和主张实证分析的工程学这两大内容，只是到了边际革命以后尤其是新古典经济学支配地位的确立，伦理学内容才与工程学内容相分离，进而随着伦理学内容逐渐被舍弃，主流经济学的研究内容也就日益狭隘化。为此，豪斯曼和麦克佛森就指出，“也许真正的挑战不是证明经济学和伦理学的联系，而是寻求分离这两者的可能性，把经济学作为一种客观的社会科学来研究。”[12]同时，实证经济学和规范经济学在现代经济学中之所以日益相分离，其根源在于西方社会根深蒂固的“事实与价值”二分法思维。问题是，人类社会中的事实和价值果真能够且应该分开吗？举个例子，当人们说“市场机制是有效率的”这句话时，这究竟是描述性的还是评价性的？一般地，现代主流经济学将之视为一个实证描述。问题是，如何界定效率呢？很大程度上，对效率内涵的设定本身就预设了特定的目的。在人类社会中，我们根本不能想象仅仅依靠事实就可以解决有关价值的问题，也无法仅仅诉诸价值评估就能解决具体的事实问题。正因如此，经济学科要走上成熟，就应该把实证经济学和规范经济学结合起来。

然而，现代主流经济学却认为，事实和价值是相互独立且可以分离的不同问题。相应地，实证经济学和规范经济学在现代经济学界就遭到了割裂，而主流经济学则热衷于可以攀附“硬性”思维自然科学而推崇实证研究。在现代主流经济学看来，“所谓‘规范经济学’不过是把实证经济学应用于那些需要直接做价值评判的相关方面而已。所以，对意识形态的研究、对经济学家价值观的研究与理解经济学或经济学方法论毫无关系。”[12]不过，这种标准观点显然低估了规范经济学的价值和意义：一方面，即使当经济学家试图给出达成某些目标的“纯技术”的建议时，实际上也很少只是一个纯技术的问题；另一方面，即使实证经济学偏重于事物间作用机理的探究，它也主要局限于功能性联系，乃至因变量和自变量往往可以随意置换。正是由于流行的实证分析局限于功能性联系，从而在发展预测和实践指导方面的效果往往就差强人意无能为力。连萨缪尔森都说，经济科学不能告诉我们哪一种政治观点是正确还是错误的，试问：又如何指导实践呢？

其实，自从边际革命将经济学导向构建数理模型和进行计量实证的道路以降，经济学科的性质就逐渐发生蜕变，最终成为一门解释性而非预测性的学科，进而也就无法承担起指导社会实践的任务。当然，一些经济学人也致力于将实证结果运用于社会改革的指导，这又是如何做的呢？一般地，这种功能与自然主义思维结合在一起，基于自然主义思维而设立不受干预的自然秩序作为

“应然”标准；相应地，现代主流经济学就倾向于合理化实证结果，以实证分析来为社会现实辩护，尤其为市场经济辩护。由此我们也就可以明白，主流的实证经济学为何会得出具有强烈现实辩护性的理论，为何会如此缺乏批判和否定的精神，为何会嵌入强烈的保守主义倾向；进而也就可以明白，现代主流经济学理论既不可能改变现存社会，更不可能构造出更为合理的社会。特别是，像中国这类社会制度还很不健全的发展中国家，如果简单地基于这种实证分析和自然主义的结合来指导社会制度的改革，反而会强化不合理的存在，进而加剧社会秩序的失范和混乱。

可见，经济学本质上属于社会科学，它无法像自然科学那样揭示或发现一个稳定的规律，相反，它应该研究的主要是，社会经济现象何以产生，社会事物何以变化，未来又如何发展等。同时，社会事物在演化过程中，事物的内在本质如物理学中的奇怪吸引子一样左右着其发展轨迹，相应地，通过洞悉事物的本质就容易揭示社会事物的发展路径或“规律”。因此，经济学要真正成为一门“极高明而道中庸”的致用之学，就不应仅限于“实然”层面，而应根植于“应然”之中。一方面，“实然”属于对社会事实的描述，而对“实然”的考察往往依赖于实证分析。显然，“实然”研究就需要运用相应的计量工具，需要对相关实证结论做理论检验。另一方面，“应然”根本上属于一个价值判断问题，“应然”探究中往往嵌入了认知主体的理念和视角。显然，为了更全面甄别事物的“应然”本质，就应该尽可能多地契合人类所积累的知识[13]。尤其是，由于纯粹实证分析根本上不能得出任何政策主张，从而也就无法为社会实践提供指导。因此，作为一门致用之学，实证经济学无论如何都不能完全取代规范经济学的地位。

三、从本质到现象的研究路线

上面强调实证分析要与规范分析相结合，只有确立起规范的标准，实证才可以有的放矢，才能为社会实践提供指导。然而，长期以来，主流经济学都将规范分析和实证分析割裂开来。既然如此，它又何以指导社会实践呢？一般地，这主要有两种思维：（1）诉诸于自然秩序和市场机制，认为摆脱人为（主要是政府）干预的市场自然可以解决问题，这是新古典自由主义信奉的“无形的手”原理；（2）诉诸于发达国家的制度安排和经验，认为发达国家的现在就是发展中国家的未来，这也是普遍得到接受的社会发展一元进步观。同时，这两种思维都根基于单一的自然主义思维，并深深嵌入在现代主流经济学之中。受此影响，不少经济学人就简单地认为，那些已经在自然科学的应用中获得较为成功的方法思维、应用目标和评估标准等也同样适用于社会科学领域，适用于对社会经济活动的分析。果真如此吗？

实际上，现代主流经济学人接受和遵循的是内含严重逻辑问题的工具主义方法论。以劳森所举的例子来说明，当绵垫子上沾满灰尘时，人们往往用大棒拍打来除尘；但是，我们想一下，如果玻璃上也沾满了尘埃，我们还可以用大棒拍打来除尘吗？这就告诉我们，即使经过实践而发现某种工具对于一个特殊的工作很有作用，但这也并不能证明它可以用于解决其他相类似的问题，进而也反映出工具化的逻辑实证主义本身就存在逻辑困境。劳森就指出，“正是这样不加怀疑地依赖于这一点，使我们得以理解最近50多年来当代经济学失败的根源所在。”[14]既然如此，如何摆脱这种实证主义的逻辑困境呢？根本上，需要挖掘隐藏在现象背后的更深层次的本质，需要超越经验而对事物的内在机制、结构进行分析，而这又需要充分运用人类的知性思维。显然，这也就是经济学的本体论问题：经济学理论的根本体现在对事物本质的揭示，在于对事物间的相互作用机理以及因果关系的洞悉，进而通过考察现实与本质的偏离来思考现实社会的改进。基于这一本体论诉求，就可以提炼出一条从本质到现象的研究路线：首先，透过纷繁芜杂的现象去挖掘社会事物的内在本质；其次，借助实证等方法来详细描述和分析社会事物的现实形态；再次，通过对社会事物发展轨迹的系统考察来揭示引发事物的现实形态与其内在表象和本质相偏离的因素；最后，基于本质的解释以及现实成因的解析来确立社会事物的发展方向和改进途径[15]。

从本质到现象的研究路线可以追溯到古希腊。事实上，柏拉图就认为，所有事物的发展都是从原初的、完美的形式或理念开始的，但发展中的事物在其变化到一定程度而与原初事物的类似性减少时就开始丧失它的圆满[16]；同时，柏拉图还将理性意识独立出来，认为理性可以存在的合理性进行识别并促使它向原初的理想状态回归。同样，亚里士多德也强调，任何事物、任何运动或变化都存在一个终极原因：“目的因”，它是运动所要趋向的目标。显然，这承继了柏拉图将正义理论扩展到宇宙的做法：不仅在社会中每个不同等级的公民都有其自然的地位，而且物理世界也存在相似的等级和种类。两者的不同主要体现为：柏拉图将形式或本质或始基都看成是先天存在的，从而是与感性的事物相分离的；亚里士多德则认为，感性事物将朝其终极的原因或目的运动，因而这些事物与其本质或形式是统一的。即亚里士多德认为形式或本质存在于事物之中，而柏拉图却认为它们先于或外在于事物。亚里士多德的逻辑依据是，事物的本质就体现为这样一种潜能，它是某种触动事物变化或运动的内在源泉，并将在运动或变化过程中得以呈现；正是在这个意义上，在发展过程中逐渐呈现的事物的形式或本质，就与其发展目标或最终状态相统一[16]。这样，亚里士多德就用乐观主义取代了柏拉图的悲观主义，从而也就不再诉求对理想国的构建。

从本质到现象这一研究路线在经济分析中的广泛使用则体现在古典政治经济学中，古典政治经济学家配第、斯密、西斯蒙第、穆勒、马克思等在具体经济分析中实际上使用的都是从本质到现象的研究路线[17]。其根本原因是，古典政治经济学的根本研究对象是组织，主要研究议题则集中在公共领域；为此，古典政治经济学家大多将经济学作为社会科学的一部分来研究，其理论和方法也就充满了明显的规范色彩，试图对现实世界加以评估和判断。例如，马克思学说就具有这样两大特征：（1）它积极吸收当时几乎所有的社会科学知识并从社会事物的演化过程来考察人类社会以及相应事物的内在本质，进而将本质当作社会事物的理想状态，并由此来确立它的发展方向；（2）它积极考察社会权力结构及其演变，进而揭示社会事物的发展轨迹以及现实出现面目与其本来面目间的背离，并由此来考察社会权力结构的演变对社会发展的根本性影响。同时，基于从本质到现象的研究路线，斯密、李嘉图、西斯蒙第、穆勒乃至马尔萨斯等古典经济学家在分析市场交换时，不仅关注由供求关系决定的交易价格，而是进一步剖析引起供求变动以及决定商品交换的内在原因。为此，古典经济学家大多对商品的自然价格（内在价值）和市场价格（名义价格）进行了界分，从而形成了贯穿于所有商品研究的二分法思维。

显然，这种二分法思维在对劳动工资的分析就非常明显，因而这里也以斯密的工资理论为例做一解说。斯密的工资理论沿着这样几个层次逐层展开。首先，斯密本质意义上将工资视为一个自然范畴。这充分体现在土地尚未私有、资本尚未积累的“原始社会状态”下，此时“劳动生产物构成劳动的自然报酬或自然工资”[18]，工资大小也就由劳动生产率决定。其次，斯密又进一步考察了现实工资。这集中体现为雇佣社会的工资，此时劳动者只能获得其劳动生产物的一部分，工资大小甚至只能维持基本生活的需要。最后，斯密由此就发现工资的现实与其本质间的分离。在本质层面上，每个人可以完全占有自己的劳动产物，工资大小就与其生产率保持同等比例增长；而在现实世界中，人们并不能完全占有自己的劳动产物，工资大小也就与劳动生产率的发展相脱节。由此，就带来一个关键问题，现实工资是如何决定的？斯密就此展开了深入的剖析。

斯密区分了劳动商品的市场价格和自然价格，并着重分析了作为劳动商品之市场价格的工资的影响因素。主要表现为：（1）工资成为商品的生产费用的一部分，对工资劳动者的需求随着预定用来支付劳动工资的基金的增加而成比例地增加，这里暗含了工资基金说；（2）现实世界的劳动工资主要取决于劳资双方所订的契约，而契约工资的大小就在于雇主和雇佣工人之间的竞争，这导向了后来的工资契约说；（3）劳动市场的讨价还价结果将取决于双方的力量，如雇主在数量上少且能支撑更长时间，法律也对雇主有利，雇主们有一种秘而不宣的团结，因而雇主在劳动市场就占有优势，这揭示了工资决定的权力原则；（4）尤其是在资本稀缺的社会中，雇主（即资本所有者）在市场竞争中往往处于极端有利的地位，乃至工人不得不满足于低微的工资水平，这也就是流行当时的“生存工资”说；（5）即使劳工的谈判力量再如何低下，他所得的工资也有基本界限：工资至少足够维持生活，这是激励理论中的参与约束，导向“最低生活费”学说；（6）基于劳动供求的分析还可以得出，最高工资水平往往不是出现在最富国家，而是出现在最快变得富裕（从而最繁荣）的国家。显然，斯密的见解与马克思是一致的，如马克思写道：“工资决定于资本家和工人之间的敌对的斗争。胜利必定属于资本家。资本家没有工人能比工人没有资本家活得长久。资本家的联合是很通常而卓有成效的，工人的联合则遭到禁止并会给他们招来恶果。”[19]

当然，无论是斯密、穆勒还是马克思，他们都不接受这种低水平的工资现状，既不认为它是合理的，也不认为它是不可改变的，而是致力于通过社会权力结构和法律制度的修正来不断提高社会工资水平。例如，斯密就致力于分析劳动供求双方力量的改变，并以此提出提高工资的基本途径。（1）随着资本的不断积累以及经济的快速发展，对劳动的需求也会相应增加，进而也就导致工资水平的提高。因此，不同于当时流行的“工资基金说”或“最低生活费说”，斯密不仅认为工资是可以提高的，而且赞成较高的工资水平。斯密所持的理由是：一方面，工资水平的上升本身就是社会财富增进的结果和标志，“对工资劳动者的需求，必定随着预定用来支付劳动工资的基金的增加而成比例地增加”；另一方面，较高的工资水平可以增强工人们的健康和体力，激励工人们尽力工作，这成为效率工资的滥觞。（2）随着允许成立工会等法令的制定和通过，工人的谈判力量就可以随之提高，进而也就会出现有利于工人的收入分配。很大程度上，这成为后来美国制度学派如加尔布雷斯等提出抗衡力量的思想来源。

工资水平随着社会发展而提高，在现代社会中也得到明显的证实。事实上，在现代资本主义社会中，当一个企业因采用新技术而提高劳动生产率时，工资水平往往会通过两条途径而得到提高。（1）如果这种新技术逐渐为竞争对手所掌握，在正常的市场竞争下，技术革新将导致社会生产率的普遍提升，使产品成本下降和市场价格下跌；在这种情况下，即使名义工资不变，实际工资水平也会因市场价格的下降而提升。（2）即使这种新技术难以为竞争对手所掌握，在不完全市场竞争导致价格存在下行刚性的条件下，那些采用新技术的企业或产业就可以获得超额利润；在这种情况下，尽管整体价格水平上升，但工资水平往往会因现代工会的分享利润要求而在生产率上升的范围内得到提高。

显然，从本质到现象的研究线路根本上不同于现代主流经济学使用的理性选择分析框架。一般认为，马歇尔的供求分析框架有机地将古典经济学注重供给成本的价值理论和边际效用学派强调需求效用的价值论统一起来，进而在“马歇尔交叉”基础上构建出一个局部均衡的理论体系，进而也就为后人认识和解释价格等经济现象的决定和变动过程提供了分析框架。相应地，不少经济学人都以供求分析框架来界分古典经济学和新古典经济学，以供求分析框架的形成作为现代经济学的标志，进而，以此作为经济学进步的证据，不少经济学人就把古典经济学家致力于从国际甚至劳动成本角度探求内在价值的思路称为误导性的，将古典经济学理论体系视为片面的。果真如此吗？其实，前面已经指出，马歇尔并不是供求分析法的最早使用者，在此之前，斯密、马尔萨斯以及马克思等都曾使用它来剖析社会现状。不同的是，古典经济学并不停留在现状（市场价格）的解释上，而是努力从更深层次上探究现状背后的东西；相反，马歇尔则致力于统合所有曾经出现过的供求论、生产费用论和边际效用论，并在此基础上提炼出一个统一（市场）价格理论，由此就代替或取消传统的价值论分析。

很大程度上，正是由于新古典经济学集中关注的是现象，其价格理论就存在根本缺陷。首先，它往往体现为一个同义反复。具体体现为：一方面，在分析供求的数量和变动时将之视为价格的函数；另一方面，在寻求市场均衡的价格时又将之视为供求的函数。这就带来了问题：哪个是因变量？哪个是自变量？既然新古典价格理论根本上无法解决价格的决定问题，阿尔钦就告诉他的学生说："价格是由什么决定的，远不如价格能决定什么来得重要。"[20]其次，它根本上无法解释现实的动态发展。事实上，既然每个厂商都按照均衡价格进行生产和销售，那么，市场价格长期上又如何会出现变动呢？马歇尔将均衡价格视为价值，进而将不同阶段的商品价值视为供求作用的结果；但同时又认为，在不同的时间跨度上，供给和需求在商品价值的形成中所起作用的主导性存在差异。通常来说，时间越短，供给就越难以改变，相应地，需求对商品价值的影响就越大；相反，时期越长，供给就越容易变动，生产成本对商品价值的影响将愈为重要。也即，马歇尔认为，边际效用和生产费用共同决定了商品的价值，而生产费用所起作用是根本性的。显然，马歇尔的认知与古典经济学存在明显的共通性，只是其信徒们在偏离古典经济学的道路上越走越远。正因如此，尽管马歇尔承袭了古典经济学思维而关注现实问题和政策，但其知识狭隘的继承者们则更关注逻辑上的严谨，从而忽视了马歇尔经济学中的现实关怀和人本主义精神。

可见，基于从本质到现象的研究路线，我们就可以对社会经济现象做全面而深入的认识，相反，如果仅仅基于供求框架来分析现象，获得的认识就免不了肤浅和片面。事实上，按照批判实在论的观点，社会经济本体可以抽象为三个层次：（1）经验和事件层次，是一种经验层次上的现实，主要是就人们的经历和印象、事件和事件的状态而言的；（2）结构和机制层次，是指社会的各种规则、传统、惯例、规范、关系和认知结构等；（3）人性层次，由人性中的永恒本质、显著特性和基本趋势所构成[21]。但是，现代主流经济学却仅仅关注事件层次的经验性规则，并基于还原的人性假设进行解释。相应地，现代主流经济学的研究主要表现为：（1）基于自然主义思维而集中于私人领域的供求均衡分析，从而不仅把社会制度视为既定的，在制度既定的前提下对现状做功能性的分析；（2）基于逻辑实证主义而热衷于对社会现状的计量实证分析，从而在伦理自然主义和实证自然主义价值观下为自由市场辩护，为强者利益服务。例如，基于供求分析逻辑以及伦理自然主义思维，人们往往把通过市场交换获得的收入都视为合理的：为什么企业家可以一夜暴富，就是因为他们对社会的贡献大；为什么经理人员能够取得高得惊人的买断年薪，也就是因为他们对社会的贡献大；而为什么保姆、清洁工的工资如此之低，也是因为他们对社会几乎没有做出什么贡献。但显然，这实际上是把现实中的“实存”视为“应该”了，从而抹杀了其中隐藏的不公正和剥削关系，无法揭示整个社会分配体制的不合理性。

四、设定可实现的理想状态为参照系

马克思将哲学的任务定位为认识和改造世界。当然，认识和改造世界不只是哲学的任务，而是几乎所有社会科学的任务，更是作为致用之学的经济学科的根本任务。问题在于，如何能够有效地认识和改造世界？一般地，认识世界本身就是服务于改造世界这一根本目的，而改造世界则体现了对理想世界的认知，从而必然会打上强烈的个人印记，必然依赖于个人多设定的改革目标。那么，如何确定合理的改革目标呢？古典政治经济学采用了从本质到现象的研究路线：只有洞悉事物的应然本质，才能识别事物的现实缺陷；只有剖析实然事物的异化成因，才能提出解决现实问题的治标之策。在这一分析路线中，事物本质就被视作一种理想状态，它不仅用于对现实事物异化程度的衡量，而且作为现实事物未来发展的参照系。正是将本质确立为事物发展的理想状态，我们就可以评估事物实然形态的合理性，就可以剖析现实社会制度的内在缺陷；通过系统剖析实然状态何以如此的成因，我们就可以有针对性地寻找改进和完善现实制度的有效途径。

然而，现代主流经济学却逐渐将经济学的理论和应用区分开来，并逐渐朝两个基本方向发展。（1）理论经济学致力于构建基于严格逻辑的数理模型，从而将自身打造成一门类似几何学那样的公理体系。显然，这种公理体系根本上是形而上的，甚至是一种概念体系，而无法指导人们的日常行为和经济体系的运行，甚至经济学本身也不再被视为一门经验科学。（2）应用经济学则热衷做数据的计量处理，从而将实证经济学从经济学中独立出来。显然，这种实证经济学强调对社会经济现象做客观性的描述而不是预测，进而以某些“客观”的解释为主流经济学理论提供支持，甚至实证分析也只承担解释这一项功能[13]。

正是由于越来越偏重数理模型和实证分析，现代主流经济学家的根本作用也就越来越退缩在解释功能上；进而，为了方便对现实世界描述和解释，也需要设定某种基准或参照系，这种参照系也就是现代主流经济学中的先验假设。例如，完全竞争就为理解和评估现实市场提供了参照系。

由此，我们就可以发现古典政治经济学和现代主流经济学在分析逻辑上的共性：分别基于本质探究和先验抽象而为其分析设定了前提假设。显然，这个前提假设既可以作为认识和构建理论的基础或基准，也可以作为分析和解释现实的标尺或参照系。但同时，古典政治经济学和现代主流经济学所设定的前提假设在性质上存在根本性差异：前者基于本质探究而为改造现实世界设定一个理想状态，后者基于先验抽象而为解释现实世界预设一个参照标准。事实上，如果混淆这两类假设在性质和功能上的差异，将不仅不利于对两类经济学互补性、差异性的理解和认识，而且也无助于政治经济学的理论发展[22]。也就是说，在我们试图对古典政治经济学和现代主流经济学之间进行架桥时，我们不能停留在“两类经济学都存在前提假设”这一点上，而应该对两类假设的丛植差异做清晰区分。只有这样，才能真正辨识出古典政治经济学的高次元思维，才能理解和推动经济理论对社会实践的指导。同时，才能真正理解现代主流经济学逐渐蜕化为解释性学科的深层原因，才能洞悉现代经济学理论何以陷入严重危机之中。

首先，两类前提假设设立的根本目的不同。一般地，古典政治经济学的根本目的在于发现和解决现实社会中的问题，为此，它就采取这样的研究路线：一方面，通过挖掘事物的内在本质而确立起一种理想状态；另一方面，通过剖析社会力量结构以及相应的社会制度而考察实存事物的发展。显然，内在本质就构成了对社会事物的本体论认知，它不仅可以成为认识社会经济现象的参照系，而且还成为改造现实社会的目标方向。正是从这个角度上说，古典政治经济学中基于事物本质所构设的可以称为本体论假设，它具有强烈的现实性和可实现性。与此不同，现代主流经济学的主要目的在于描述和解释社会经济现象，为此，它就采取这样的分析路线：一方面，基于抽象分析而先验地设立一些假设前提作为观察和解释现实世界的参照系；另一方面，在此假设下又借助形式逻辑和计量分析来描述和解释社会经济现象。显然，先验假设构成了对社会现象的解释性认知，它仅仅局限于解释现实的方便，而无法为社会改造提供方向性指导。正是从这个角度上说，现代主流经济学中基于先验抽象所构设的只能是解释论假设，它往往与现实无关，甚至也根本无法成为现实。

其次，两类前提假设设立的思维途径不同。一般地，古典政治经济学采用了社会科学的综合性思维：它注重对大量而具体的经验事实进行概括和提炼，倾向于从人类社会的历史演化过程中洞悉其未来发展的基本趋势，并把事物发展所达致的最终结果视为进行现实改造的理想状态。同时，人类社会发展往往又遵循否定之否定的规律，最终达致的理想状态也必然会在以前的历史阶段中得到某种程度的展现；相应地，这种思维路径就特别注重系统地考察影响事物发展的各种因素，从事物演变的历史轨迹中寻求和洞识相类似的理想状态。正是基于这一思维，古典政治经济学的本体论假设就源于对现实世界的观察和调查，源于对事物演化中各种形态的提炼。与此不同，现代主流经济学则积极模仿自然科学的研究思维：它重视想象力和逻辑推理的训练，进而倾向于在经济分析中大众使用严谨的数学工具和形式逻辑。例如，在物理学中，无摩擦状态就是一种想象，通过小球在平滑平面上直线运动的试验也永远得不出均衡状态。相应地，现代主流经济学的先验假设也主要源于想象，而不是社会实践或生活经验的提炼。

正是由于现代主流经济学的假设是抽象的，也是永远不能实现的，因而简单地按照经济学的理论逻辑根本就无法解决具体的现实问题。举一个关于经济学家的讽刺画：一个物理学家、一个化学家和一个经济学家被困在一座孤岛上，他们身上只有一个肉罐头，却没有任何工具，因而如何打开这个肉罐头就成了问题。于是，物理学家就用石头和树枝做了一个杠杆系统对罐头施压，化学家则用燃烧树皮和树枝的办法把罐头放入水中煮沸，但遗憾的是，这两个方法都没能打开罐头。这时，站在一旁的经济学家非常自信地提出了一个解决问方案，“让我们假定有一个开瓶器”。问题是，从哪里可以以及如何才能获得开瓶器，经济学家却不闻不问。回到现代主流经济学，作为其基石的一般均衡就依赖于人类的完全理性和市场的完全信息这两大条件。问题是，人类如何才能有完全理性？市场如何才能有完全信息？显然，不解决后两个问题，就不能简单地依靠市场竞争来解决现实问题。也正是由于现代主流经济学缺乏解决问题的功能，因而后来就转向了解释功能这一层次？问题是，现代主流经济学果真提供了合理的解释了吗？

现代主流经济学进行研究的一般程序是：首先是构设某种向往的均衡状

态，其次是分析该均衡状态下的各变量（因素）之间的关系以及由此获得的相关结论，最后就是以这种想象的均衡状态为基准对现实社会加以解释和评估。例如，就竞争市场而言，现代主流经济学首先构设出一种一般均衡状态，进而分析这种一般均衡状态下各个市场要素间的数量关系以及各个市场主体间的互动行为，由此得出福利经济学定理、帕累托优化、资源最优配置以及边际生产力分配净尽定理等结论，由此也就可以对市场机制加以辩护，或者提出完善市场的建议。现代主流经济学人大多认为，只要真正理解均衡状态，就能逻辑清晰地分析不均衡的情形。果真如此吗？例如，现代主流经济学在一般均衡状态得出了有效市场说，但问题是，迄今为止的现实市场运行或者发展中国家的市场化改革是帕累托有效的吗？面对现实市场中暴露出的种种问题，现代主流经济学往往简单地将之归咎于现实市场还不是完全竞争的市场，从而需要更进一步推进市场化的改革。问题在于：一般市场均衡本身就是建立在根本不可能实现的一系列条件之上，如主体的充分理性、行为的同时性、偏好次序的连贯性、生产集合的凸性以及信息的完全性等。例如，市场主体根本上就是有限理性的，市场信息根本上也是偏在的。更进一步地，即使市场均衡会出现，它往往也是多重的。相应地，人类社会或市场竞争中也就会出现多样的帕累托状态，又如何预测那种帕累托有效的出现呢？

正是由于现代主流经济学在虚构的引导假设下进行分析，从而就难以深入到经济活动的实际过程之中，反而退化成为一种“我向思考”的逻辑游戏；相应地，这种分析也就难以真正发展和解决现实社会的具体问题，反而基于实证自然主义和伦理自然主义而将现实合理化，从而导致学说变得日益庸俗化。事实上，在先验预设下做纯理论构建的取向在古典主义后期已经开始盛行了，马克思将这些学者就称为“庸俗经济学家”；相应地，马克思批判道：“不要像国民经济学家那样，当他想说明什么的时候，总是置身于一种虚构的原始状态。这样的原始状态什么问题也说明不了。国民经济学家只是使问题堕入五里雾中。他把应当加以推论的东西即两个事物之间的例如分工和交换之间的必然关系假定为事实、事件。神学家也是这样用原罪来说明恶的起源，就是说，他把他应当加以说明的东西假定为一种具有历史形式的事实。”[19] 例如，马克思坚持从人的劳动及劳动对财富的创造出发来揭示商品或资本以及人类社会的本质，但现代主流经济学却舍弃了对劳动的本质分析而代之以劳动负效用假设；

进而，它将劳动视为与资本等同质的生产要素，将劳动视为共同生产过程中的一个投入要素，这样，基于生产要素之间的替代和交换的思维就把价值转换成交换比例以及价格问题。

现代主流经济学将其理论体现建立在非现实的前提假设的基础上，其重要的方法论基础就是弗里德曼的“理论合理与否与假设的现实与否之间存在不相关性”命题：经济假说是否合理在于它是否成功预言未来，而与其显而易见的错误假定无关。正是这一命题鼓励了现代经济学人将已知的虚构实体置入其解释性假说中，而偏离了从发生的因果联系中探寻其内在本质的科学要求。显然，这种做法也遭到众多经济学方法论专家的批判。例如，劳森就指出了正确抽象化的两大原则：（1）必须要与真实的发生机制相关，而不能理想化那些出于解释方便或具有启发性的虚构假设上；（2）必须与事物的内在本质有关，而不能只是关注那些最普遍的性质并由此做高度的概括。即经济解释贵在从经济现象中抽象出内在本质，再以科学方法加以探究[23]。同样，博伊兰和奥戈尔曼也区别了原因探究和解释假说，并由此提出的因果关系整体论，它强调在先验和经验之间进行架桥，致力于从经验中发现本质并获得超验的认识。显然，这种思维实际上也就嵌入在从本质到现象的研究路线中。

可见，古典政治经济学设立的理想状态比新古典经济学的先验假设更有意义：从本质到现象的研究路线将经验和超验联系了起来，不但可以探究长期的理想状态，也可以通过权力结构等因素考察现实的变异性；相反，基于先验的引导假定往往会形成不同的解释共同体，且这种引导假定既不可证实也不可证伪。正是基于从本质到现象的研究路线，马克思系统地审视了现实世界，深刻地批判资本主义制度，进而从本质的探究中为改造现实社会确立“应然”方向；与此不同，基于先验的引导假设，现代主流经济学倾向于以演绎结论作为对比现实的参照物，从而主要局限于解释层次而不是为社会实践提供理论指导，或为社会改建提供方向。为何会形成这种研究路线的差异呢？又在于经济学理论被赋予的根本目标存在显著的不同。马克思经济学不承认现状的合理性，而是认为现实事物或多或少地出现了异化，从而致力于现实世界的改造；为此，它就必须挖掘事物的内在本质，由于规定了可以实现的理想状态。相反，现代主流经济学则基于肯定性理性而合理化了社会现实，从而致力于对这些现实何以如此进行解释而不再是为了推动社会发展和现实改造；为此，它就努力为方便观察和解释而预设某种参照基准，这种参照系根本上也就不是那个转化为现实的理想状态。

五、契合归纳和演绎的回溯法

上面的分析都指出，对事物本质的揭示是认识和改造世界的基础。事实上，一个理论之所以能够逐渐发展成熟并广为接受，绝不仅仅在于它提供了一个自圆其说的解释，而是能够给出更为可信和合理的本体论认识，并由此构建出一套更接近事物内在本质的认知体系。相应地，一个好的经济学理论也应该体现为对本体的揭示而非对现象的解释，揭示出社会经济现象之间相互作用的因果机理而非体现量之相关性的功能性联系。问题是，如何才能揭示出事物的内在本质以及事物间相互作用的因果机理呢？一般来说，自然事物的本质和社会事物的本质是不同的：自然事物往往是由一定的物质组成的，因而其本质就体现在它的实在结构；社会事物往往是一种无形的社会结构，因而其本质主要体现在它的根本目的。为此，这里继续就探究事物本质及其因果关系的基本方法做一阐述。

首先，由于事物本质和因果关系是内在的，因而就很难借助于形式逻辑和数学推理而获得，相反需要依赖人的智性思维。事实上，亚里士多德将知识或科学分为两种：（1）直观的知识，它体现了把握事物的“不可分的形式”、本质或本质属性，是一切推论的原初前提和最初源泉；（2）推论的知识，它是一种“因果”的知识，由能够推论的陈述和三段论的推理一起组成[16]。显然，推论的知识是否为真，依赖于前提（直观的知识）是否为真。为此，这就要求对各种前提进行依次证明，从而使真的问题以另一步骤转移到一组新的前提上来，以此类推，直至无穷；结果就只有假定一些前提是真的，这就是“基本前提”。这意味着，全部科学知识也就包含在基本前提之中。很大程度上，现代主流经济学的数理模型都设定了不言自明的“公理”假定，由此得出的论断也依赖于这些假定。所以，波普尔就指出，纯数学和逻辑并没有给我们提供任何关于世界的信息，而只是发展了描述它的手段[16]。问题是，如何获得这些“基本前提”呢？根本上，这些“基本前提”应该来自对事物本质的本体论认识，而不能是想象的虚构。

其次，现代主流经济学主要通过计量实证方法来寻求基本前提，这是逻辑实证主义的基本特色。例如，弗里德曼提出这样一些观点：（1）研究中最为重要的工作在于是基于某种推理方法来对大量资料加和、分类、组织，由此加深对资料的理解并从中抽象出一种假说；（2）假说的有效性不在于其假设是否真实、是否有用，而在于能否为经验所证实；（3）为经验所证实的假说就成为基本原理，以此为基础所获得的推理结论也就是可信的[24]。但显然，其中潜含了这样两个问题：（1）错误的假设前提和错误的逻辑推论也有可能获得正确的结论；（2）现实条件往往如此复杂而难以完全为假设所刻画。尤其是，事物本质和因果关系往往隐藏在现象背后，而不是一个经验性的认识，相应地，它根本上无法通过实证分析而获得。布罗姆利就指出，“如果上述的规律仅仅是由推断律组成——所谓推断律，就是仅仅由统计的齐一性得出的假说，那么，这一诊断就并没有对观察到的事实进行解释。”[25]波普尔则进一步强调：“经验虽然对我们在科学上的努力可能很重要，但它却从不能用来建立任何观念或理论上的真理，无论某些人可能如何强烈地直接地感受到它一定是真的或它是‘自明’的。这样的直观甚至不能用作一种论证，尽管它们可能鼓励我们去寻找论证……科学的路上铺满了各种被抛弃的理论，它们都曾一度宣称是‘自明的’。”[16]

再次，计量分析根本上是基于小规模的数据，从而必然无法获得因果关系的认知。究其原因，现实世界中的大多数事件都是随机的，都是各种因素共同作用的结果。例如，美国两位统计学家霍华德·维纳和哈里斯·泽维林在盖茨基金会 17 亿美元的资助下调查研究最成功的院校有哪些特点，其结论之一就是著名院校规模普遍较小。证据之一，在宾夕法尼亚州对 1662 所院校的调查中，排名前 50 的院校里有 6 所规模较小，是普通院校的 3 倍多。但是，卡尼曼却指出，这个因果分析是毫无意义的，所得到的结论也是错误的。事实上，如果那些向盖茨基金会提交报告的统计学家调查过最差学校的特点，将会发现那些较差学校也比水平一般的学校的规模小[26]。同样，一项对美国 3141 个县的肾癌发病率进行的调查显示，发病率低的县差不多都是位于中西部、南部和西部人口稀少的乡村，这些区域按照惯例由共和党管辖。那么，能否由此认定共和党的政策有效地防控肾癌这一结论呢？事实上，按照卡尼曼的看法，某县的人口稀少既不会引发癌症也不能避免癌症，但会使癌症发病率比人口稠密地区更高或更低，如果这个县的癌症爆发时正好在某特殊年份赶上抽样调查就会出现发病率高的结果，而如果在前一年做调查就很可能就是相反的结果。所以，卡尼曼说，小样本事件往往比大样本事件更容易产生极端结果，而观察结果完全依赖于调查方法[26]。

显然，上面的分析表明，演绎和归纳都存在逻辑的缺陷，由此发展而来的数理分析和计量实证也必然无法真正获得本体论认识。那么，我们究竟如何认识事物的本质呢？如何对本体展开探究呢？古希腊的柏拉图和亚里士多德等人诉诸直观的把握：人类运用与生俱来的理智能力可以识别本质，进而辨析何种本质主义的定义更为合理。同样，康德也认为，人类头脑中先天拥有将感官所提供的杂乱无章的感觉材料整理成普遍“形式”能力，并将人脑中的这种共同结构称为“先验知觉”，它由直觉和理解形式组成：先验的直觉和外在感官将各种感官材料综合成时间和空间的秩序，然后综合的结果在范畴（理解力形式）的加工整理下就被带入普遍性和必然性的因果关系之中，因而整个复合体就统一在“先验认识”之中[27]。问题是，我们如何运用这种智性能力呢？显然，这又来自对经验事实的思考，经验为理论概念提供了内容和形式。正如波普尔指出的，“科学并不寻问科学家如何获得他的观念，它只是对能被每个人验证的论据感兴趣。”[16]为此，我们就需要在演绎和归纳之外寻找获得本质认知的路径，而源于归纳的计量模型对相关的数据进行论证，源于演绎的数理模型则是从中进一步获得衍生知识。

承袭亚里士多德的本质主义的理智直观理论，康德、黑格尔等人都主张通过现象来寻求本质，而更为充分的阐述在胡塞尔的纯粹现象学方法中。胡塞尔指出，现象学的根本方法是反思分析，它将哲学探索的真正课题定位为通过殊相而闪耀的理想的本质[28]。如何透过现象来探究事物的本质呢？这就要不带偏见地将“现象还原”，从而获得纯粹的感知；同时，这种感知不仅来自于经验，更是要借助人的知性思维。自此以后，康德的先验认识论也为一大批学者所继承和发扬。例如，米塞斯从康德的先验认识论发展出了先验的人类行为学，巴斯卡和劳森等则借鉴康德使用的“超越（Transcendental）”一词发展了超验实在主义学说（Transcendental Realism）。其中，“先验”是对康德哲学的承袭，而“实在论”则是对康德哲学的发展。进而，“超验实在主义”还与“批判自然主义（Critical Naturalism）”相结合而形成“批判实在论（Critical Realism）”，由此对各种实在认知进行系统的审视。按照劳森的理解，包括经济学在内的社会科学应该致力于揭示事件背后的深层结构和根本的因果关系，而决不能仅限于发现事件表层的"恒常关联性"。为此，劳森提出并比较了两种实在主义：经验实在主义（Empirical Realism）和超验实在主义（Transcendental Realism）。

经验实在主义认为，有关社会事件的知识来自于我们的经验或印象，它根植于休谟的因果分析之中。正是由于特殊性的知识被限制在经验的原子实践中，一般性知识就体现在对事件规律性的如下阐述："只要 X 事件发生，Y 事件就发生。"但劳森认为，经验实在主义犯了两个错误：（1）运用经验范畴来去界定整个世界，强用一个认识论的范畴去完成本体论的任务，这就犯了巴斯卡称之的"认识的谬误（Epistemic Fallacy）"；（2）只有被人们经历或者给予人们可能的体验才被视为现实的核心特征，只有经历了的东西才被视为真实的，这就忽略了将某物归于真实的因果标准。超验实在主义则强调，世界不仅由事件以及我们对之的经验或印象所组成，而且由（不可减小的）结构和机制、力量和趋势等组成；而且，后者往往构成了我们经验中实在事件的基础，统治着或创造出现实中的事件，尽管它往往无法观察到。按照超验实证主义的观点，科学的根本目标就在于揭示出那些决定表面现象的内在结构或作用机制。从这个意义上说，规律或规律陈述所表达的与其说是事件的规律性，不如说是对这样的结果及其作用方式的准确描述；而且，如果研究无法揭示事物表象的内部机理和结构，那么，这种作用也就仅仅体现为一种趋势而非现实，它是关于一种结构及其运作方式的一个超事实的说明[29]。

问题是，如何挖掘这种内部结构和机理？如何揭示事物本体以及相互之间因果关系并将之上升到理论层面呢？劳森采用了一种回溯推理或外展推理，它借助于类比和隐喻从事物的表象回溯到其深层结构，从而揭示结构、事件与经验之间的因果关系和机制。同时，回溯法借鉴了实用主义创始人皮尔斯提出的溯因推理（Abduction）。皮尔斯认为，归纳法和演绎法都无法创造出新的思想，而溯因推理则弥补了这两种传统方法的缺陷，它试图通过用一种新的概念框架来观察和解释事物，从而对事物做出新的解释。事实上，几乎所有的科学思想都是运用溯因推理方法而获得的，这一思维有助于把握知识的创造和知觉的火花，点燃吸纳事实的火种[30]。皮尔斯写道："溯因推理的启示闪现于我们目前。它是一种调查活动，尽管是极有可能错误地洞察。确实，我们头脑中以前有过不同的假设，但是，正是那种把我们原来从未想过要放到一起的东西结合起来的想法，在我们的冥想过程中带来新的启示。”[30]进一步地，回溯法则以批判实在论的多层实在论为基础，从可经验观察到的事件中揭示客观存在的非经验的或深层的结构、机制和趋势，从而直接从现象层次抽象出相关的因果机制。

溯因推理法要求将各种相互联系的事物放在一起并通过思维转换和融合而形成对事物内在结构的深刻认识。一般地，溯因法体现为从结果和规则中推出事件的逻辑，即“规则＋经验事实”→事件。这一逻辑过程充分体现出与演绎法和归纳法的差异。一方面，演绎法体现为基于规则（公理）和事件（假设和应用性假定）而产生出一个可供检验的结果并由此推出可能的理论命题。即“规则＋事件”→结论。显然，演绎法的问题在于：（1）由此所推出的结论依赖于公理假设和应用性假定，从而并没有新知识的产生；（2）从事演绎法的学者往往将公理假定当作基本信条而自我满足于将研究建立在逻辑的有效性上，从而没有实际考察前提假定是否有效，而那些可供经验检验的结论也遇到太多的检验难题。另一方面，归纳法体现为基于事件（假设）和结果（观察的现象）而获得规则（一般性命题）的逻辑过程。即“事件＋结果”→规则。显然，归纳法的问题在于：（1）它是对已有假设的证明，而不是一种逻辑推理；（2）总存在没有考虑的特殊个体，从而潜含着归纳谬误[31]。

由此，我们也就可以看出溯因法的重要特色：一方面，不像演绎法那样准备提供一个放之四海而皆真的普适理论，它致力于为解释而提供一个更为合理的理论；另一方面，不像归纳法那样试图从特殊结论推出一般法则，它致力于从影响中寻求原因以提供解释。以具体例子来说明。（1）给定一个规则命题：由不均衡的力量博弈决定的社会制度和分配规则是不公正的，而不公正的社会社会制度和分配规则将导致相同的劳动不能获得相同的收入；（2）给定一个观测现象：现实市场中付出相同劳动的个体所获得的收入往往相差悬殊。由此，就可以得出这样的结论：现实市场中的收入差距体现了分配规则的合理性而不是努力水平或劳动贡献的大小，由不均衡的社会力量结构产生了不公正的分配规则，从而导致现实市场收入分配的不合理。显然，溯因法体现了从结果到原因的推理[31]。当然，溯因法只能获得一种猜测性的论断，但这却是理论研究中最为值得重视的方法；究其原因，溯因法有助于克服归纳法和演绎法的缺陷，有助于形成假设和新的分析框架，从而为形成新概念、形成假说和验证假说提供依据[32]。

事实上，溯因法致力于以从事物的表象回溯到事物的深层结构，并由此剖析事物的内在本质，揭示事物之间的因果关系和作用机制，从而可以更好地构建出不断完善的理论体系。一般地，一个完美的理论有两大要求：（1）内在逻辑一致性，它强调理论体系必须具有自成一体的严格逻辑关系；（2）理论与现实间的一致性，它强调理论必须根基于经验。显然，就归纳法而言，它主要在实现理论与现实间的一致性方面表现得较好，但也可能没有把握与未来相关的因果机理而缺乏预测性；就演绎法而言，它主要在实现理论的内在逻辑一致性方面表现得较好，但也可能因假设缺乏真实性而导致结论与现实脱节。也就是说，纯粹的归纳或纯粹的演绎都无法实现经济理论的两大要求。为此，一些经济学家尝试将归纳和演绎结合起来而形成完整的假设—演绎分析路线，包括这样循环往复的系列过程：假设→演绎→理论→经验证明→归纳→修正假设→……[33]这实际上就是波普尔的证伪法。不过，这也存在问题，绝大多数理论都是由多种假设联合而成的，从而证伪主义就面临着杜恒—奎因难题（duhem-quine thesis）：当理论被经验证伪时，往往很难确定究竟是哪种假设存在问题。为此，拉卡托斯在波普尔证伪主义基础上进一步发展出了科学纲领，它允许新理论可以摆脱零星的证伪检验，直到它凭借新的资料而逐渐达到相对成熟的阶段。

由此，我们还可以对检验一门学科是否是硬科学的两大标准做一审视。（1）内部标准。根据这个标准，一个理论是否具有科学性，首先必须阐明现象之间的因果联系，探明事物之间作用的内在机理。（2）外部标准。根据这个标准，研究对象的可控制性和实验的可重复性在科学发展史上被赋予了优先地位，以至于“硬科学”和“实验科学”往往作为同义词出现。关于这两大标准在经济学中的适用性，需要做进一步的辨析：（1）经济学理论的检验更重要的是依据内部标准，要解释因果机理，并提供一个相对完善的逻辑体系。究其原因，经济学在进行实验室检验上面临许多困难，因而经济学要像其所声称的那样具有“硬科学”的特征几乎是不可能的。（2）经济学所依据的内部标准绝不等同于自然科学中的形式逻辑，从而不能简单地鼓吹数学逻辑的推理。究其原因，尽管数学逻辑具有内部严密性，但它在具体应用中往往并不严密，在表达具有感性特征的个人行为时尤其如此[33]。尤其是，基于数学逻辑获得的认知往往是封闭的和僵化的，从而会窒息理论的进一步发展；与此不同，溯因法则以开放多元的视角看到理论的发展，将理论置于动态的辩证否定之中，并借助经验事实而不断检验和修改。

可见，经济学的理论根本上在于对事物的内在本质的认知，这显然不能局限于数学逻辑的使用，因为它往往体现为一种量的相关性或者功能性联系，而不能自动揭示事物的实在结构和内在本质。正如劳森指出的，“科学研究的首要目标绝不是阐明/预见事件，而是认识和理解支持并控制事件的力量和趋势等。而这种认识是政策分析和有效活动所要求的全部。比方说，医学研究的最终目标不是预测病人皮肤上的病斑的形式，而是辨明引起这一状况的病毒或原因，并开出有效的治愈药方。”[14]那么，如何揭示事物的内在本质呢？这就需要将归纳分析和演绎分析契合起来而形成溯因推理法。事实上，尽管溯因法迄今为止在经济学界得到的关注还非常少，但在科学知识探索中，它却是最常用的方式。布罗姆利认为，“一个经济学家，如果他是先观察某个具体的人类行为——具体的经济结果，而后再试图解释这些行为或结果，那他就是在使用溯因法”；而且，一般地，“当我们观察到周围世界的某种经验的规律性现象（或者某种新发现的不规律性现象），并试图为这些观察到的现象建立某种合理的解释（即事件）时，我们就是在进行对溯因式信念的探求。”[25]很大程度上，正是基于溯因法，我们应该且可以基于知识的契合而不断推动理论的进步，而不是试图在特定库恩范式下构建一个形式优美的普世公理。

六、结语

作为一门着眼于公共领域的学科，政治经济学所应使用的研究方法显然不同于关于私人领域的新古典经济学：一方面，公共领域中的任何社会事物都不是外在于行为主体的，而是人类创造的产物，都体现了一定的人类目的，从而必须引入规范的分析；另一方面，公共领域中的任何社会事物都不是个人理性选择的结果，而是众人共同作用的结果，都体现了明显的强势者偏好，从而必须引入本质的剖析。事实上，政治经济学要承担起认识和改造现实世界的任务，就不能简单停留在对现象的描述和解释上，尤其不能基于肯定性理性思维而将现实社会经济合理化，而是要深入认识现象背后的事物本质，尤其要基于批判理性思维来发现现实社会经济的问题。这就是从本质到现象的研究路线，基于这一路线，就可以正确认识事物的“变”与“常”的关系，才能正确认识事物的“体”与“用”的关系：从各种变化形态中挖掘体现本质的“常”和“体”，同时又以体现本质的“常”和“体”来辩证看待体现为各种具体形态的“用”和“变”，从而实现熊十力所讲的“体用不二”。

显然，要洞悉事物的内在结构和本质，就需要借助人的知性思维，进而需要运用契合归纳与演绎的回溯法。然而，现代主流经济学却割裂了实证分析和规范分析，并集中于事物表象之间的功能联系和数字关系而忽视事物的本质，它或者偏于“极高明而不道中庸”的形式逻辑推演，或者偏重于“道中庸而极不高明”的纯粹计量实证。正因如此，现代主流经济学的研究就难以发现现实世界中存在的问题，更无法找到解决问题的根本举措。其实，数学工具和计量手段的进步虽然有助于提高常规性的分析，却无法提高我们的思想和洞见，反而往往成为窒息思维的不利因素。究其原因，由于技术分析得到过分的推崇，青年人就会忽视乃至轻视前人的洞见。从现实表现看，正是由于现代主流经济学倾向于使用越来越复杂的数学技术，结果，在一整套的分析范式和写作格式支配下，思想的萌生和理论的发展却遭到严重窒息；而且，一篇经济学论文所使用数学技术越复杂，其内含的思想往往也就越缺乏。徐复观在《不思不想的时代》一文中就指出，“越是现代化的地方，便越是不思不想的地方”，究其原因，“现代人不追问‘为了什么’？而只追问‘怎么办’……‘怎么办’，当然也是一种思想的运用；但这种思想的运用，常以感官为主，把思想拘限在事物的表层上，局限在事物的孤立的个体上；作为思想特性的向深度与广度的推展扩大，在这种强调之下，是发挥不出来的。”[34]现代经济学研究的处境也是如此，在一整套分析技术的开发和使用下，现代经济学也进入了不思不想的时代。

参考文献

[1] 朱富强．为何“经济学”本质上应是“政治经济学”［J］．学习与探索，2016（11）：131－139.

[2] 霍奇逊．资本主义、价值和剥削［M］．于树生，陈东威，译．北京：商务印书馆，2013.

[3] 博特莱特．金融伦理学［M］．静也，译．北京：北京大学出版社，2002.

[4] 朱富强．现代主流经济学的效率概念是价值无涉的吗？效率原则的实践后果及科

斯中性定理反思［J］. 学术研究，2009（10）：79－84.

［5］哈耶克 . 致命的自负［M］. 冯克利，等，译 . 北京：中国社会科学出版社，2000.

［6］朱富强 . 收入再分配的理论基础：基于社会贡献的原则［J］. 经济学家，2014（08）：5－14.

［7］朱富强 . 进步还是后退？经济学数量化历程中的科学性审视［J］. 首都经济贸易大学学报，2009（02）：111－118.

［8］朱富强 . 实证经济学是否是一门客观性学科？实证分析中主观性和规范性探微［J］. 经济社会体制比较，2009（01）：146－152.

［9］朱富强 . 经济学是一门科学吗？基于科学划界标准的审视［J］. 福建师范大学学报，2009（03）：57－65.

［10］朱富强 . 经济实验如何才会更有效：兼对杜宁华先生批判的回应之一［J］. 上海财经大学学报，2018（01）：114－129.

［11］朱富强 . 实证经济学中" 致命的自负"：实证分析的合理性、可信性及有用性质疑［J］. 社会科学战线，2008（07）：47－55.

［12］豪斯曼，麦克佛森 . 经济学、理性和伦理学［M］. //豪斯曼 . 经济学的哲学［M］. 丁建峰，译 . 上海：世纪出版集团/上海人民出版社，2007.

［13］朱富强 . 经济学能否蜕化为一门纯粹解释的实证学科？基于实证分析的解释合理性之反思［J］. 学术月刊，2010（04）：69－77.

［14］劳森 . 一个经济学的实证主义理论［M］. //巴克豪斯 . 经济学方法论的新趋势［M］. 张大宝，等，译 . 经济科学出版社，2000.

［15］朱富强 . 从本质到现象：比较制度分析的基本路线［J］. 学术月刊，2009（03）：79－87.

［16］波普尔 . 开放社会及其敌人（第二卷）［M］. 郑一明，等，译 . 北京：中国社会科学出版社，1999.

［17］朱富强 . 马克思经济学的基本分析思维及其实践价值：古典经济学与新古典经济学的研究路线之比较［J］. 福建论坛，2011（05）：8，9－16.

［18］亚当·斯密 . 国民财富的性质和原因的研究（上卷）［M］. 郭大力，王亚南，译 . 北京：商务印书馆，1972.

［19］Marx K. Economic and Philosophic Manuscripts of 1844［M］. New York：Prometheus Books，1988.

［20］张五常 . 科学说需求（经济解释卷一）［M］. 北京：中信出版社，2010.

［21］贾根良 . 西方异端经济学主要流派研究［M］. 北京：中国人民大学出版社，2010.

［22］朱富强 . 约定主义、解释共同体以及两大流派的分析特质：马克思经济学和西方

主流经济学的引导假定之比较［J］. 清华政治经济学报，2013（07）.

［23］博伊兰，奥戈尔曼．经济学方法论新论［M］. 夏业良，主译．北京：经济科学出版社，2002.

［24］弗里德曼．实证经济学方法论［A］. 豪斯曼．经济学的哲学［C］. 丁建峰，译．上海：世纪出版集团/上海人民出版社，2007.

［25］布罗姆利．充分理由：能动的实用主义和经济制度的含义［M］. 简练，等，译．上海：上海人民出版社，2008.

［26］卡尼曼．思考，快与慢［M］. 胡晓姣，等，译．北京：中信出版社，2012.

［27］马尔库塞．理性与革命——黑格尔和社会理论的兴起［M］. 程志民，等，译．重庆：重庆出版社，1996.

［28］胡塞尔．欧洲科学危机和超验现象学［M］. 张庆熊，译．上海译文出版社，1988.

［29］朱富强．经济学中因果分析的认识论思考：超验实在主义与经济理论的“发现”［J］. 福建论坛，2010（06）.

［30］霍奇逊．演化与制度：论演化经济学和经济学的演化［M］. 任荣华，等，译．北京：中国人民大学出版社，2007.

［31］朱富强．计量结果的基本特性及其实践价值——兼论经济理论的评判标准和发展路向［J］. 天津师范大学学报（社会科学版），2014（02）：36-45.

［32］贾根良．西方异端经济学主要流派研究［M］. 北京：中国人民大学出版社，2010.

［33］谢拉.C. 道．经济学方法论［M］. 杨培雷，译．上海：上海财经大学出版社，2005.

［34］徐复观．中国人文精神之阐扬［M］. 李维武，编．北京：中国广播电视出版社，1996.

How to Recognize and Reform the Real World: The Research Logic and Methodology of Political Economy

Zhu Fuqiang

Abstract: What economics tries to explore basically is the social matter that belongs to the public domain, and it needs to undertake the task of recognizing and reforming the real world. Therefore, the theory research of economics must adopt the four strong realistic methods. (1) Unifying empirical analysis with normative analysis. It emphasizes the combination of "to be" based on the empirical analysis on phenomena and "should be" based on the normative analysis on nature, so as to can conclude the two major contents of engineering and ethics. (2) Obeying to the research route from essence to phenomenon. It emphasizes the combination of the ontology based on internal structure and the epistemology based on external phenomenon, so as to can go deep into the essence problem behind the phenomena. (3) Establishing achievable ideal state for the premise of theory. It stresses to take the essence of things as reference to examine the actual problems and guide its development in future, so as to can distinguish the two main hypotheses of ontology and interpretation. (4) Applying the reproduction combining inductive and deductive analysis. It emphasizes to make full use of the intellectual thinking to improve the experience knowledge up to the transcendental system and deepen the understanding of ontology, so as to effectively compensate the defects of empirical induction and abstract deduction. Only based on these four methods, economics can be a kind of applicative science of "the unity of the wise and the mean", so as to achieve the double goal of recognizing and reforming the real world.

Keywords: Normative analysis Assumption Ontology Retroduction Economics methodology

CLC number: G633. 23 Document code: A

I. Introduction

Despite historical origin or academic characteristics, the fundamental research area of the economic discipline is within the public domain, which includes wealth creation, division of labor, income distribution, welfare improvement, social norms, etc. Therefore, "political economy" is the original as well as the appropriate name for this discipline[1]. Meanwhile, socio-economic phenomena and problems in the public domain origins from individual behaviors and their social interaction under certain social relations. Thus, it is necessary to pay attention to the social relation among individual preference and behavior, institutional changes, and collective actions, to introduce ethic and just social concerns, as well as to be embedded into the analysis of law, sociology, political science, ethics and philosophy. Therefore, the name of "political economy" is consistent with social economics, public economics, institutional economics, collective economics and humanistic economics. Unfortunately, since the marginal revolution, mainstream economics has shifted its research focus to the private sector, exploring the allocation of resources under a given system and individual behaviors in isolated situation. Accordingly, on the one hand, it has established a series of sophisticated mathematical models on the basis of a reductionism thinking; on the other hand, based on ethical naturalism and positive naturalism, it prefer to describe and explain the reality. The result is, however, modern economics has gradually been separated from the disciplines such as management, ethics, and political science. It has increasingly converged on the natural sciences such as mathematics and physics, and has even become a branch of applied mathematics. Accordingly, the modern mainstream economics has become more and more abstract. Economic theories have become increasingly apart from reality. The modern mainstream economics have disintegrated into intellectual games of those who prefer mathematic logic and skills, and are no longer the knowledge to discover and solve problems.

In fact, the research thinking and method of a discipline should be compatible to its research object and content. For example, it is the individual behaviors focusing on the private sphere that lead neo-classical economics to the analysis of the formal logic and functionalism. Then, focusing on the social issues in the public domain, what characteristics should the research methods of economic disciplines have? At the same time, neo-classical economists changed the name of the economic discipline from "political economy" to "economics" for their dislike of politics, and tried to abandon moral and ethical factors so as to construct pure theoretical economics. Did it really make it? Hodgson pointed out that the neo-classical school has not cut off the associated relationship with ideology. While they remain silent on their value judgments, these value standards are playing a worse role behind them. In terms of political practice, the neo-classical school essentially advocated that political and government intervention should be excluded from economic activities. If Smith and Ricardo had tried to use theoretical tools to prove the so-called superiority of the market mechanism, the neo-classical school simply wanted people to accept it unconditionally. They remain politically silent, but they are latently defending the status quo in silence[2]. In particular, as a practical discipline, does modern mainstream economics take the responsibility of "to learn and transform the world"? Hodgson continued to write: Although the neo-classical orthodoxy is dominant in the field of economics, it lacks the directness, substantiality, and reality of Marxism. Mainstream economics tends to be an empty form of algebraic formalism in terms of "theory", and to be a kind of lifeless naive empiricism in terms of "application". Constructing such a theory has almost become a pure logic game[2]. This paper makes a systematic exploration of the methodologies that should be used in political economy and even economics.

II. The Consilience between Phenomena Demonstration and Essential Norms

Since taking the promotion of human welfareas the basic goal, the research content of economics includes engineering and ethics these two mains aspects. (1) The engineering content focuses on the relationship between human and nature, including the optimal allocation of resources and isolated individual choice behaviors, etc.; (2) The ethical content pays attention to the relationship among different persons, including the social distribution of resources and the social interaction among people. Correspondingly, there are some relevant requirements of different research methods. (1) The study of engineering content is mainly concerned with the technical relations of human dealing with natural objects. Obviously, this is related to the level of productivity and instrumental rationality, and which is more suitable for empirical research, as well as abstract analysis based on mathematical logic. (2) The study of ethical content mainly involves the social interaction among people. Obviously, this embeds certain social needs and value judgments, which is more applicable to normative analysis and the comprehensive analysis on the basis of knowledge consilience.

In general, the allocation of resources involving value judgments reflects the purpose of social development, while the allocation of resources not involving value judgments belongs to the category of instruments and tools. At the same time, the use of tools cannot be separated from purpose setting. For example, a basic tenet of modern mainstream economics is that the goal of a company is to maximize shareholder value. In reality, this creed itself is also a normative proposition about how business activities should behave[3]. Therefore, although modern mainstream economics tends to view economics as a purely technical, non-value-related science, it only cares about method and means, rather than its purpose; but it is clear that this view oversimplifies the complicated social facts, neglects the purpose itself embedded in the creation and development of social affairs. In fact, even if modern mainstream economics concentrates on analyzing technical issues, it will inevitably slip from the proposition of "to be" to the proposition of "should be". For example, the principle of equalizing various marginal replacement rates involved in optimization takes social efficiency as its goal, while social efficiency itself implies certain values[4].

Therefore, although modern mainstream economics emphasizes the empirical nature of economics and advocates to abandon the ethical factors in economics; however, it cannot be achieved at all. The reason is that any socio-economic phenomenon occurs in a certain social relationship and is involved in the relationship of interest among people. Hardin pointed out that ethics is the study of the allocation of resources[5]. For example, modern mainstream economics often declares that its three major research contents are "what to produce", "how to produce" and "for whom to produce", but apparently these already cover two major aspects of engineering and ethics. (1) If "what to produce" and "how to produce" belong to problems of engineering, then "for whom to produce" belongs to an ethical problem, which involves the allocation of social resources among human. (2) Even in terms of "what to produce," it depends on the comparison of interpersonal utility, and is involved with the choice of interpersonal utility, so that it is necessarily related to the relationship among people; (3) Even in terms of "how to produce", technology is chosen by certain powerful people and will inevitably reflect the interests of specific individuals or groups. Therefore, existing production organizations also have obvious social characteristics[6]. Unfortunately, modern mainstream economics analyzes the allocation of resources based on individual choices under a closed and static framework, so as to focus on the so-called "efficiency" issues, rather than ethical relations.

At the same time, as an essential social science, the economic discipline has such dual features. (1) As the object of research, the socio-economic phenomenon is not external to the cognitive subject just as the natural phenomenon, but is the product of human behaviors. Meanwhile, the cognition of economic phenomena from the subject is not separated from their own experience and feelings. Therefore, the theoretical study of economics has a characteristic of strong subjectivity. (2) People's exploration of socio-economic phenomena is not just the application of certain unchangeable principles as is done by the natural sciences, but the in-depth knowledge of human's purposes. It aims at transforming the unreasonable status quo in order to promote the development of human society. Therefore, the study of economics itself is strongly normative. In other words, whether it is social science or economics as social science, its theory itself is full of subjectivity and normative nature: subjectivity reflects the private knowledge and the inherited social habits of an individual, and the normative nature reflects the social care and perspective of individuals[7].

Therefore, although modern mainstream economics emphasizes empirical analysis and considers empirical analysis as objective and scientific, in reality, this cannot be achieved at all. The reason is that any designs of social systems and policy proposals involve the selection of means and goals, and all of them definitely reflect a certain value orientation. In fact, in the process of empirical analysis, whether it is the choice of data or the choice of analytical tools, whether it is the choice of dependent variables or independent variables, it is full of subjectivity. To a large extent, the economists' purpose is to persuade others when they choose the econometric analysis during their research. For this reason, on the one hand, they hope to find out those evidences that help to support his own point of view; on the other hand, high emotional words are also used when explaining their findings to others[8]. At the same time, in terms of the nature of this discipline, economics not only fails to meet the scientific standards required by logical positivism[9], but fails to reach the "science" height of natural sciences. Accordingly, the theoretical development of economics is not mainly based on the external standard of the controllable experiments, but is based on the logical system of the internal standards[10]. Unfortunately, modern mainstream economics has focused on the "confirmation" of modern economic theories within the framework of neoclassical and Keynesian economics, and provided defense for this "positivist" analysis based on scientism.

Both of the above analyses have shown that the objectivity of econometric analysis is only a fiction. At the same time, economics is by no means merely an empirical science. After all, economics is a science of applied Learning, it needs to solve specific problems related to social reality, but not just the description of phenomena. In general, the theoretical system of economics has two basic requirements: first, it should come from life experience, and second, it must raise experience to the level of transcendentalism, so as to achieve a theoretical system of "the unity of the wise and the mean". At the same time, the results of empirical research are often policy-related. It shows, to a certain extent, that whether the policy has promoted or hindered the completion of value goals. Obviously, purely empirical research cannot solve policy and value problems without some prior value proposition; the reason is that pure empirical research is independent from any specific ethical positions or value judgments, and any policy advice is based on specific goals or a specific position. To this end, the theoretical study of economics must combine empirically-based "what to be" and normative-based "what should be": purely "positivist" that does not explore "what should be" is meaningless, while the "normative" arguments not knowing "what to be" is also an armchair strategy[11].

The explanation is as follows. First, empirical analysis must be made on the basis of normative exploration. Just think: If we do not explore the problem of "what should be", even if we understand "what to be", we just stay on the pure "empirical level", and how can we propose any suggestions for the improvement to the reform of the social system? This will only be confined to the far-fetched stereotyped writing like the current Chinese economists. Second, normative exploration should also be oriented toward empirical analysis. Just think again: If we do not have a full understanding of "what to be", even if we already understand "what should be", what practical things can this guide us to do? This will only make us stay at the unrestricted "ism" debate like traditional economists. On the contrary, combining empirical analysis with normative analysis can form a complete research line from the essence to the phenomenon: on the one hand, empirical analysis is used to explore the deviation of phenomena from nature and its causes; on the other hand, to reveal intrinsic essence and development requirements of social issues on the basis of normative analysis can help us find the direction and approach for the improvement of the existing system.

The history of economics also shows that the normative ethics and the empirical engineering are unified within the economic discipline. However, due to the increasingly narrowing research content of neo-classical economics and then the gradual abandonment of the content of ethics, the separation of ethics and engineering finally occurred. So, as Hausman and McPherson pointed out, maybe the real challenge is not to prove the connection between economics and ethics, but to seek the possibility of separating the two, and to regard economics as an objective social science[12]. In modern mainstream economics, the separation between positive economics and normative economics fundamentally origins from the dichotomy thinking between facts and values rooted in western society. But in fact, the fact-value dichotomy itself is ineffective. For example, is the sentence "market mechanism is efficient" descriptive or evaluative? Modern mainstream economics treats it as an empirical description, but it is clear that the connotation of efficiency itself takes the specific purpose of the cognitive subject as its premise. In fact, in human society, there is no question about value that can be solved through facts. There are also no problems that can be solved simply by assessing their value. For this reason, mature economic discipline should put positive economics and normative economics together.

However, modern mainstream economics believes that the issues of facts and values are not only separated but also independent. Therefore, economics gradually separated positive economics from normative economics, and increasingly focuses on empirical research in pursuit of natural science objectivity. According to the standard view of modern mainstream economics, the so-called "normative economics" is no more than the application of positive economics to relevant aspects that require direct value assessments. Therefore, the study of ideology and the values of economists have nothing to do with the understanding of economics or economic methodology[12]. But it is clear that this standard view is overstated: (1) When economists are consulted for the advice on "pure technology" that achieves certain goals, few of them will get a purely technical problem; (2) Even though econometrics focuses on the exploration of the relationship between things, it is mainly based on functional connections, and thus often arbitrarily replaces dependent variables and independent variables. It is precisely because the ideological analysis of modern mainstream economics is mainly limited to functional linkages that it is often incapable of making predictions. Samuelson admits frankly in his preface to the textbook *Economics* that economics cannot tell us which political view is correct.

In fact, it is precisely because neoclassicism has gradually turned to the path of mathematical modeling and econometrics, the nature of the economic discipline has undergone a marked transformation: it is no longer predictive but explanatory, and thus does not take the task of guiding social practice. Of course, it is undeniable that some mainstream economists are indeed keen to apply the results of empirical analysis to guide social reforms, but this function is often combined with the naturalistic thinking of western society; at the same time, modern mainstream economics estabilshed its standard of "should be" based on naturalistic thinking, which often rationalizes the empirical results and defend the reality by using empirical analysis. Because of this, mainstream positive analysis has obvious characteristics of conservatism and compromise. It forms the theory of chanting for the reality and lacks the spirit of criticism and negation. Obviously, this theory cannot change the existing society, and is impossible to create a reasonable society. Particularly, in the underdeveloped societies whose social systems are still unsound, if we rely on this combination of empirical analysis and naturalism to guide social reforms, we will inevitably exacerbate imbalance and confusion in the entire society.

Obviously, as a social science, economics cannot explore a constant law like natural sciences, but needs to explain questions of how social phenomena occur, what factors determine the changes in social things, and how things will develop in the future, so on. At the same time, in the evolution process of social things, the intrinsic nature of them, like the strange attractors in physics, determine the development tracks of them, so that by understanding their nature, it is easy to reveal the path or "law" of the development of things. Therefore, if economics really wants to become an applicative science of "the unity of the wise and the mean", it should not be limited to the level of "what to be", but should be deeply rooted in "what should be." On the one hand, "whatto be" is an examination of the social status quo and reflects the results of empirical analysis. Obviously, such an analysis often requires certain measurement tools. At the same time, it also needs to test the empirical conclusion about "what to be". On the other hand, "what should be" is a kind of value, which embodies the concept and perspective of the cognitive subject. Obviously, to fully understand "what should be" requires in-depth survey combined with the knowledge accumulated by human beings[13]. In particular, a purely empirical analysis cannot provide any policy advice at all, and thus cannot provide guidance for social practice. Therefore, as an applicative science, positive economics can by no means replace the position of normative economics.

III. A Research Route from Phenomena to Essence

The above emphasizes that empirical analysis should be combined with normative analysis. Only by establishing normative standards, can empirical evidence be targeted so as to provide guidance for social practice. However, for a long time, mainstream economics has separated normative analysis and empirical analysis. Since it is so, how does it guide social practice? Generally speaking, there are two main ways of thinking. (1) Resorting to the natural order and market mechanism, since thinking that market can solve the problem naturally getting rid of the artificial (mainly government) intervention, and this is the principle of "invisible hand" advocated by neoclassical liberalism. (2) Resorting to the institutional arrangements and experience of developed countries, since taking the developed countries today as the future of developing countries, and this is the monistic view of social development accepted universally. Furthermore, these two kinds of thinking are rooted in a single naturalistic thinking and deeply embedded in modern mainstream economics. Affected by this, modern mainstream economists often take it for granted that some methods, goals, and criteria of reasoning have been proven to be effective in specific natural science fields, so they will be definitely applicable to all other scientific fields, especially social and economic analyses. Is that true?

In fact, modern mainstream economists accept and follow an instrumental methodology that contains serious logic problems. For example, a big stick can remove the dust from the mat, but this does not mean that it is also suitable for the dust on the glass; accordingly, even if it is found through practice that a tool is useful for a particular job, this does not mean that it can be used to solve other similar problems. Lawson pointed out that it is precisely this unreasonable reliance on this reasoning that allows us to understand the causes of the failure of contemporary economics in the past 50 years[14]. Obviously, to get rid of current dilemma of positive logic, it is necessary to make an in-depth exploration of things behind the phenomenon, and to use human intellectual thinking to go beyond the empirical analysis to explore the nature of things, which is the ontological issue of economics. In fact, the fundamental purpose of the theoretical study of economics is to reveal the essence of things, so as to clarify the logical mechanisms and causal relationships between the developmental roles among things. Furthermore, a basic aspiration to guide social practice by exploring the essence of things can refine the research path from essence to phenomena: first, to explore the essence of social affairs through complicated phenomenon; second, to analyze the current status of things; third, to analyze the causes of the current situation and the factors that cause appearance and essence to be separated from each other; finally, to find ways to correct the alienation of things[15].

The research route of "from essence to phenomenon" can be traced back to ancient Greece. In fact, Plato believed that the development of all things begins with the original, perfect form or idea, but things in the process of their development start to lose their perfection when they change to a certain extent and the similarities with the original forms decrease[16]. At the same time, Plato also made the sense of rationality independent, and he believed that rationality can be identified by its existence and help it to return to its original ideal state. Similarly, Aristotle also emphasized that there is an ultimate reason for the change of anything at any movements: "the reason of purpose," which is the goal of the movement. Obviously, this inherited the practice of Plato's extension of the theory of justice to the universe: not only every citizen of different ranks in the society has their natural status, but also the physical world has similar levels and categories. The main differences between the two are as follows: Plato saw the form or the essence or the foundation as the inherent existence, and thus they are separated from the sensible things; while Aristotle believed that the sensible things will move to its ultimate cause or purpose. Therefore, these things are the same as their nature or forms. That is to say, Aristotle believed that form or essence existed in things themselves, while Plato thought that they existed before or outside things. In Aristotle's view, all movements or changes mean the realization (or actualization) of the potential inherent in the nature of things. The essence including all the potential is something intrinsic to the changes of things or the internal source of movements. Therefore, the form or essence of anything in the process of development is the same as its development goal, purpose or final state[16]. In this way, Aristotle replaced Plato's pessimism with optimism, thus no longer appealing for the construction of an ideological country.

The full use of the research route of "from nature to phenomenon" in economic analysis can be traced back to classical political economy. The classical political economists such as Petty, Smith, Mill, Marx, etc. actually used the study route that goes from essence to phenomenon[17]. The reason is that the research object of classical political economy is organization, and the research topics are concentrated in the public domain; for this reason, classical political economists mostly study economics as part of social science, and their theories and methods are obviously full of normalization, and they try to evaluate and judge the real world. For example, Marx's study has two characteristics: (1) He absorbed almost all the social scientific knowledge of that time and explored the essence of things in light of the evolutionary history of social things. He considered this essence as a reasonable and ideal development direction in the future. (2) He made full use of the power structure to analyze the differences between the original appearance of the object and its reality, and analyzed the influence of the evolution of the power structure on the development of social things. At the same time, classical economists such as Smith, Ricardo, Mill, and Malthus not only focus on the exchange of commodities and the price decided by the exchange, but the internal reason for the decision and influence of the exchange of goods. For this reason, these classical economists all distinguish the natural price (intrinsic value) and the market price (nominal price) of the commodity, andthus forming a dichotomy thinking that runs through their research on all commodities.

Obviously, this dichotomy thinking in the analysis of labor wages is very obvious, so here also take Smith's wage theory as an example to explain. When Smith analyzed the wage theory, he did it from one aspect to another. First, Smith explored the nature of wage. In this regard, he saw it as a term within the natural category. This is fully embodied in the "state of primitive society" where land has not been privately owned and capital has not yet been accumulated. At this time, wages are the total remuneration of the workers gained through labor[18]. Therefore, it is determined by productivity, that is, "products of labor constitute natural rewards or natural wages for labor." Second, Smith did not remain at this metaphysical level, but further observed the status quo of wages. Obviously, in the employment society, workers cannot own all the products, but only obtain a part of them, and what they obtained can only meet the basic needs of life. The last, Smith also discovered the separation of the reality of wage from its essence. In fact, if everyone can fully own his own product of labor, wages will grow at the same ratio as his productivity; however, in modern employment society, people cannot completely obtain their own labor products, and thus wages won't be in line with productivity. Thus, a key question is how the actual wage is determined. For this, Smith has carried out an in-depth analysis.

Smith distinguished the market price and the natural price of labor products, and focused on the analysis of the factors that influence the wages that mean the market price of labor goods. The analyses are follows. (1) Wages become part of the cost of production, and the demand for wage proportionately increases with the rise of wage funds, which implies wage fund theory. (2) In reality, "the wages of workers depend on the contract set by the employer and the employee." The amount of wages depends on, to a certain extent, the competition between the two sides. This is the origin of the "wage contract theory". (3) Employers have an advantage in the bargaining in the labor market because they are small in quantity and can last longer. The law is also partial to them. Employers have a secretive unity that reveals the power principle of wage decision. (4) In particular, the capital owner was in an extremely favorable position in the competition at that time, so the workers had to be satisfied with the low "survival wages". (5) At the same time, there is also a basic boundary of wages: they must at least be enough to sustain life; this is Participation Constraint in the Incentive Theory that leads to the "subsistence" theory. (6) According to the relationship between supply and demand of labor, the highest wage does not exist in the richest countries, but in the most prosperous ones that are becoming the fastest growing affluent. Obviously, these insights of Smith's and Marx's argument have strong commonality, as Marx wrote: Wages are determined through the antagonistic struggle between capitalist and worker. victory goes necessarily to the capitalist. The capitalist can live longer without the worker than can the worker without the capitalist. Combination among the capitalists is customary and effective; workers' combination is prohibited and painful in its consequences for them[19].

Of course, Smith, Mill or Marx did not accept this low level of wages, and they believed that wage levels can be continuously increased by means of the correction of social power structure and legal system. In this regard, Smith further explored ways to increase wages, which mainly depend on changes in the forces of the two sides. (1) If capital accumulation increases and the economy develops rapidly, it will increase the demand for labors and promote the increase of wages. Therefore, Smith did not believe that wage cannot be increased as said by the advocates of "wage fund theory" or "subsistence theory", and he, on the contrary, agrees to high wages. On the one hand, Smith saw rising wages as a result and a sign of social wealth growth. "The demand for wage labors must increase in proportion to the increase in funds that are set to pay for labor wages." On the other hand, high wages can promote the health and physical strength of workers and encourage workers to try their best to work. This has become the beginning of efficiency wage. (2) Smith also pointed out that if an agreement such as the establishment of the trade union is allowed, the negotiating power of workers can be intensified, thereby facilitating the distribution workers. This has become a mental source of countervailing power.

It also have been clearly confirmed in modern society that wage levels have improved along with the development of society. Actually, in modern capitalist society, when an enterprise increases labor productivity due to the adoption of new technologies, the wage level is often improved through two ways: (1) If this new technology is gradually mastered by competitors, technological innovation will lead to a general increase in social productivity in the normal market competition, which will result in a decrease in product costs and a drop in market prices. Under this circumstance, the real wage level will increase as market prices decline even if nominal wage does not change; (2) If this new technology is gradually mastered by competitors, under the condition that incomplete market competition leads to downward rigidity of prices, enterprises or industries that adopt new technologies can obtain excess profits. Under this circumstance, wages tend to increase due to the demand of modern labor union's sharing profits within the range of rising productivity despite the increase in the overall price level.

Obviously, the analysis route of "from essence to phenomenon" used by the classical political economy is fundamentally different from that of the neo-classical economics which only focused on the status quo. The prevailing view is that Marshall combined the cost-value theory of classical economics emphasizing the supply with the utility value theory of the marginal school emphasizing the demand, and established an economic theory with partial equilibrium based on supply and demand and the "Marshall cross" formed by these two curves. This framework of supply and demand analysis provides a theoretical basis for late comers to understand and analyze the process of determining and changing economic phenomena such as price. Correspondingly, some scholars believe that the supply and demand analysis framework constitutes the differences between classical economics and neoclassical economics, and represents the progress of economics. They even consider that neoclassical theory is by far the best economic theory, and that the way in which classical scholars sought intrinsic value was misleading. However, as is pointed out earlier, the supply and demand analysis of the status quo is not firstly used by Marshall. On the contrary, the classical economists, Smith, Malthus, and Marx have actually used this method; but classical economics did not only stay in the decision of status quo (market price), but also dig deeper into the essence behind it, while Marshall integrates the previous theories such as supply and demand theory, the production cost theory, and the marginal utility theory, and transforms it into a price theory to replace or cancel the theory of value.

To a large extent, it is precisely because neoclassical economics focuses on phenomena that its price theory has fundamental flaws. (1) When analyzing supply and demand, it considers them as a function of price; while when seeking equilibrium prices, it regards it as a function of supply and demand. Obviously, this is a tautology. Which decides which? It is precisely because the price theory of neo-classical economics cannot solve the problem of price determination at all that Alchian taught his disciples that "what determines prices is much less important than what prices can determine"[20]. (2) Since in a short term, each manufacturer is producing and selling products at an equilibrium price, how does the long-term price change? In fact, in Marshall's view, although all kinds of value theories are the result of interactions between demand and supply, the roles of demand and supply in balancing the formation of prices are also different due to different length of time. Generally, the shorter the period of consideration is, the greater the impact of demand on value will be, while the longer the period is, the more important the impact of production costs on value will be. In other words, under the premise that the marginal utility and production costs jointly determine value, Marshall pays more attention to the role of production costs.

Obviously, there are some obvious commonalities between Marshall's cognition and classical economics, but Marshall's followers deviate from the road of classical economics and go further and further. Therefore, although Marshall inherited classical economics thinking and focused on practical issues and policies, but his successors are confined to logical repairs, while ignoring Marshall's realistic concerns and humanistic spirit.

It is clear that we can make a comprehensive and in-depth understanding of the socio-economic phenomena on the basis of research path of "from essence to phenomenon" On the contrary, if we only analyze the phenomena based on the supply and demand framework, the understanding will be superficial and one-sided. In fact, according to critical realism, the ontology of social economy can be abstracted into three levels: (1) The level of experience and events, which is the reality at the level of experience, and is mainly about people's experiences, impressions, events and the state of events. (2) The level of structure and mechanism, which refers to various rules, traditions, conventions, norms, relationships, and cognitive structures of the society. (3) The level of human nature, which consists of the eternal nature of human, significant features and basic trends[21]. However, modern mainstream economics only focuses on the empirical rules at the level of event and explains it based on the hypothesis of reductive human nature. Correspondingly, the research of modern mainstream economics mainly includes the following. (1) Focus on the balanced analysis of supply and demand in the private sector based on naturalistic thinking, which not only regards the social system as an established one, but also makes an analysis of function on the premise of the established system. (2) Focus on the quantitative analysis of the status quo based on logical positivism, while defending the status quo and serving the interests of the strong under the ethical positivist values. For example, based on the analytical logic of supply and demand and the thinking of ethical positivism, people tend to consider the income obtained through market exchange as reasonable. Why entrepreneurs can get rich overnight? Because they contribute so much to the society. Why managers can achieve amazingly high buy-out annual salary? The reason is the same. And why the salaries of nannies and cleaners are so low? Because they have made almost no contribution to the society. But obviously, this actually regards the "existence" as "should be", which obscurs the hidden relation of exploitation among them and fails to reveal the unfairness of the entire social distribution system.

Ⅳ. Setting a Realizable Ideal State as the Frame of Reference

Marx emphasizes that the task of philosophy is not to know the world but to change it. Of course, it is not only the task of philosophy but also the task of almost all social sciences to recognize and transform the world, and it is the fundamental task of the economic discipline of the study. The question is, how to effectively recognize and transform the world? Generally, to know the world is the previous step to change the world, a process that is bound to be marked by an individual's features. A man must conceive a reform target first before he changes the world. So the question is: how to decide a reform target. The method of classical political economy is to study from essence to phenomenon. One should understand the essence of things before he knows the defects of the world, and should discover the reason of alienation before effective solutions. Apparently, under this circumstance, the essence of things is seen as an ideal state not only used to measure how an objective thing alienates, but also deemed a basic frame of reference for things' further development. The assumption of such an ideal state allows us to comment on the rationality of the current situation and to analyze the internal defects of our realistic system. Accordingly, by revealing the reason why the realistic system alienates, we can find the effective means in a well-directed way to improve the system.

However, modern mainstream economics are gradually divided into a field of theory and a field of application, and mainstream theoretical economics develops in two ways. (1) Establishing a pure mathematical model of axiomatic systems. Such systems are merely a form of subject thinking or a conceptual product. It does not require economics to provide a reliable guidance for the actions of economic agents or the operation of economy as a whole. It does not even see economics as a science of experience any longer. (2) Separating empirical economics form economics. This direction emphasizes that empirical economics is a subject of objective description instead a subject of forecasting, and after the promotion by people such as Friedman, such objectiveness has become a common view in mainstream economics[13]. These economists pay more and more attention on mathematical models and empirical analysis, the function of theoretical economics is gradually narrowed and it is only used to explain the world. Meanwhile, a frame of reference is needed for explanations and descriptions. This is the priori hypothesis in mainstream economics.

Apparently, two schools of economics, classical political economy that focuses on the exploration of the essence of things and the modern mainstream economics that underlines priori hypothesis, both presume an premise condition. It can be used as a base or a benchmark for the study of theories and the establishment of theoretical systems, and a frame of reference for realistic analysis and explanation. However, based on different aims of theoretical research, the ideal state in classical political economy and the presuppositions in modern economics are different in nature. Unfortunately, some current scholars try to connect the two schools of economics just because of "theoretical hypothesis", the only thing in common, and then to provide a platform for the communication between them. Consequently, theses scholars obscure the difference of the two kinds of hypothesis both in nature and in function. The outcome brings difficulties when we study the complementarity and otherness of the two economics, and does no good to the development of the theories of political economy[22]. In other words, although two economics both have "presuppositions", we need to distinguish the differences between the hypotheses of two economics. Only by doing so, can we truly understand why classical political economy, of which Karl Marx is one of the representatives, is used as a theoretical guidance for our social practice, while modern mainstream economics is gradually regressing into a subject of explanation and has fallen into a theoretical crisis which is increasingly severe.

First, the two hypotheses are not set for the same purpose. Political economy aims to solve realistic problems, so it analyzes things in this way: on the one hand, by analyzing the essence of things, it sets an ideal state; on the other hand, by analyzing social systems and the structure of social forces, it reveals the alienation of reality. In this way, the ontological cognition that reflects essence becomes not only the frame of reference to analyze social phenomena, but also the direction in which we change the alienated reality. Therefore, the ontological hypothesis based on the cognition of essence is strongly realistic and realizable. Unlike political economy, modern mainstream economics aims to explain social phenomena. This is how it analyzes things: it analyzes and explains social and economic phenomena with abstract thinking and mathematical tools, and sets a hypothetical condition as a benchmark. Such priori hypothesis mainly aims to make explanations easier instead of to give guidance or a direction for the transformation of our society. Therefore, this hypothesis based on the need to explain things is disconnected with reality, and more importantly unrealizable.

Second, the two kinds of hypotheses are not set through the same process of thinking. The synthesis of social science used by political science, which focuses on the summarization of facts and experience, underlines the trend of further development of mankind in its history of evolution and regards the final state as the ideal one. Of course, such an ideal state always complies with the law of the negation of negation, and, to some extent, once appeared in the past. Accordingly, this process requires people to spend more time on investigating various influence factors and explore the ideal state which once possibly existed. Therefore, the ontological hypothesis of political economy comes from the observation and research of the real world. It is an abstraction of the evolution history of things. Modern mainstream economics, unlike political economy, spares no effort to introduce the thinking mode of physical science which stresses the application of mathematical tools and the training of logical reasoning and imagining. Obviously, the frictionless state in physics is an example of imagination and we can never see a little ball's uniform motion on a smooth surface. Similarly, instead of a product of practice or experience, the assumption of modern economics is a product of imagination which comes out of mere thoughts.

Since the abstract hypothesis of modern mainstream economics is unrealizable, no realistic problems can be solved according to the theories and logic of the economics. Imagine a caricature where a physicist, a chemist and an economist are trapped on an isolated island. They have only one can of meat but no tools, so the question is how to open the can. The physicist makes a lever system with rocks and sticks and tries to open the can while the chemist burns barks and sticks to heat the water which is to boil the can, but neither of the plans opens the can. At that time the economist confidently proposes a solution, "Let's suppose that there is an opener". However, the economist does not care where and how to get the opener. For instance, the general equilibrium relies on people's perfect rationality and the market's complete information, but the question is how to achieve such a state. Obviously, if we cannot achieve such a state, the realistic problems cannot be solved merely by market competition. Since the modern economics cannot solve problems, it serves as an economics to explain things. However, does the modern mainstream economics truly make sense?

The typical research framework of modern mainstream economics is: to suppose a state of equilibrium, then to study the situation under the state and to make conclusions, and, from the perspective of the supposed state of equilibrium, to explain the real world. Mainstream economists think that when they understand the equilibrium, the situations of disequilibrium are more logically explicit and easier to understand. Is that so? For example, according to the general theory of equilibrium, the production and exchange of the market will be under a state of Pareto Optimality when the market is under the ideal state supposed by mainstream economists. But why is not the real market a Pareto Efficient one? The explanation of the economists is: the real market is not the one of complete competition. Then new questions appear. (1) Which Pareto state comes when there is the state of multiple equilibrium? (2) The needs of a balanced market are hard to meet, including the full rationality of subjects, the simultaneity of actions, the continuity of the order of preferences, the convexity of production sets and the completeness of information, etc. For example, information can never be complete because the market price itself is a paradoxical signal: price reflects supply and demand while it cannot reflect the search cost, otherwise there will be no information search.

Modern mainstream economics analyzes the market on the basis of its fictional hypothesis, so it cannot be used to go deep into the real process of economic activities. It solves no real problems but uses positivism to rationalize the reality, and thus the economics become more and more vulgar. Hence, Marx criticized such economics—the construction of pure theory based on priori hypothesis, which was very popular among vulgar economists at that time—and he said: Do not let us go back to a fictions primordial condition as the political economist does, when he tries to explain. such a primordial condition explains nothing. He assumes in the question away into a gray nebulous distance. He assumes in the form of fact, of an event, what he is supposed to deduce-namely, the necessary relationship between two things-between, for example, decision of labor and exchange. Theology in the same way explains the origin of evil by the fall of man; that is, it assumes as a fact, in historical form, what has to be explained[19]. " For example, Marx insists to discover the nature of things from the angle of labor and the wealth created from labor, while such a way of analysis is the first thing that modern economists abandon. They use the simple relation between supply and demand to explain the mathematical connections between things and see labor as an external factor at best. In this way, they turn the problems of value into the ones of price.

Modern mainstream economics raises its theories on unrealistic assumptions, of which the important methodological basis is Friedman's opinion: "whether a theory is reasonable or not has nothing to do with whether the supposition is realistic or not". That is to say, an economic hypothesis is reasonable when it can successfully predict the future and it does not matter that the assumption is obviously wrong. Such a proposition encourages mainstream economists to put their explanatory hypothesis into the known fictitious entity, and let them ignore the most important thing in social science research- that one should find the essence of any individual theory as well as real scientific events according to the causal mechanism. Lawson criticizes the research for its violation of the two principles of correct abstraction: (1) Correct abstraction must stick to real mechanisms instead of idealizing hypotheses. Economists should focus on the scientific exploration of the internal mechanisms that really exist instead of on idealization, heuristic fiction and extroverted empiricism. (2) Correct abstraction must be related with the essence, not only the features most commonly seen. Economists should attach importance to the individuals and the events from daily economic life, the individual and the nature and trend of economic structures[23]. The highly-generalized methodology should not be abused. In other words, the real economic explanation should first abstract the essence of economic life from the economic phenomenon and then study it scientifically. But it is clear that mainstream economics has turned economic explanations into merely correct predictions of the future, and it is based on the wrong way of abstraction.

It is clear that the ideal state of classical political economy is more meaningful than the priori hypothesis of neoclassical economics. The research route from essence to phenomenon connects experience and transcendence, which lets economists not only explore the long-term ideal state, but also examine the variability of reality through factors such as power structure. Thanks to the research route from essence to phenomenon, Marx rethought about the real world. He criticized the capitalist system and tried to set the "should be" state of the society by finding the essence, which is also the direction in which the alienated real world needs to be developed; On the contrary, the research route of modern mainstream economics is fundamentally different from this one. Its theory is based on the priori hypothesis and regards the conclusions based on the hypothesis as the benchmark, instead of seeking the ideal state of society through the exploration of essence. Therefore, it cannot provide policy guidance. The difference, of course, lies in the fact that the fundamental goal assigned to economic theory by the two is different: Marxism economics does not recognize the reasonableness of the situation, but the fact that the reality is more or less alienated, so Marx made effort on the transformation of the real world; Therefore, he must explore the essence of things and the preset ideal state can be realized. On the contrary, modern mainstream economists rationalize the real social system through the balance of supply and demand and thus focus on the interpretation of reality rather than the transformation of reality. For this reason, the economics sets up a standard frame of reference only for the convenience of observation, which is an ideal state, unrealizable in itself, that these economists never expect to come true.

V. The Retroduction Method Synthesizing induction and deduction

All the analyses above have shown the fact that the revelation of the essence of things is the basis to know and change the world. In fact, the reason why a theory becomes more and more mature and widely accepted is not only that it provides a self-consistent explanation, but also, fundamentally, that it can provide more reasonable ontological knowledge, so as to construct a cognitive system closer to the inner essence of things. Accordingly, a good economic theory should reveal things but not explain phenomena. It should reveal the intrinsic causality of social economic phenomena rather than the functional relationship outside. It should reveal the mechanism of the interaction between things rather than the correlation of the quantities. The question is, how do we reveal the intrinsic essence of things and the way things interact with each other? In general, the essence of natural things and the essence of the society are different: natural things are composed of certain matter, and thus the essence is embodied in real structures; Social things are often a kind of intangible social structure, so the essence is mainly reflected in their fundamental purposes. Therefore, this paper continues to explain the basic research methods of the essence and causality of things.

First of all, since the essence and causality of things are intrinsic, it is difficult to obtain them by means of formal logic and mathematical reasoning. On the contrary, it relies on people's intellectual thinking. In fact, Aristotle divides knowledge or science into two kinds: (1) intuitive knowledge, which embodies the "indivisible characteristics", essence or essential features of things, is the original premise of all deductions and thus the original source of all deductions. (2) the knowledge of inference, which is a kind of "cause-effect" knowledge, and is made up of statements that can be deduced and the reasoning according to three-section theory[16]. Obviously, whether the knowledge of deduction is true or not depends on whether the premises (intuitive knowledge) are true. Accordingly, this requires proofs of the various premises in turn, so that we have to prove a new set of premises by another step, and make it an infinite circle; in the end, we can only assume that some premises are true and need not to be proved. This is the "basic premise", which means that all scientific knowledge is included in the basic premise. To a large extent, the mathematical models of modern economics rely on some self-evident "axioms". The question is how do you get these basic premises? Ultimately, these "basic premises" are an explanation of the essence of things. Popper says, "the pure mathematics and logic proved by promises do not give us any information about the world, but merely develop the means to describe it[16]."

Second, modern mainstream economics mainly seeks for the basic premise through empirical measurement methods, which is the basic characteristic of logical positivism. For example, Friedman believes that the most important thing for research is to propose an inference method to classify and organize the actual data, thereby deepening people's understanding and drawing a hypothesis from it; meanwhile, it is usefulness rather than authenticity that decides the validity of a hypothesis; finally, the hypothesis proved by experience becomes the basic principle so that reasoning conclusions obtained based on this are also credible[24]. The question is that wrong assumptions and wrong logical inferences may also lead to correct conclusions, not to mention that actual conditions cannot be fully characterized by assumptions. In addition, the essence and causality are often hidden behind the phenomenon instead of being a simple empirical understanding, thus accordingly, it cannot be obtained through empirical analysis. Bromley wrote: If the above laws are merely made up of inference laws, i. e., hypotheses derived solely from statistical homogeneity, in that way, the diagnosis does not explain the observed facts[25]. Popper said, these experiences, important as they may be for our scientific endeavours, can never serve to establish the truth of any idea or theory, however strongly somebody may feel, intuitively, that it must be true, or that it is "self-evident"[16].

Third, econometric analysis is based on small scale data, which is bound to be unable to get causal cognition. The reason is that most events in the real world are random, and they are the result of co-actions between a various factors. For example, two American statisticians,

H. Wainer and H. Zwerling, investigated the characteristics of the most successful colleges and universities under the $1.7 billion support by the Gates foundation, and one of the conclusions was that the size of the famous universities was generally small. One evidence is that six of Pennsylvania's top 50 institutions were smaller, more than three times the size of the average, in a survey of 1, 662 institutions. However, Kahneman pointed out that this causal analysis is meaningless and the conclusion is wrong. In fact, if the statisticians who report to the Gates foundation have investigated the characteristics of the worst schools, they will also find that the worse schools are also smaller than the standard schools[26]. Similarly, a survey of the incidence of renal cancer in 3141 counties in the United States showed that the counties with low incidence were mostly in the rural areas in the Midwest, South and West, which were traditionally ruled by the Republican Party. Can we conclude that the Republican policy is effective in preventing and controlling renal cell carcinoma? In fact, according to Kahneman, there is little population in a county that neither causes cancer nor can avoid cancer, but it will make the incidence of cancer higher or lower than that in densely populated areas. If the county's cancer breaks out in a particular year, there will be a high incidence of the incidence of the disease in a particular year, and if the first one is in the previous one. A survey of the year is likely to be the opposite. So, Kahneman says, small sample events are often more likely to produce extreme results than large sample events, and observations are entirely dependent on investigation methods[26].

The above analysis reflects logical defects in both deduction and induction, so that mathematical analysis and measurement evidence developed from them definitely cannot obtain ontological understanding. So how do we understand the essence of things? How to explore the ontology? Plato, Aristotle and other philosophers in ancient Greece appealed to intuitive assurance: human beings possess a sensible and intuitive ability, with which we can understand the essence and find which definition of essentialism is correct. Similarly, Kant believes that the human mind naturally owns the universal "form" of organizing the senseless and chaotic sensory materials and calls this common structure in the mind "a priori perception", consisting of intuition and understanding: transcendental intuition and external senses synthesize various sensory materials into temporal and spatial order, and then the integrated results are brought into causality of universality and inevitability under the processing of categories (comprehensive forms). Therefore, the entire complex is unified in "a priori understanding"[27]. The question is how do we use this intellectual capacity? This obviously comes from thinking about empirical facts, for which provides content and forms for theoretical concepts. As Popper pointed out, Science does not ask how he has gotten his ideas, it is only interested in arguments that can be tested by everybody[16]. As a result, a path to acquire essential knowledge shall be found out beyond deduction and induction, which is different from the inductive econometric model to demonstrate the relevant data and the deductive mathematical model to further gain derived knowledge.

Inheriting Aristotle's rational intuiationistic theory of essentialism, Kant and Hegel all advocated the pursuit of essence through phenomena, which are fully elaborated in Husserl's pure phenomenological approach. Husserl pointed out that the fundamental method of phenomenology is reflective analysis, for it positions the real subject of philosophical exploration as the essence of ideals that shine through particularity[28]. How to explore the essence of things through phenomena? It is needed to "restore the phenomenon" without prejudice, and thus obtaining pure perception, which not only comes from experience, but also requires human intellectual thinking. Since then, Kant's transcendental epistemology has also been inherited and developed by a large number of scholars. For example, Mises developed a transcendental human behavior from Kant's priori epistemology, while Baska and Lawson developed the Transcendental Realism from the term "transcendental" used by Kant. The meaning of transcendental realism contains two points: "transcendental" shows a partial inheritance over Kant's philosophy, while "realism" shows a difference from it. Meanwhile, the combination of "Transcendent Realism" and "Critical Naturalism" formed "Critical Realism". Correspondingly, Critical Realism also owns the same two major characteristics: "criticism" embodies the general characteristics of its philosophy, while "realism" shows critical realism still belongs to the realism camp. Lawson emphasized that the goal of social sciences (including economics) is to confirm the deep results and underlying causality behind observed events, far beyond discovering the "constant relevance" on the surface. Thereby Lawson proposed and compared two kinds of realism, i. e. Empirical Realism and Transcendental Realism.

Empirical Realism refers to viewpoints about the reality of events and our knowledge of relevant experiences or impressions, rooted in Hume's analysis of causality. According to Empirical Realism, if specific knowledge is confined to the atomic practice in experience, the only possibility of general knowledge is to elaborate the event in this form with regularity: "As long as X occurs, Y happens." But Lawson believes that empirical realism has made two mistakes: (1) Use experience categories to define the entire world, and use an epistemological category to accomplish the task of ontology, which is what Baska calls "epistemic fallacy"; (2) Regard experience that owned by people or offering people possibilities as the most central feature of reality, thus ignoring the causality criteria of categorizing something as true, but only acknowledging what is experienced. Transcendental Realism believes that the world is not only composed of events and our experiences or impressions about them, but also consists of (indispensable) structures and mechanisms, forces and trends; although the latter may not be able to be observed, it constitutes the basis of real events in our experience, governing or creating real events. According to transcendental positivism, the goal of science is to elaborate the structure or mechanism of action that determines the surface phenomenon. Therefore, the regularity or its statement must be an accurate description of such a result and its mode of action instead of the regularity of the event. Moreover, if the internal mechanisms and structures are rarely exposed in the study, this effect is embodied as a trend rather than a reality, a description of a structure or a matter and its mode of operation beyond the facts[29].

The question is how to excavate this internal structure and mechanism? How to reveal the ontology of things and their causality with each other and raise them to the theoretical level? Lawson advocates reduction or outreach reasoning, which traces from the appearance back to the deep structure of things through analogy and metaphor, thereby revealing the causality mechanism between structure, events and tests. Reduction draws on abduction proposed by the founder of pragmatism, Pierce, who believes since neither inductive nor deductive methods can ever create any possible ideas, abduction complements these two traditional methods, attempting to observe and interpret things through a new conceptual framework to make new interpretations of things. In fact, all ideas of science are obtained through abduction, for it helps to grasp the creation of knowledge and the spark of consciousness, thus lighting the fire of facts absorption. Pierce wrote: "The revelation of abduction flashes in front of us. It is a survey activity despite of highly likely misleading insight. Indeed, we once possessed different assumptions in our minds. But it is the idea to combine things that we had never thought of putting together that brings new inspiration in our meditation process[30]." Further, based on multilayered realism of critical realism, reduction discovers objectively existing non-experienced or deep structures, mechanisms and trends starting from events observed by experience, thereby abstracting related causal mechanism directly from the phenomenon level.

Based on such abduction, a variety of interconnected things can be put together to gain a deeper understanding of their internal structure through transformation and fusion of thinking. In general, abduction launches events from results and rules, namely: rules + empirical facts → events. Obviously, on the one hand, abduction method is different from deduction method, for the latter produces a testable claim based on rules (axioms) and events (hypotheses and applied assumptions) and deduces possible theoretical propositions; i. e., rules + events → conclusion. The problems of the deductive method are: (1) Its conclusions depend on assumptions of axioms and application, thus with no new knowledge produced; (2) Scholars engaged in deductive methods tend to regard hypothesis of axiom as basic belief and gain self-satisfaction through establishing research on the validity of logic, so that validity of assumptions is not studied in advance, while conclusions that can be empirically tested also encounter too many relevant problems. On the other hand, the abduction method is also different from the induction method, for the latter obtains the rule (general proposition) process based on the event (hypothesis) and the result (observed phenomenon), i. e., event + result → rule. The problems of induction are: (1) it is a proof of existing hypotheses, not a logical reasoning; (2) there are always special individuals not being considered, thus existing potential inductive fallacies[31].

Accordingly, characteristics of abduction are: (1) different from deduction preparing to provide a universal theory, it tries to provide a more reasonable theory for interpretation; (2) different from induction trying to deduce general rules from specific conclusions as well, it seeks out reasons from influences to provide explanations. For example, I. given a rule proposition: an unbalanced power game determines unfair social systems and distribution rules, thus leading to that the same labor cannot obtain the same income; II. given an observational phenomenon: individuals in the real market who pay the same labor often receive very different incomes. Therefore, it can be concluded that the income gap in the real market reflects the rationality of the distribution rules rather than the level of effort or the contribution of labor. Unequal distribution of social forces leads to unfair distribution rules, thus leading to unreasonable distribution of income in the real market. Obviously, abduction reflects the reasoning from the result to the cause. Although it can only obtain a speculative assertion, it is the most important method in theoretical research, for it can help overcome the defects of induction and deduction and create assumptions and new analytical frameworks so as to provide basis for producing new concepts, forming hypotheses and verification hypotheses[32].

Actually, abduction is committed to tracing from the appearance back to deep structure of things, thus analyzing their intrinsic essence, revealing causality and mechanisms of action between the things, so that a constantly improving theoretical system can be better built. Generally speaking, a perfect theory owns two major requirements: (1) inherent logical consistency, which emphasizes a theoretical system must possess a self-contained and strict logical relationship; (2) the consistency between theory and reality, which emphasizes that the theory must be based on experience. Apparently, induction mainly performs better in achieving consistency between theory and reality, but may also lack predictability for not grasping causal mechanism associated with the future; as regards deduction, it mainly performs better in achieving inner logical consistency of the realization theory, but may also lead to a disconnect between the conclusion and the reality for assumption's lack of truthfulness. In other words, pure induction or pure deduction cannot fulfill the two major requirements of economic theory. Therefore, some economists try to combine induction and deduction to form the hypothesis-deduction method, containing a series of cyclical processes: hypothesis → deduction → theory → empirical proof → induction → modified hypothesis →...[33] This is actually Popper's method of falsification. But there are also problems with this method. Since most theories are formed by a combination of multiple hypotheses, falsificationism is faced with the Duhem-Quine Thesis: when the theory is verified false by experience, it is always difficult to determine which assumption is problematic. Therefore, Lakatos further developed a scientific program based on Popper's falsificationism, which allowed new theories to escape sporadic falsification tests until it gradually reached a relatively mature stage with new data.

Therefore, we can also review two standards testing whether a discipline is a hard science. (1) Internal standard. According to this standard, even if it is possible to perform an acceptable reinterpretation of the functional interpretation model, the causal explanation model is given priority. In other words, the scientific nature of a theory lies in clarification of the causal links between phenomena and exploration of the internal mechanism of the interaction between things. (2) External standard. According to this standard, the controllability of subjects and the repeatability of experiments are given priority in the history of scientific development, thus "hard science" and "experimental science" often appear as synonyms. The applicability of these two standards in economics needs further analysis. (1) The test of economic theory relies more on internal standard to explain the causal mechanism and provide a relatively complete logic system. To figure it out, that economics faces numerous difficulties in carrying out laboratory tests, thereby it is hardly possible to possess characteristics of "hard science" as it claims. (2) The internal standard on which economics is based are by no means equivalent to the formal logic in the natural sciences, thus the reasoning of mathematical logic cannot be simply advocated. To figure it out, despite the internal rigor of mathematics logic, strict specific applications can always hardly be achieved, especially when expressing personal behaviors with perceptual features[33]. In particular, the cognition obtained based on mathematical logic is often closed and rigid, thus stifling further development of the theory; in contrast, abduction sees the development of theory with open and diversified perspective, puts the theory into dynamic dialectical negation, gets tested and modified with the aid of empirical facts.

To conclude, the theory of economics fundamentally aims to reflect the cognition of the intrinsic nature of things, which obviously cannot be confined to the use of mathematical logic, for it is often embodied as a quantitative correlation or functional connection instead of automatically revealing the real structure and inner essence of things. As Lawson pointed out, "The primary goal of scientific research is not to clarify/forecast events, but to recognize and understand forces and trends that support and control events. This recognition equals to all required for policy analysis and effective activities. For example, the ultimate goal of medical research is not to predict the form of lesions on patients' skin, but to identify the virus or cause and to develop an effective cure[14]." So, how do you reveal the intrinsic nature of things? The answer is to combine inductive analysis with deductive analysis to form abduction. In fact, although abduction has so far received little attention in the economics circle, it is the most common method in scientific knowledge exploration. Bromley believes that "an economist, if he first observed a specific human behavior-a specific economic result, and then tried to explain such behaviors or results, he is actually using abduction"; and in general, "when we observe the regularity of certain experience in the surrounding world (or some newly discovered irregularity) and try to establish some reasonable explanation for them (i. e., events), actually we were searching for retrospective beliefs[25]." Apparently, based on abduction, we can maintain an open academic attitude, continuously advancing the theoretical progress through the integration of knowledge instead of trying to construct a beautiful universal axiom under a specific framework.

VI. Epilogue

As a discipline focusing on the public domain, the research method used in political economics is obviously different from the neo-classical economics in the private sector. On the one hand, any social thing in the public domain is not external to the subject but a product created by mankind, which embodies a certain purpose of mankind, so that normative analysis must be introduced. On the other hand, no social things in the public domain are not the result of individual rational choice, but of the joint action of all people and reflects obvious strong preferences, thus essential analysis must be introduced. In fact, since political economy assumes the task to recognize and reconstruct the real world, it cannot simply remain in the description and interpretation of phenomena, especially in rationalizing the realistic social economy based on affirmative rational thinking, but must go deep into the essence of things behind the phenomenon, especially in discovering the problems of real social economy based on critical rational thinking. This is the study route from the essence to the phenomenon, based on which we can correctly understand the relationship between the "change" and "constancy" and between the "substance" and the "function" of things: excavate "constancy" and "substance" reflecting essence from various changes, meanwhile the "function" and "change" of various concrete forms shall be dialectically regarded through "constancy" and "substance" embodying essence, so as to realize "the integration of substanceandfunction" stated by XiongShili.

Obviously, to build an ontological understanding of the inner structure and essence of things requires forming a back-tracking method combing induction and deduction by means of human intellectual thinking. However, modern mainstream economics has fragmented empirical analysis and normative analysis and focused on the functional connections and numerical relationships between the appearance of things, rather than the essence of things. It is biased towards either the formal logic of "extremely high-minded but not moderate" or the purely empirical evidence of "moderate but extremely unintelligent". As a consequence, the study of modern mainstream economics can hardly discover problems in the real world, not to mention to find the fundamental solutions. Actually, advance of mathematical tools and measurement methods can only help improve routine analysis, rather than our thoughts and insights, which even usually become an unfavorable factor in suffocating thinking. To conclude, young people may ignore or even despise insights of predecessors due to the highly praised technical analysis. From the perspective of reality and performance, it is precisely because modern mainstream economics tends to use more complex mathematical techniques, emergence of ideas and development of theories have been severely suffocated under the control of a whole set of analytical paradigms and writing formats. Moreover, the more complex mathematics techniques used in an economics dissertation, the more often there is a lack of ideas. XuFuguan pointed out in his article "The Time I Do Not Want to Think": "People in more modern places tend to choose not to think." This is because "Modern people usually ask 'How to do' instead of 'What for' … 'How to do' is of course an application of ideas; however, the use of such ideas often focuses on the senses, which limits the thinking to surface of things and to isolated individuals. The expansion of the depth and breadth of ideological characteristics cannot be realized under such emphasis[34]." So does the situation in modern economics, for it also enters the unintended era under the development and use of a whole set of analytical techniques.

References

[1] Zhu Fuqiang. Why "Economics" should Essentially be "Political Economy" [J]. Learning and Exploration, No. 11, 2016, 131-139.

[2] Hodgson. Capitalism, Values, and Exploitation [M]. translated by Yu Shusheng and Chen Dongwei, Commercial Press, 2013.

[3] Boatright. Ethics in Finance [M]. translated by Jingye, Peking University Press, 2002.

[4] Zhu Fuqiang. Is the Concept of Efficiency in Modern Mainstream Economics Worthless? Practical Consequences of Efficiency Principle and Reflection on Coase's Neutral Theorem [J]. Academic Research, No. 10, 2009, 79-84.

[5] Hayek. The Fatal Conceit: Errors of Socialism [M]. Translated by Feng Keli et al., China Social Science Press, 2000.

[6] Zhu Fuqiang. The Theoretical Foundation of Income Redistribution: Principles based on Social Contribution [J]. Economist, No. 8, 2014, 5-14.

[7] Zhu Fuqiang. Is the Theory of Economics in Development, Stagnation or Retrogradation? A Survey on Mathematical Economics with Scientificity [J]. Journal of Capital University of Economics and Business, No. 2, 2009, 111-118.

[8] Zhu Fuqiang. Is Empirical Economics an Objective Subject? Exploration of Subjectivity and Normativeness in Empirical Analysis [J]. Comparative Economic & Social Systems, No. 1, 2009, 146-152.

[9] Zhu Fuqiang. Is Economics a Science? A Survey Based on the Criterion of the Demarcation of Science [J]. Journal Of Fujian Normal University, No. 3, 2009, 57-65.

[10] Zhu Fuqiang. How could Economic Experiments Be More Effective? A Response to Mr. Du Ninghua's Critique [J]. Journal of Shanghai University of Finance and Economics, No. 1, 2018, 114-129.

[11] Zhu Fuqiang. The Fatal Conceit in Positive Economics: Rethinking the Rationality, Reliability and Serviceability of Positive Analysis [J]. Social Science Front, No. 7, 2008, 47-55.

[12] Hausman and McPherson. Economics, Rationality, and Ethics [M]. // Hausman (Eds.), The Philosophy of Economics, translated by Ding Jianfeng, Century Publishing Group / Shanghai People's Publishing House, 2007.

[13] Zhu Fuqiang. Can Economics Degenerate into a Purely Empirical Discipline? Rethinking the Rationality of Interpretation Based on Empirical Analysis [J]. Academic Monthly, No. 4, 2010, 69-77.

[14] Lawson. A Positivism Theory of Economics [M]. //Barkhouse (Eds.), New Directions in Economic Methodology, translated by Zhang Dabao et al., Economic Science Press, 2000.

[15] Zhu Fuqiang. From Essence to Phenomenon: A Comparative Study of the Basic Route of Institutional Analysis [J]. Academic Monthly, No. 3, 2009, 79-87.

[16] Popper. The Open Society and Its Enemies (Volume II) [M]. translated by Zheng Yiming et al., China Social Sciences Press, 1999.

[17] Zhu Fuqiang. Basic Analytic Thinking and Practical Value of Marxian Economics: A Comparison of the Research Routes between Classical Economics and Neo-classical Economics [J]. Fujian Forum, No. 5, 2011, 8, 9-16.

[18] Adam Smith. An Inquiry into the Nature and Causes of the Wealth of Nations (volume I) [M]. translated by Guo Dali and Wang Yanan, The Commercial Press, 1972.

[19] Marx K. Economic and Philosophic Manuscripts of 1844 [M]. New York: Prometheus Books, 1988.

[20] Zhang Wuchang. Economic Explanation, volume I: Explain Demand Scientifically [M]. CITIC Press, 2010.

[21] Jia Genliang. A Study of the Main Schools of Western Heterogeneous Economics [M]. China Renmin University Press, 2010.

[22] Zhu Fuqiang. Analytic Characteristics of Contractism, Interpretive Community, and Two Major Schools: Comparison of Marxist Economics and Western Mainstream Economic Assumptions [J]. Tsinghua Review of Political Economy, July 2013.

[23] Boylan & O Gorman. New Directions in Economic Methodology [M]. translated by Xia Yeliang, Economic Science Press, 2002.

[24] Friedman M. The Methodology of Positive Economics [M] //Hausman M. D. The Philosophy of Economics: An Anthlogy. Ding Jianfeng, translation. Century Publishing Group/ Shanghai People's Publishing House, 2007.

[25] Bromley. Sufficient Reason: Volitional Pragmatism and the Meaning of Economic Institutions [M]. translated by Jian Lian et al., Shanghai People's Publishing House, 2008.

[26] Kahneman D. Thinking, Fast and Slow [M]. China CITIC Press, 2012.

[27] Marcuse H. Reason and revolution: Hegel and the rise of social theory [M]. Cheng Zhiming, etc., translation. Chongqing Publishing House, 1996.

[28] Husserl, E. Die Krisis der Europaischen Wissenschaften und die Transzendentale Phanomenologie [M]. Zhang Qingxiong, translation. Shanghai Translation Publishing House, 1988.

[29] Zhu Fuqiang. The Epistemological Reflection of Causal Analysis in Economics: Transcendental Realism and "Discovery" of Economic Theory [J]. Fujian Forum, No. 6, 2010.

[30] Hodgson. On Evolutionary Economics and the Evolution of Economics [M]. translated by Ren Ronghua et al., China Renmin University Press, 2007.

[31] Zhu Fuqiang. The Basic Nature of Econometric Conclusion and Its Signification for Practice: On the Criterion of Value and the Direction of Development for Economic Theory [J]. Journal of TianJin Normal University, No. 2, 2014, 36 - 45.

[32] Jia Genliang. A Study of the Main Schools of Western Heterogeneity Economics [M]. China Renmin University Press, 2010.

[33] Sheila C. Dow. Economic Methodology [M]. translated by Yang Peilei, Shanghai University of Finance & Economics Press, 2005.

[34] Xu Fuguan. The Exposition of Chinese Humanistic Spirit [M]. edited by Li Weiwu, China Radio, Film and TV Press, 1996.

主流财政理论中社会角色缺失的困境及其出路*

——基于政府、市场与社会三维视角

严维石

摘　要：英美财政理论成为主流财政范式，是建立在市场与政府两维认知基础上，认为市场失灵自然须政府干预。其本身蕴含政府越位和财政扩张的机制，最终无法摆脱财政赤字宿命，财政政策的“扩张—赤字—紧缩—扩张”重复上演。政府干预代替社会互惠功能引起政府边界扩张和预算不堪重负。更为严重的是，这将削弱个体社会互助和社会情感，提高整个社会运行成本。让政府财政救助成为最后且最低保障将促进社会互助互惠行为回归，使得市场、社会与政府各就各位，各司其职。财政赤字、财政可持续和财政政策连续性等问题才可能在此基础上得到根本解决。

关键词：英美财政理论　两维世界　财政赤字　三维世界

［**中图分类号**］F881.9　［**文献标识码**］A

大陆财政理论先于经济学称为独立学科，然而古典、新古典经济学与凯恩斯宏观经济学发展使得大陆财政理论逐步边缘化，取而代之，马斯格雷夫等人[1]的英美财政学已经是财政学主流教材，有趣的是，主流的英美财政学却成为现代宏观经济学的一部分和一个子学科。财政学与经济学关系的“颠倒性”变迁是学术探讨的问题[2]。大陆财政学边缘化与英美财政学占据主流并没有得

* 基金项目：中央财经大学中国财政发展协同创新中心课题“财局与政局关系研究项目”（项目编号：011250315002）。

［作者简介］：严维石，广东财经大学经济学院教授，主要从事企业劳动理论、财政理论研究。

到学术界普遍认同，对此问题的质疑与批判一直存在。伴随而至的让“大陆财政”回归的冲动与财政学重建的努力从没有停止过[3][4]。这里不关注大陆与英美财政理论比较与评价，而是面对现实财政赤字和财政可持续问题，研究主流财政理论面临的困境，据此探讨摆脱困境的出路。

一、当代主流财政理论与财政赤字

财政学术史表明，大陆财政理论发展到英美财政的历史逻辑在于范式转换。布坎南和马斯格雷夫的财政理论成为英美财政理论的主流，相对而言，后者的理论因“可操作性”比较强而被广泛应用与实践，现已成为财政学教材的主要内容。他们俩人之间的公开理论辩论被视为主流英美财政理论的派系理论交锋，不同国家观点的争辩。他们争论的焦点是，政府财政政策如何干预经济[5]？布坎南认为，政府财政干预经济要谨慎，依据其公共选择理论通过政治市场竞争实现公共财政有效配置；而马斯格雷夫则是将大陆财政积极干预传统通过凯恩斯的宏观经济理论框架变成一个“可操作”理论体系，将市场失灵视为政府财政干预的理由，甚至作为应该干预的证据。布坎南将政府财政政策归为利益集团在政治市场上博弈的结果，而马斯格雷夫则自然地将政府当作公众利益的代表。

然而，他们的财政理论有一个共同点，即在市场与政府两维世界里构建财政理论。布坎南强调政府财政的政治市场博弈特性，但他希望通过公共选择机制限制政府财政决策使得财政更加有效，并不排斥政府财政干预经济。很显然，在市场与政府两维的世界里，经济问题解决途径就是一个非市场即政府的二元结构，这是布坎南与马斯格雷夫等英美主流财政理论的共同特征，仅在如何应用财政政策以及积极程度方面有差异。这里无须赘述凯恩斯关于政府财政干预经济的理由，也就不需要再去争论市场与政府的二元关系。但是一个财政现实是，财政赤字一直是大多数国家面临的现实经济问题，为什么各国财政都逃不过赤字的宿命？难道仅仅是“民主政治”所致[6]？

（一）基于市场与政府两维世界的财政赤字机制

以布坎南和马斯格雷夫为代表的当代主流财政理论对政府的理解不尽相

同，但他们的理论同属于市场与政府两维世界框架体系。他们将社会职能转化为政府职能，这样造成效率损失，同时使政府财政不堪重负，也在一定程度上消解了社会互助与社会同情。最典型的问题就是社会救助与社会保障。社会救助、社会医疗保障和养老保障本应属于社会互助范畴，不牵涉到政府财政，然而各国社会救助、医疗和养老保障都变成政府职责，最终成为政府救助、医疗和养老政府保障。政府越界进入社会领域对于财政学来说不是一个新鲜事，大陆财政干预社会领域是其一大特色。英美财政介入社会事务在一定程度上与经济衰退、萧条有关，同样，凯恩斯宏观经济学难辞其咎。接下来，解析当代主流财政理论与其实践的赤字宿命以及相关机制。

首先，“非市场即政府”。在市场与政府的两维世界里，市场不能解决的问题就得政府解决。显然，现代政府需要解决的问题越多，财政开支就越大。这种两维世界的认知不仅仅属于普通公众，甚至政府高层或重要政治人物也认可这种两维观点。然而，人类社会发展史表明，人类社会化生活早于政府出现。也就是说，在相当长的时间里，人类社会并没有政府，这种无政府状态运行很长时间，政府及其机制是人类对社会越来越复杂化的一种应对。这并不意味着政府出现之前的社会机制完全无效。换言之，政府及其机制不是取代社会机制，而是应对社会机制无法有效应付的新情况或者新问题。这种两维认知经过大陆财政理论发展而得以强化，大陆全能型财政政策实施使得政府边界不断外扩，侵蚀社会功能，弱化社会个体自我应对能力。显然，这种社会认知使得从摇篮到坟墓的社会保障系统并非依托于社会，而是依附于政府财政。依附于政府的所谓社会保障系统不一定是经济社会发展的阿喀琉斯之踵（Achilles′ Heel），然而毋庸置疑，它是经济社会变革的掣肘。

其次，市场化促进社会职能进一步弱化和政府职能扩张。在市场与政府的两维世界里，在自利个体共同作用下，市场逐步占据社会领域中有利润的空间领域，不进入或者抛弃没有利润空间的那部分，这就进一步弱化了社会功能。例如，商业银行发现在一个居民数量规模不足够大的小社区开办一个从事存贷与结算业务的分行是有利可图的，但是对这个社区中小企业因无法提供抵押品的贷款则是无利可图且风险较高的。随着企业创新与市场机制的完善，一些社会互助与社会互惠行为确实可能被更加有效的市场交易机制取代。在两维世界里，政府职能也“自然”扩张，财政开支广度与强度也不断增加。

再次，人口老龄化逐步揭开政府财政扩张的赤字隐患。现在或曾经的经济不断成长的经济体有一个共同的经验，即与经济发展相伴的社会人口不断老年化。发达经济体的社会人口老年化毋庸赘述，像中国这样的发展中国家也已经表现出“未富先衰”的老年化趋势。人类寿命延长反映社会进步，但应对人口老龄化引起的经济社会问题是一个尚未破解的难题。与人口寿命延长相伴的“少子化或无子化”人口趋势使社会人口结构加速老龄化。抚养小孩与赡养老人最大的不同是，随着小孩成长，负担变轻，最终他们会独立自主；而随着老人年龄变大，负担渐重。因此，人口寿命延长与少子化叠加推高社会抚养比，“养老靠谁?”问题就凸现出来了。养老及其相关服务的产业化可以解决相应的供给问题，满足老人养老服务需求靠谁支付呢？在“非市场即政府”的两维世界里，人口老龄化所带来问题会让任何支撑社会保障的政府财政不堪重负，这种趋势将削弱财政收入增长，同时加速财政开支，财政赤字将如约而至。更为麻烦的是，人口老龄化将使得民主社会改革当前政府财政支撑的社会保障体系变得越来越困难，代际不公问题越发严重，西欧高福利社会政策改革举步维艰就是一个佐证。

最后，经济全球化将进一步恶化老龄社会的政府财政。老龄化引发的财政困难使得政府财政支撑的社会福利保障变成“镜中花水中月”。在经济全球化背景下，资本和劳动力跨国流动越来越便捷，老龄化国家的资本和年轻劳动力在其本国的税负随着老龄化推进而越发沉重，资本和劳动外流是一个不可阻挡的趋势。资本与劳动流失反过来削弱该国经济竞争力，进而制约经济增长和恶化财政收支平衡。

总之，基于市场与政府两维世界的财政理论与实践避免不了财政赤字的宿命，无论是英美财政还是大陆财政。基于市场与政府两维认知的相关理论及其实践削弱社会互助与互惠行为的社会功能，也就无法破解财政赤字难题。相对积极的马斯格雷夫财政理论与比较保守的布坎南财政理论都没有办法跳出市场与政府两维世界的财政困境。因为此时政府财政早已经越界进入本该由社会完成的社会领域，而且越界程度日趋加重。让政府对社会越俎代庖，损失的不仅仅是经济效率，对社会互助与互惠行为等基本社会机制的破坏已经伤害社会肌体，修复社会肌体困难重重。

（二）主流财政理论应对财政赤字

无论是马斯格雷夫还是布坎南的主流财政都清楚财政赤字问题。深受凯恩斯宏观经济学影响的马斯格雷夫财政理论认为，逆周期财政政策发生的财政赤字随着经济复苏与增长逐步缓解，实现周期性财政平衡。现在主流财政学教材里的基本理论框架与凯恩斯宏观经济政策理论一脉相承，在 IS-LM 或者 IS-LM-BP 的框架里，财政收支政策是如何调节宏观经济。新古典宏观经济学发展与宏观经济实践都表明，凯恩斯式的宏观财政政策对经济调控的效果并不像凯恩斯宏观经济学与主流财政理论预期的那样好，倒是其调控后的产业结构失衡等后遗症非常明显，马斯格雷夫财政理论的科学性与有效性缺乏现实证据支持与理论说服力，依然是一个假说。在这个方面，相对消极的布坎南财政理论并不会更胜一筹，基于个体理性决策理念，他强调财政尊重公众意见，采用“同意计算”，也就是说，财政政策须在公众一致同意前提下进行，从而实现帕累托改进。对财政政策进行全民公决的有效性令人质疑，这样的财政政策决策成本难以接受，采取代议民主制对重大财政政策进行决策已经在很多国家实践多年，但是财政赤字依然阴魂不散而且与日俱增。这里尚没有考虑财政效率问题。

模糊政府与社会职能边界让政府财政行为越界，继而消解社会职能，财政赤字就不可避免，应对方式往往是采取断崖式的财政紧缩，然后进入新一轮循环。财政紧缩的短期见效特性在一定程度上掩盖了政府职能越界扩张的弊端，个体责任与社会职能被政府侵蚀，长期使个体依赖于政府而缺乏责任感，进而让社会互助与互惠行为失去动力，稀释社会同情与社会凝聚力。

（三）以社会共同需求为核心的财政理论

中国大陆财政学家也在不断探索财政职能边界问题，如何振一[6]和李俊生等[8][4][9]提出并论证以“社会共同需要”划分财政职能边界。这一理论创新值得提倡，但以社会共同需要作为财政活动起点和归属的财政理论需要将社会角色纳入其中，让社会功能发挥应有作用，否则它依旧使得财政政策陷于市场与社会两维困境，同样无法摆脱财政赤字的命运。以公共选择方式将社会共同需要变成政府财政政策的理论探索[4]需要面对国内外的财政压力与财政赤字现实。麻烦在于，动态调整社会共同需求界定以及相应决策将是一个耗费成本的过程，这个博弈过程可能相当复杂。

阿罗的社会选择不可能定律将使社会共同需求界定过程可能在经济上变得

不可行。这样就可能使得政府为了节省社会共同需求界定与决策成本而实施直接政府干预。财政收入和财政支出调整的公共选择偏向性极易造成财政赤字。增加以税收为主的财政收入政策经过公共选择很难通过，而增加特定财政开支而不改变其他开支的财政支出政策则可以通过公共选择过程而实施，最后财政赤字难以避免。用特定税收与特定财政开支捆绑的预算平衡方案来应对社会共同需求的调整，也会因财政效率问题而受到批评。社会共同需求理论将面对如何有效缓解过度财政压力与巨额财政赤字问题。

二、社会角色回归与三维世界的财政职能

前面阐述的是市场与政府两维世界的财政理论及其政策如何引发财政赤字问题。也就是说，不考虑财政效率问题，在两维世界里，财政赤字是一个自然，也是必然结果。市场与政府的二元结构使财政政策持续性与连贯性无法实现，财政赤字是一个无法摆脱的宿命。在两维世界里，政府财政越界削弱了互助与互惠行为的社会职能，使得财政压力不堪重负，最终引发财政赤字。应对财政赤字和改善财政政策连贯性与持续性的关键是，让社会角色回归，使市场、社会和政府各就各位，各司其职。用三维世界认知构建的财政理论才可能有效解决三维现实世界中的财政问题。为此，下面将阐述在市场、政府和社会的三维世界内讨论人际间交换方式，并说明在这三维世界中，人际间按照不同方式进行交换，相关成本与产生的效果也不尽相同，用其中的一种交换方式代替另一种方式会产生负面影响和效率问题。

（一）三维世界中的个体交换方式

在现实社会中，个体合法获取他人劳动产品与服务的方式不外乎以下三种：

一是市场交换。这是用于产权比较明晰的商品与服务，在市场竞争中，交易双方通过讨价还价达成交易，并以一定方式实现银货两讫。很多时候，在产权界定成本比较高或者信息引起的不确定性较大的情况下，这种方式的成本比较高，不是一个有效方式。因此，在市场经济最成熟的国家里，也长期存在大量的非市场交换方式，这在一定程度上表明，非市场交易方式长期存在是效率使然。

二是政府转移。即政府通过政府权力以货币或其他形式将物品与服务由一些公民转移给其他公民，也就是宏观经济学上的转移支付。这种以政府转移为媒介的交换方式使交易双方本身不参与交易，不存在相互间的权力责任问题。受转移方因某种历史或社会情结获得转移的物品与服务；而转移方则是由于法定的纳税义务或者缴费要求提供物品与服务的转移所需资金。政府媒介隔离转移双方，使转移双方不能在物品与服务转移过程中得到情感体验，受转移方获得转移物品与服务不会感激任何人，他不知道自己所获物品的转出人是谁？他也不会感激政府官员，他知道这些物品与服务不是他们提供的。这样会使他们认为接受转移物品理所应当，无须承担相应责任或者“负债感”。逐步将接受转移的权力或待遇作为骄傲资本的社会氛围挫伤劳动积极性和刺激社会慵懒行为。

三是社会互助。它包括社会互惠行为和利他行为。这是人类社会生活的古老方式，比前两种交换方式要早得多，与人的社会生活相伴而生。但是，这种交换方式往往被学者忽略，甚至视而不见。市场经济成功实践使得经济学家对市场交换效率顶礼膜拜，它也成为高效交换的代名词。然而，互惠行为与利他行为的社会互助交换方式在一定范围内是一种较高效率的交换方式，相对于市场交换，社会互助交换既不依赖交换媒介，也不需要界定产权，更不要给付等价与及时交割。另外，这种交换通常涉及同情、责任、感动与感恩等社会情感体验，施助方与受助方在交换过程中满足相应的社会情感需求。更为重要的是，这种情感体验将会使有关各方都认识到他们有责任为这种社会互助做出贡献。这种社会互助交换本身不能完全防止机会主义行为，但社会互助一般是连锁性的，前后社会互助存在关联性，从而衍生出一系列的社会互助，在一系列社会互助中，机会主义行为者将被甄别、警告和驱除出互助群体。相对于政府转移，社会互助有助于遏制搭便车的机会主义行为，增强个体社会责任感以及积极有为的生活情操，可以接受社会互助，但是随时准备成为施助者。当然，这种交换没有在大范围内自然衍生出来，社会互助交换机制往往适用于社区等小群体，市场交换在更大范围内的交易效率优势就体现出来，如国际贸易等。

显而易见，在市场、社会和政府的三维世界里，不同维度的交换方式是不同的，交换成本与效率也是不同的，更重要的是，交换产生的影响也不尽相同。它们不是相互取代而是互补关系，用一种交换代替另一种交换方式可能事与愿违。当前财政理论及其实践就是让不同互补方式发生替代引起混乱的现实案例。

当代主流财政理论将现实三维世界的经济问题置于市场与政府的两维框架中加以分析解决的思路就决定了由此理论指导财政实践效果。包括财政学在内的经济学忽略社会维度，在市场与政府的两维世界里分析解决经济问题，使得经济问题变得日益复杂化。财政赤字就是一个典型例子。

（二）社会角色回归，市场、社会与政府各司其职

市场、社会与政府履行职能是不同的，其履行职能的方式也是不相同的，当然，履行职能的目标与结果也不尽相同。它们之间不是替代关系，而是互补关系。其中的任何角色缺位都难以有效弥补，显然社会职能被政府越俎代庖不仅使得政府财政不堪重负，也削弱社会互助与互惠行为等社会性行为，伤害社会情感与凝聚力。解决市场与政府两维世界的财政问题需要正本清源，即让社会职能回归，使市场、社会与政府各司其职。那么，究竟市场、社会与政府如何各就各位呢？

首先，市场优先原则。国内外经济史表明，市场是配置资源有效机制，个人获取生存发展的资源通过市场获得的方式可以有效防止机会主义行为。这就是为什么市场经济成为大多数国家经济形态的原因。各国在任何时期都必须高效配置资源以应对面临的资源稀缺压力。市场交易使得交易双方在产权明晰的前提下实现责权利相结合，市场交易遵循自愿、自由交易，因此交易结果是，资源配置到实现价值最高的去处。市场经济的有效推广是现代经济社会垫脚石，在市场、社会与政府职能分工上坚持市场优先原则，主要理由：一是个体通过市场合法获得生存发展所需的商品与服务必然履行“银货两讫”责任。这样就使交易双方权利义务对等，激励个人通过向市场提供自己的劳动或服务最终获得自己所需。二是市场交易使交易不局限于社区或某个有效区域，在更大范围内配置资源获得更高的回报。相对社会互助与互惠行为社区性和政府服务的地域性，市场在时间和空间上要更加广阔，很多市场交易发生于跨地域、跨国度的个体之间，进而使个体可在更大范围内，也可能更好地获得所需之物。三是市场交易方式使相关交易成本无需第三方而是由交易双方承担。市场交易

双方自行搜寻对方，进行相关交易谈判与交割，一般不存在外部性，也就不牵涉第三方。因此，市场交易一般不涉及人际间“超经济”财富转移，当然就不存在人际或代际不公问题。

然而，这也不意味着在任何时空中，市场都是个体获得生存发展所需之物的最有效机制。市场交易依赖于交易对象产权清晰程度，同时需要给付等价。划分产权不仅是有成本的，有时这种成本会非常高，给付等价也会产生相关成本。在划分产权很复杂的情况下，市场机制可能不再是有效机制。

其次，让社会的互助与互惠行为功能充分发挥作用，实现个体的社会性需求。在社区邻里与亲朋好友之间获得生存发展所需之物不一定通过市场方式进行，而是可以通过社会互助或者互惠行为等社会方式实现物品与服务的交换。这种交换不需要清晰划分产权，也不需要给付等价的“银货两讫”，在特定地域或人群间，社会性互助与互惠行为是一种高效交换机制。更为重要的是，这种社会性机制可以履行高效经济功能，也可满足个体社会性情感需求，促进社会同情与提高社会凝聚力。但是这个机制发挥作用需要长期性，不是任何个体都能进入这种社会互惠机制的。社会互助与互惠行为机制的建立依赖于频繁互惠合作以及由此产生声誉。前后社会互助与互惠行为之间存在关联，前一次社会行为中的施助或施惠者可成为下一次类似社会行为受助或受惠者，这种关联性就是一个防止个体的机会主义行为机制，社会互助与互惠行为频率越高，互助与互惠机制越有效。另外，这种互助与互惠机制并不要求双方施助施惠对等，而是限制人为的机会主义行为，如参与社会残障人士的救助者并不要求或者指望被救助者日后回馈。被这种社会机制抛弃的个体往往不是由其财富状况和生理特征所决定的，而是其道德品行使然。基于这种社会机制的社会保障才能发挥其应有功能，社会保障不必然保障每一个个体，而是帮助参与这种社会机制的个体，此机制核心是自愿基础上的互助与互惠，参与这个机制个体主要不是为了获得保障权益，而是实现互助与互惠的社会情感需求。这样的机制是有弹性的，没有规定谁一定付出多少，也没确切保证谁将从中获益多少，随时调整使得该机制可持续发挥作用。当然，随时调整不是一个个人意志行为，而是互助与互惠群体的共识，不存在机会主义行为。

最后，政府提供最后且最低的个人生命安全网，避免人道灾难。被排除市场交易机制与社会互助互惠机制之外的个体生命安全威胁可能引发人道灾难，政府应当责无旁贷地成为他们生命安全的最后屏障。也就是说，政府财政支持对任何社会个体救助是最后、最低的选择。最后选择就意味着被救助者已经被市场交易和社会互助与互惠机制抛弃，换言之，他曾努力通过市场交易机制或者社会互惠机制解决生命安全问题，但因自身缺陷无法取得成功。具备身心条件的政府救助申请者应承诺重返市场与社会时间，救助期间重返社会行动计划等。而最低的选择则表示，政府财政救助水平仅仅维持生命安全，与参与市场活动的个体生活水准与社会互助与互惠机制提供的生活水平不可同日而语。政府财政的最低救助才能使其成为个体的最后选择，促使政府救助者尽可能重返社会，参与市场活动。

（三）市场、社会与政府各司其职后的财政政策

社会互助与互惠行为的弱化源于政府越位，政府越界行动必然引起相应的政府财政负担。显然，为了防止政府越位，在政府财政支出上进行限制是必要的，限制财政开支约束政府越界行为是可行途径，社会互助与互惠行为才能回归，社会功能得以修复。具体而言，主要包括如下举措。

一是政府财政退出社会保障体系。各国都需要将目前“名义上的社会保障，实质上的政府保障体系”转变成真正意义上的社会保障体系。大多数社会保障体系都会面临入不敷出的窘境。表面上，这是现行劳动制度与人口老龄化叠加使然，实际上，出于各种原因，各国建立社会保障制度偏离社会互助与社会互惠性质，使政府财政深度介入社会保障，从而实质上将社会保障转变成政府保障。这样破坏了传统社会保障的微观基础和家庭结构，也在事实上加剧了人口老龄化进程。因此，政府偿还历史旧账后退出社会保障系统有助于修复社会功能和微观家庭结构，进而强化社会保障能力。

二是政府财政救助遵循最后与最低原则。为了让市场发挥基础性资源配置作用和修复家庭与社会的互助与互惠功能，对任何个体来说，获得政府财政救助必须是最后选项。也就说，他们必须尽其所能地通过市场或家庭与社会机制解决生存发展问题，不到万不得已决不申请政府财政救助。需要说明的是，这样安排可能引发某些个体发生生命安全危机，这是让市场充分发挥作用和家庭与社会履行职能的代价。况且，没有一个保障体系能够保证所有生命绝对安

全，每个个体切实履行家庭与社会责任是最有效社会保障体系的前提。最低原则是防止机会主义行为的必要环节，过高且易得的政府救助将抑制市场作用，侵蚀家庭和社会机能。

三是基础类和民生类财政政策由地方实施，中央协调。市场和社会无法解决的基础类和民生类政府开支由地方政府通过地方税收解决，中央政府进行必要协调。这样可以利用地方和一线的信息优势，而且可以通过减少外部性提高效率。更加重要的是，居民自由迁徙使实施此类财政政策的地方政府间竞争加剧，进而促进地方政府提高财政政策的科学性和效率，否则居民迁徙可能导致一些地方政府失去税基。

四是让购买第三方服务成为政府财政支出、救济的主要方式。政府可以直接提供相应的产品与服务给特定人群，政府直接建立相应实体来提供物品与服务将面临效率问题，管理这个实体将使政府力所不能及。在市场购买第三方服务可使政府节省相应成本，提高财政效率。

三、建议与展望

主流财政理论受制于市场与政府两维世界认知，政府越界行为不可避免，财政赤字意料之中。大陆财政与英美财政都会陷入财政赤字的宿命。财政政策的“扩张—赤字—紧缩—扩张”循环成为现代国别经济史的一个线索。摆脱财政赤字宿命需要限制政府越位行为，让市场、社会和政府各就各位，各司其职。在市场、社会和政府三维世界中，让政府财政承担最后且最低保障才可解决财政赤字、财政政策连续性和持续性问题。

在一段时间内，让财政救助成为最后与最低的保障会使社会公众难以接受的。另外，财政决策者和实施者的工作惯性可能不会让政府救助与扶持行动成为最后支持，过去政府行为的积极性经验和习惯使得政府不愿意等待。或许，在沉重的财政赤字和持续财政压力下，这种等待才可成为可能。

被政府行为与财政政策侵蚀的个体责任、家庭结构与社会互助与互惠机体的修复不会一蹴而就，需要很长时间才能唤醒个体责任心和社会同情，逐步培育家庭和社区互助与互惠机制。因此政府越位的退出可能引起社会一定程度的不适性并不意外。

参考文献

［1］理查德·马斯格雷夫，佩吉·马斯格雷夫．财政理论与实践［M］．邓子基，邓力平，译校．北京：中国财政经济出版社，2003.

［2］严维石．基于轴心原理的大陆与英美财政理论范式比较［J］．广东财经大学学报，2015（03）：12－18.

［3］马珺．财政学：两大传统的分离与融合［J］．经济理论与经济管理，2012（10）：63－73.

［4］李俊生．盎格鲁-撒克逊学派财政理论的破产与科学财政理论的重建——反思当代“主流”财政理论［J］．经济学动态，2014（04）：117－130.

［5］詹姆斯·M. 布坎南，理查德·马斯格雷夫．公共财政与公共选择：两种截然不同的国家观［M］．类承曜，译．北京：中国财政经济出版社，2000.

［6］郭剑鸣．民主理性蜕化与西方“政治性赤字”的膨胀［J］．学术月刊，2010（11）：5－11.

［7］何振一．理论财政学［M］．北京：中国财政经济出版社，1987.

［8］李俊生，王雍君，等．社会共同需要——财政活动的起点与归宿［M］．北京：中国财政经济出版社，2011.

［9］李俊生，姚东旻．互联网搜索服务的性质与其市场供给方式初探——基于新市场财政学的分析［J］．管理世界，2016（08）：1－15.

The Dilemma and Way-out of Social Role Lacking in Mainstream Fiscal Theory: on a Three-dimensional Perspective of Government, Market and Society

Yan Weishi

Abstract: American and British fiscal theories have become mainstream fiscal paradigm, which is built on the two-dimensional cognition of market and government that market failure warrants government intervention. Because it has an endogenous mechanism of government offside and fiscal expansion, this paradigm therefore cannot escape the destiny of fiscal deficit with the recurrence of "expansion-deficit-contraction-expansion". The replacement of social reciprocity by government intervention leads to the expansion of government boundary and budget overload. More seriously, this weakens mutual support and attachment among individuals, thus increases the social operating cost. Reshaping government fiscal aide as minimal security and last-resort will facilitate the comeback of reciprocal behavior & mutual aid and the functional division of market, society and government. Based on this, the issues of fiscal deficit, sustainability and policy continuance can be resolved at the root.

Keywords: American and British fiscal theories Two-dimensional world Fiscal deficit Three-dimensional world
CLC number: F881.9 Document code: A

The fiscal theories of the European mainland had preceded economics as an independent discipline. However, the development of classical, neo-classical economics, and Keynesian macroeconomics had gradually marginalized the theory of mainland finance. Instead, the British and American public finance of Musgrave and others[1] has been regarded as the mainstream textbooks of this discipline. Interestingly, the mainstream British and American public finance has become a part and a sub-discipline of modern macroeconomics. "inverted" change in the relationship between public finance and economics is an academic issue[2]. The marginalization of public finance in the mainland and the British and American finance being the mainstream have not been widely recognized in the academic circle. There has always been questioning and criticism of this issue. Accompanied by the impulse of letting the "Mainland Finance" return and the effort of reconstructing the public finance have never stopped[3][4]. This thesis does not focus on the comparison and evaluation of the fiscal theoretical path between the mainland and the UK and US, but study how do mainstream fiscal theories face challenges of and the solution to the actual fiscal deficits and fiscal sustainability issues.

I. Contemporary Mainstream Fiscal Theories and Fiscal Deficit

The history of fiscal theories shows that the logic of the development from the mainland fiscal theories to the Anglo-American finance is the change of paradigm. The fiscal theories of Buchanan and Musgrave become the mainstream of the Anglo-American fiscal theories, which, relatively, has been widely used and practiced because of its strong "operability". It has now become the main content of the textbooks for public finance. The open theoretical debate between them[5] was regarded as a theoretical dialogue among different factions of the mainstream Anglo-American fiscal theories. In fact, their understanding of nation is different. The focus of their argument is how government fiscal policy intervenes in the economy? Buchanan believed that government fiscal intervention in the economy should be cautious and that government should achieve effective distribution of public fiscal resources through political market competition based on the public choice theory; while Musgrave turned the active intervention in mainland finance into an operative theoretical system through Keynesian macroeconomic theoretical framework and treated market failure as a reason or even an evidence for government fiscal intervention. Buchanan classified the government's fiscal policy as a result of interest groups competing in the political market, while Musgrave naturally regarded the government as a representative of the public interest.

However, their fiscal theories have one thing in common: they construct fiscal theory in the two-dimensional world of market and government. Buchanan emphasized the game characteristics of political market of government finance, but he hoped that the government's fiscal decision-making could be limited by the public choice mechanism, so as to make public finance more effective. He did not exclude the government's fiscal intervention in the economy. Obviously, in the two-dimensional world of market and government, the solution to economic problems is a choice of either market or government. This is the common feature of Buchanan's and Musgrave's Anglo-American mainstream fiscal theories, and differences only appear in how they are applied and the degree of active application. There is no need to state here about Keynes's reasons for the government's fiscal intervention in the economy, thus there is no need to argue about the relationship between the market and the government. However, a fiscal reality is that the fiscal deficit has always been a real economic problem faced by most countries. Why is it that public finance of almost all countries fail to escape from suffering deficit? Is it just due to "democratic politics"[6]?

a. A Fiscal Deficit System Based on a Two-dimensional cognition of Market and Government

In the contemporary mainstream fiscal theories, Buchanan and Musgrave show different understandings of the nation, but they both belong to the framework of the two-dimensional cognition of the market and government. They regard social functions as governmental functions, which results in a loss of efficiency and makes the government financially overwhelmed, as well as weakens social assistance and social sympathy to some extent. The most typical case is social assistance and social security. Social assistance, social health insurance, and pension security should be in the category of social mutual assistance and have nothing to do with government public finance. However, these have become government responsibilities in almost all countries. It has not been a new viewpoint in public finance circle that the government does duties of social groups. Fiscal intervention in the social sphere is the major feature of the mainland public finance. British and American governments' intervention in social affairs is partly related to the economic recession and depression, as well as Keynesian macroeconomics. Next is the analysis of the fate of deficit of contemporary mainstream fiscal theories and practices and their relevant mechanism.

First of all, "no market is government". In the two-dimensional cognition of market and government, government have to solve the problems that cannot be done by the market. Obviously, the more problems the modern government needs to solve, the greater the fiscal expenditure will be. The two-dimensional cognition belongs to the public, as well as the high-level government officials or important political figures. However, the history of human society shows that human socialized living appeared earlier than the government. In other words, for a very long time, there were not governments in human society. This state has been lasting for a long period. The government and its mechanisms are a response to the increasing complexity of society. This does not mean that the social mechanism before the appearance of government is completely ineffective. In other words, the government and its mechanisms are not to replace social mechanisms, but to respond to the fact that social mechanisms cannot effectively cope with new problems under new situations. Two-dimensional cognition has been strengthened by the development of the mainland fiscal theory. The implementation of the mainland's all-encompassing fiscal policy has made the government's border continuously expand, covered social fields and weakened the individual's efforts. Obviously, this kind of social cognition makes the "from cradle to grave" social security system rely on the government, rather than the society. The so-called social security system attached to the government is not necessarily the Achilles' Heel of economic and social development. However, it is undoubtedly a constraint on economic and social reforms.

Secondly, marketization leads to further weakening of social functions and expansion of government functions. In the two-dimensional cognition of market and government, the market gradually takes up profitable space in the social sphere under the joint function of self-interested individuals and does not enter or abandon the part without profit. This further weakens social functions, for example, commercial banks find it profitable to set up a branch to work on deposits and settlements in a small community, but it is unprofitable and with high risk when the community's SMEs fail to provide collateral for loans. With the gradual innovation of enterprises and the improvement of market mechanisms, some social mutual assistance and social reciprocal behaviors may indeed be replaced by some more effective market trading mechanisms. In the two-dimensional cognition, government functions also "naturally" expand, and the breadth and intensity of fiscal expenditure consistently increase.

Furthermore, the aging of the population has gradually revealed the underlying danger of government fiscal expansion. There is a common experience in current or former growing economy that the population that accompanies economic development continues to age. There is no need to state the aging of the population in developed economies. Developing countries like China have already had the trend of population aging before people getting rich. The extension of human life span reflects social progress, but the economic and social problems caused by aging population have not yet been solved. The demographic trend of "having less children or even none" combined with the extension of life expectancy has accelerated the aging of the population. The biggest difference between raising a child and caring the elderly is that as children grow up, the burden becomes lighter, and eventually they become independent; while as the elderly age, the burden becomes heavier. Therefore, the prolonged life expectancy of the population and declining birthrate increase the ratio of social support, and the problem of "who to rely on to care the old?" has become apparent. Caring the old and the industrialization of services related to this issue can solve the problem of supply. But who will pay for the elderly-caring services? In a two-dimensional cognition, it will be overwhelmed for any government finances that support social security when facing problems caused by the aging population. This trend will hinder fiscal revenue growth and accelerate fiscal expenditure. The fiscal deficit must come as expected. What is even more troublesome is that the aging population will make it more and more difficult for the democratic society to reform the social security system supported by the current government finance, and the problem of generational inequality will become more and more serious. The difficulty in the reform of social welfare policies for the high-welfare Western Europe society is a proof.

Finally, economic globalization will further aggravate government public finance in aging society. The fiscal difficulties caused by the aging population have made the social welfare supported by the government finance impossible. In the context of economic globalization, the cross-border flow of capital and labor has become more and more convenient. The capital and young labor force in the aging countries have become more and more taxed with the increasingly aging population. Capital and labor outflow is an inevitable trend. The loss of capital and labor will in turn weaken the country's economic competitiveness, which will further constrain economic growth and worsen fiscal balance.

In short, the fiscal theories and practices based on the two-dimensional cognition of market and government cannot avoid the fate of the fiscal deficit, whether it is the Anglo-American finance or the mainland finance. Relevant theories and practices based on the two-dimensional cognition of market and government has weakened the social mutual assistance and reciprocity, so it is impossible to solve the problem of fiscal deficit. The relatively active Musgrave fiscal theory and the conservative Buchanan fiscal theory have no way out of the financial dilemma in the two-dimensional cognition of market and government for the reason that government finance have already crossed the border into social areas that should have been completed by society, and it is intervening in more and more affairs with increasing intensity. To let government meddle in social issues will not only cause a loss of economic efficiency, but a deep destruction of basic social mechanisms such as social mutual assistance and reciprocal behaviors, which are hard to be repaired.

b. Mainstream financial theory responds to fiscal deficits

Both Musgrave and Buchanan bear fiscal deficit in mind. The Musgrave fiscal theory deeply influenced by Keynesian macroeconomics believes that the fiscal deficit arising from counter-cyclical fiscal policies will gradually ease as the economy recovers and grows, achieving a periodic fiscal balance. The basic theoretical frameworks in the current mainstream fiscal textbooks are in line with Keynes's macroeconomic policy. In the IS-LM or IS-LM-BP framework, how fiscal revenue and expenditure policy regulate macroeconomics. Both neoclassical macroeconomic development and macroeconomic practice have shown that Keynesian macroeconomic fiscal policy is not as effective as is expected in Keynesian macroeconomics and mainstream financial theories in terms of regulating the economy. On the contrary, it has a series of apparent residual, for example, the imbalanced industrial structure. Musgrave's fiscal theory remains a hypothesis for its lack of realistic evidence and theoretical persuasiveness in its scientificity and effectiveness. In this respect, the relatively cautious Buchanan fiscal theory will not be superior to that of Musgrave. Based on the individual rational decision-making philosophy, he emphasized that respects should be given to public opinions when making fiscal decisions, and "calculation with agreement" need to be adopted. That is to say, fiscal policy must be made with the joint agreement of the public, so as to achieve Pareto improvement. The effectiveness of a national referendum on fiscal policy is questionable because of the cost beyond imagination. The adoption of a representative democracy for making decisions on major fiscal policies has been practiced in many countries for years, but the problem of fiscal deficit is still lingering and increasing. The issue of financial efficiency has not yet been considered here.

A vague boundary between governmental and social functions makes the government's fiscal behaviors cross the border to dissolve social functions, and thus the fiscal deficit is unavoidable. A cliff-like fiscal austerity is taken in response to this, and then a new round of cycle begins. The short-term effect of fiscal austerity, to a certain extent, can cover up the drawback of the government's meddling in social issues. If individual responsibility and social functions are consistently covered by the government, individuals will, in the long run, rely on the government and lack the sense of responsibility. As a result, social mutual assistance and reciprocity will lose incentives. Social sympathy and cohesion will also be weakened.

c. Fiscal theory based on the common needs of the society

Domestic fiscal experts are also constantly exploring the boundary of fiscal functions. He Zhenyi[7] and Li Junsheng[8][4][9] proposed and demonstrated that the division of fiscal functions should be based on "common social needs". This theoretical innovation is worthy of advocacy, but the fiscal theory taking the common needs of our society as the starting point and the final goal of fiscal activities needs to include social roles and allows the society to play its due functions. Otherwise, it will still make fiscal policy fall into the two-dimensional predicament between the market and the society and it will also be impossible to get rid of the fiscal deficit. The theoretical exploration of turning common social needs into governmental fiscal policy through public choice[4] needs to face the financial pressure and fiscal deficit both at home and abroad. The trouble is that to dynamically adjust the boundary of common social needs and make relative decisions will be a process that costs a lot. This game process may be quite complicated.

The fact that Arrow's impossibility theorem will make the process of defining social common needs economically infeasible. This may allow the government to implement direct interventions in order to save the cost of defining and deciding common social needs. The preference of the public choice in terms of fiscal revenue and expenditure adjustments will, to a large extent, cause fiscal deficits. To increase the tax-based fiscal revenue policy can hardly be agreed by the public. While the fiscal expenditure policy in which specific fiscal expenditure is increased without changing other expenditures can be implemented through the public choice process, which will definitely lead to fiscal deficit in the end. By using budget-balancing plan that combines specific fiscal revenue and expenditure in response to the adjustment of common social needs will also be criticized in consideration of fiscal efficiency. The theory of common social needs will face a problem of how to effectively alleviate excessive fiscal pressure and huge fiscal deficits.

II. The Return of Social Roles and the Fiscal Function of Three-dimensional World

The above explains how the fiscal theories and policies in the two-dimensional world of market and government caused fiscal deficits. In other words, regardless of fiscal efficiency, fiscal deficit is a natural and inevitable result in the two-dimensional world. The dual structure of market and government makes the sustainability and coherence of fiscal policy impossible, and the fiscal deficit is inescapable. In the two-dimensional world, the government's meddling in social affairs has weakened the social functions of mutual assistance and reciprocity, causing unbearable fiscal pressure and eventually triggering fiscal deficits. The key to coping with fiscal deficits and improving the continuity of fiscal policy is to let social roles return again, so that the market, society, and government will undertake their own duties. Only when using fiscal theories set in the way of three-dimensional world cognition can we effectively solve the fiscal problems in the three-dimensional world. Such being the case, the following part will be the discussion of interpersonal exchanges in the three-dimensional world of market, government, society, and an explanation that in this three-dimensional world, interpersonal exchanges are performed in different ways, and the related costs and effects are not all the same, so it will bring negative effects if we replace one way with another.

a. Ways of individual exchange in the three-dimensional cognition

In the real world, there are three ways in which an individual legally obtains products and services from others.

The first one is market exchange. This is used for goods and services with clear property rights. In the market competition, both parties conclude a transaction through bargaining, and both of them can get what they want in a certain way. In many cases, it may not be an effective way for its cost will be relatively high due to high cost of defining property rights and great uncertainties of information; therefore, in countries with the most mature market economy, there are also a large number of cases in which non-market exchange method is practiced. To a certain extent, the long-term existence of non-market trading method shows it is efficient.

The second one is government transfer. By using its power, government makes an order to transfer goods and services from some citizens to others through money or other ways, that is, transfer payment in macroeconomics. This kind of exchange method using government transfer as a medium makes both parties of the transaction not participate in the transaction, thus issues related to mutual rights or responsibilities doesn't exist. The transferred party obtains the transferred goods and services because of a certain historical or social complex; while the transferring party transfers the capital due to the statutory tax liability or the payment required for the transfer of goods and services. The government acts as a medium to keep both parties of transfer having no access to emotional experience during the process of transfer. The transferee will not be grateful to any person for the goods and services he obtains because he does not know who transferred those to him? He will not be grateful to government officials because he knows that these items are not provided by them. They would think that accepting these goods is their rights and they need not take liabilities and the sense of "debt". The social atmosphere that takes the transferred power or treatment as a kind of capital dampens the enthusiasm of labor and stimulates social laziness.

The third one is social assistance. It includes social reciprocity and altruism. This is an ancient way of human social life which is much earlier than the first two ones and it is accompanied by human social life. However, this way of exchange is often ignored by scholars. The successful practice of market economy has made economists pay homage to the efficiency of market exchange, which has become the synonymous of efficient exchange. However, the mutual exchange of reciprocal and altruistic behaviors is a relatively efficient way of exchange within a certain range. Compared with market exchange, social mutual assistance exchange does not rely on exchange media, and need not to define property rights and even need not to pay parity and give timely delivery. In addition, this kind of exchange often involves social and emotional experiences such as sympathy, responsibility, affection, and gratitude. Helpers and recipients meet their social and emotional needs in the exchange process. More importantly, this emotional experience will enable all parties to recognize that they have a responsibility to contribute to this kind of social assistance. This kind of mutual social assistance exchange cannot completely prevent opportunistic behaviors itself, but social mutual assistance is generally chained, and there is a correlation between periods before and after social assistance, which leads to a series of social mutual assistance. Thus, opportunistic actors will be identified, warned, and driven out of such groups. Compared with government transfer, social assistance helps to curb opportunistic behaviors, enhance social responsibility of individuals, and bring a positive attitude towards life. People can accept social assistance as well as be ready to become helpers. Of course, this type of exchange has not been derived at a large scale for social mutual exchange system is often applied to small groups like a community. Thus, the market exchange has an advantage of efficiency in transactions at a larger scale, such as international trade.

Obviously, in the three-dimensional cognition world, the exchange of different dimensions is different, so do exchange costs and efficiency. More importantly, the impact of exchange is not the same. They do not replace, but complement each other. Using one way of exchange to replace another can be contrary to our expectations. The current fiscal theories and practices are examples of situations in which substitutions occur in the supplementary way of exchange.

The method that current mainstream fiscal theories put the economic problems of the three-dimensional world into the two-dimensional framework of the market and the government so as to solve them determines the effect of fiscal practice guided by this method. Economics, including public finance, ignores the social dimension, and analyzes and solves economic problems in the two-dimensional cognition of market and government, making economic issues increasingly complex. The fiscal deficit is a typical example.

b. The social roles return, and the market, society and government take their own duties

The market, the society, and the government undertake different functions in different ways. Of course, the goals and results are also different. They keep a complementary relationship, rather than a replaceable one. The absence of any roles is difficult to be made up for. It is clear that the government's meddling in social issues not only makes it a burden for governmental fiscal expenditure, but weakens social behaviors such as mutual social assistance and reciprocity, harming social emotions and cohesion. To solve the fiscal problems in the two-dimensional world of market and government requires the reform from the bottom, that is, the return of social functions, so that the market, society, and government will perform their own duties. How do the market, the society and the government achieve this?

First, the market priority principle. The economic history at home and abroad shows that the market is an effective resource allocation mechanism, and that opportunistic behaviors can effectively be curbed through the market way individuals obtain resources for survival and development. This is the reason why the market economy has become the economic form of most countries. Countries at all times must allocate resources efficiently to cope with the pressure of resource scarcity. Market transactions enable both parties of transaction to achieve the combination of responsibility, right and interest. Market transactions are voluntary and free. Therefore, the result of transactions is that resources are allocated to where the highest value can be realized. The effective promotion of market economy is a stepping stone to the modern economy. We should adhere to the principle of market priority in the division of functions among the market, society, and government. The main reasons are: First, an individual must perform his responsibility of "making both sides clear" so that he can legally obtain the goods and services to survive and develop. In this way, the rights and obligations of the trading parties are equivalent, which motivates individuals to obtain their own needs by providing their own labor or services to the market. Second, the market transactions are not limited to a community or a valid area. To allocate resources within a larger area may get higher returns. Compared with the regional nature of social mutual assistance and the regional nature of government services, the market is broader in time and space dimension. Many market transactions occur among trans-regional and transnational individuals, which in turn allows individuals to get better what he needs within a larger range. Third, there is no third party involved in the cost and only both sides of the transaction need to share it through the way of market transactions. Both sides of the market transaction search for each other on their own and negotiate relevant issues. Generally, there is no externality and thus no third party is involved. Therefore, market transactions generally do not involve interpersonal "super-economic" wealth transfer. Of course, there is no interpersonal or inter-generational inequality.

However, this does not mean that in any time and space, the market is the most effective mechanism for individual survival and development. Market transactions rely on the clarity of the property rights of the transaction objects, and the need to pay the parity. Dividing property rights is not only costly, but sometimes the cost is very high, and paying the parity will also lead to related costs. In the case where the division of property rights is complicated, the market mechanism may not be an effective one.

Second, to make full use of mutual assistance and reciprocity so as to realize individual sociality. The objects for survival and development can be obtained from neighborhoods, friends and family members not necessaril y through the way of market. Instead, they can achieve the exchange of goods and services through social means such as social mutual assistance or reciprocity. This kind of exchange does not require a clear division of property rights, nor does it require payment of the parity that "making both sides clear". In certain regions or groups, social mutual assistance and reciprocity is an efficient mechanism for exchange. More importantly, this kind of social mechanism can fulfill economic functions with high-efficiency, as well as meet the emotional needs of an individual in the society and promote social sympathy and enhance social cohesion. However, it will take a long time for this mechanism to work, and not any individual can enter this mechanism of social reciprocity. Its establishment relies on frequent mutually beneficial cooperation and the resulting reputation. There is a correlation between two social assistance and reciprocity activities, and the helpers in the former one may become the beneficiary of the next similar social behavior. This correlation is a mechanism to prevent opportunistic behaviors of individuals. The higher the frequency of social mutual assistance and reciprocal behavior, the more effective the mechanism will be. In addition, this mechanism does not require both parties to give equivalent assistance, but is to limit artificial opportunistic behaviors. For example, the rescuer who participated in activities that aim to help the disabled does not demand or expect the rescued person to give feedbacks in the future. Individuals abandoned by such social mechanism are generally not determined by their wealth status and physical characteristics, but by their moral traits. Social security based on this mechanism can play its due function. Social security does not necessarily guarantee every individual, but guarantee those who participate in it. The core of this mechanism is mutual assistance and reciprocity based on a voluntary choice. Those who join it are not mainly for the purpose of guaranteed rights and interests, but to meet the emotional needs through mutual assistance and reciprocity. Such a mechanism is flexible. It does not stipulate how much people must pay, and it does not guarantee exactly how much you will benefit from it. It can be adjusted at any time so that the mechanism will be continuous and effective. Of course, adjustment at any time does not depend on individual willingness. Such being the case, opportunistic behaviors will not exist in mutual assistance and mutual benefit groups.

Finally, the government provides the last and lowest safety net of an individual's life to avoid humanitarian disasters. Threats of individual life safety that are excluded from market trading mechanisms and social mutual assistance and mutual benefit mechanisms may lead to humanitarian disasters, and the government is responsible to act as the last barrier to their safety. In other words, governmental fiscal support is the last and lowest choice for any individual social assistance. The last choice means that the rescued person has been abandoned by the market transactions and social mutual assistance and mutual benefit mechanism. That is to say, he has tried to solve the problem concerning his safety through the two ways, but ends with failure for his own defects. Applicants with qualified physical and mental conditions should make a promise of the time to return to the market, the society and their action plans during the period. The lowest choice shows that the level of government fiscal assistance only maintains life safety, which cannot match with the living level provided by the market activities and the social assistance and reciprocity mechanism. Only the government's minimum fiscal aid can make it the last choice for individuals, and encourage those who need the help to return to the society as much as possible and participate in market activities.

c. Fiscal policies after market, society and government each performs its own function

Government's offside is the reason for bot corresponding government fiscal burden and weakening social mutual assistance and mutual benefit behavior. Apparently, in order to prevent government's offside, it is necessary and feasible to impose restrictions on government expenditure, thus re-strengthening social mutual assistance and mutual benefit behavior and renovating social functions. Specifically, government shall take following actions:

First, stop government finance intervening in social security system. Countries shall transfer the current ' nominally social but virtually governmental security system ' into the real sense of social security system. Most social security systems are usually faced with dilemmas that can't make ends meet, which ostensibly results from both current labor system and aging population. However, in fact, social security systems of countries usually deviate from the nature of social mutual assistance and mutual benefit so that government finance profoundly intervenes in social security and substantially convert social security into governmental security, which actually destroys micro-foundation and family structure of traditional social security and accelerates the process of aging population. Therefore, after paying off old account, government's non-intervention in social security system helps renovate social functions and micro family structure, thus enhancing social security.

Second, government financial assistance shall obey the last and minimum principle. In order to give play to market's function of fundamental resource allocation and renovate mutual assistance and mutual benefit function between family and society, it is the last alternative to receive governmental financial assistance for any individual. In other words, they have to make every effort to survive and develop through market or the mechanism of family and society and only as a last resort will they apply for governmental financial assistance. It is important to note that such arrangement may trigger a life-safety crisis for certain individuals, which is the cost for the market to play its full role and the family and society to perform its functions. Moreover, since no security system can ensure absolute safety of all individuals, the premise of the most effective social security system is that everyone can fully undertake family and social responsibilities. The minimum principle is necessary to prevent opportunism, for government assistance with high amount and availability will inhibit market, family and social functions.

Third, basic and livelihood fiscal policies shall be implemented by local government with coordination of central government. The basic and livelihood government expenditure that cannot be solved by the market and society shall be spent by local governments through local taxation, with necessary coordination from the central government, which can not only take advantage of local and firsthand information, but also reduce externalities to improve efficiency. More importantly, the free migration of residents has intensified the competition between local governments implementing such fiscal policies, thus forcing local governments to improve scientificity and efficiency on fiscal policies. Otherwise, the residents´migration may cause some local governments to lose their tax bases.

Fourth, government shall implement fiscal expenditure and relief mainly through the method of purchase of third-party services. Though the government can directly provide corresponding products and services to specific groups of people, establishment of corresponding entities to provide such products and services will certainly raise efficiency problems, which cannot be easily fixed by the government. Purchasing third-party services in the market can save the government costs and increase financial efficiency.

III. Recommendations and Outlook

The mainstream financial theory is subject to the two-dimensional cognition of market and government. The government's offside is inevitable and the fiscal deficit is expected. i. e. , Continental finances and Anglo-American finances will all fall into the fate of the fiscal deficit. The "expansion-deficit-austerity-expansion" cycle of fiscal policy has become a clue to economic history of modern individual countries. To get rid of fiscal deficits needs to limit government's offside and make market, society, and government undertakes its own functions. In the three-dimensional world, only when the government finance undertakes the last and minimum security can the problem of continuity and sustainability on fiscal deficits and fiscal policies be solved.

For a certain period of time, it's unacceptable to the public that financial assistance becomes the last and minimum security. In addition, the inertia of financial decision makers and implementers may not allow government assistance and support actions to become the last support, for the previous positive experiences and habit surge the government to take actions without waiting. Perhaps such waiting will be possible under heavy fiscal deficits and continuous financial pressure.

Individual responsibility, family structure and social mutual assistance and reciprocity organism eroded by government actions and fiscal policies will not be renovated overnight. Instead, it will take a long time to arouse individual responsibility and social sympathy, thus gradually fostering family and community mutual assistance and reciprocity mechanisms. Therefore, it is not surprising that the cease of government's offside may cause certain degree of discomfort in society.

References

[1] Richard Musgrave, Peggy Musgrave. Public Finance in Theory and Practice [M]. Deng Ziji, Deng Liping, translation, Beijing: Chinese Financial&Economic Publishing House, 2003.

[2] Yan Weishi. Comparison between Continental and Anglo-Saxon Fiscal Theories Paradigms based on Axis Principle [J]. Journal of Guangdong University of Finance & Economics, 2015 (3): 12-18.

[3] Ma Jun. Public Finance: The Separation and Mix of the Two Traditions [J]. Economic Theory and Business Management, 2012 (10): 63-73.

[4] Li Junsheng. The Bankruptcy of the Anglo-Saxon School Theory and the Reconstruction of the Scientific Fiscal Theory—Rethinking the Contemporary "Mainstream" Fiscal Theory [J]. Economic Perspectives, 2014 (4): 117-130.

[5] James Mcgill Buchanan, Richard Musgrave. Public Finance and Public Choice: Two Contrasting Visions of the State [M]. Lei Chengyao, translation, Beijing: Chinese Financial& Economic Publishing House, 2000.

[6] GuoJianming. The Degeneration of Rational Democracy and the Expansion of Western "Political Deficit" [J]. Academic Monthly, 2010 (11): 5-11.

[7] He Zhenyi. Theoretical Finance [M]. Beijing: Chinese Financial&Economic Publishing House, 1987.

[8] Li Junsheng, Wang Yongjun, etc. Common Needs of Society-Starting Point and Destination of Financial Activities [M]. Beijing: Chinese Financial&Economic Publishing House, 2011.

[9] Li Junsheng, Yao Dongmin. The Nature of Internet Search Service and Its Market Supply: An Analysis Based on New Market Finance [J]. Management World, 2016 (8): 1-15.

《新市场财政学研究》创刊说明

《新市场财政学研究》是由中央财经大学新市场财政学研究所、中国财政发展协同创新中心主办的一本财政学基础理论类期刊。本刊暂以集刊形式一年发行两期，主要刊发财政基础理论及其创新内容，试图打造中国特色财政学派的理论原发和传播平台。我们广泛欢迎跨学科（政治科学、组织社会学、公共管理）、多视角、宽进路的有关财政基本原理与中国财政实践的各类论文，来稿研究方法不限，数理建模、经验实证与定性的理论分析均可。现将创刊说明公布如下，欢迎学界同仁关注并赐稿。

一、《新市场财政学研究》——推动财政基础理论的发展繁荣

1. 创办意义。

党的十八届三中全会在《中共中央关于全面深化改革若干重大问题的决定》中提出了“财政是国家治理的基础和重要支柱”的重要论断，从而把财政在国民经济中的地位和作用提升到了一个新的高度。而国内财政学界长期对财政基础理论缺乏重视，导致财政基础理论的发展与创新滞后，从而致使财政政策与财政实践缺少与时俱进的理论基石。财政学是一门研究国家财政分配关系的综合性学科。当今学术界，盎格鲁-撒克逊学派的财政理论占主流地位。该学派从市场失灵理论出发，在逻辑上推导出政府及其财政存在的必要性。但是无论是从历史的角度看，还是从逻辑的角度看，那种“以市场失灵为政府财政的起点”的观点可能本身就是一个谬误。在这一逻辑体系中，政府财政成为弥补市场缺陷的手段，市场和政府的关系也变成对立的双方。并且，这种财政理论很难指导我国的财政实践。

同时，由于国内学界对于财政基础理论研究的忽视，财政学界完全照搬盎格鲁-撒克逊财政理论，我国财政理论体系被全盘“英美化”。而我国与英美等

国的经济理论基础及相关的政治制度的根本差异决定了对西方财政理论不能照搬。“市场失灵”理论很难解释和预测我国的财政行为。在这种情况下，财政理论很难针对我国的经济社会发展进程和需要提出必要的智力支持。另一方面，国内财政学界缺少交流财政基础理论的平台，也使得财政理论难有百家争鸣的局面。

《新市场财政学研究》是国内财政学基础理论类期刊。我们创办《新市场财政学研究》，希望能够借“新市场财政学”激发国外学界对于基础理论的探讨，提供让学者深入研讨财政基础理论的平台，从而产生高质量的研究成果，最终让财政政策、财政实践有理可依，让财政研究有章可循。

2.《新市场财政学研究》的定位。

本刊鼓励接收立足中国现实，兼具学术性、理论性的财政学研究成果。在内容上，本刊鼓励诸位学者关注财政领域，特别是基础理论方面的重大问题、热点问题以及我国财政现象。各位学者可以综合性的研究视角来拓展研究的广度与深度，研究方法包含但不限于理论分析、计量实证、数理建模、文本分析、案例分析等。

本刊物在新市场财政学理论构建之初创办，旨在为财政学的基础理论建设开辟全新的研究视角。因此我们期望国内外志同道合的学者们能够共同发展与创新这一理论，从而促进财政学基础理论的发展与繁荣，为国家的良好治理、社会经济系统的繁荣提供稳固的理论根基。本刊物更期待在诸位学者的共同努力下，孕育出具有普适性和解释力的本土化财政学基础理论，产出世界一流的研究成果，最终实现我国财政学的理论自信。

《新市场财政学研究》的创办，有利于加深学界对新市场财政学的认识，重新反思主流财政学存在的问题，更好地解决本土财政问题。“新市场财政学”是具有中国特色的财政基础理论的探索，是在紧密联系中国财政实践和其他国家财政实践的前提下构建，充分考虑了中国文化和中国思维方式在理论框架建设中的影响。《新市场财政学研究》不仅希望能为政府及其他需求者研究与探索财政问题提供更具解释力的理论方法与工具，还肩负了打造财政学“中国学派”的任务。

3.《新市场财政学研究》的命名缘由。

“新市场财政学”是作为一个新的财政理论框架、新的财政学分析与研究范式而提出的。依据财政学研究对象分类甄别，当代主流财政学属于研究市场经济条件下政府财政活动规律的“狭义”财政学，简单地说，属于“市场财政学”。作为这种市场财政学的理论基础——市场失灵理论的“失灵”以及其对公共部门、私人部门和市场之间关系认识的偏差，让我们重新回归到对经济学的有关公共部门、私人部门、市场关系的探讨，从而诞生了“新市场财政学”。新市场财政学“新”在，基于对市场失灵理论的批判和解剖的基础上，借鉴欧洲大陆学派财政理论的合理内核，重新定位公共部门、私人部门和市场之间的关系，探寻重构与完善财政理论的新财政理论分析与研究范式。在放弃了“市场失灵理论”的前提下，新市场财政学一方面为财政学理论的理论基础开辟了全新的研究视角；另一方面新市场财政学从国家治理需求的角度出发，为政府以及经济社会其他有关需求者研究与探索财政问题提供更具解释力的理论方法与工具。

为了进一步推动财政基础理论在当代中国的繁荣发展以及扩大其在西方财政理论界的影响，《新市场财政学研究》的创办就更具理论及现实意义。期刊名称继续承袭了“新市场财政学”的概念，首先与主流财政学做出区别，重新回归到对财政学的有关公共部门、私人部门、市场关系的探讨。新市场财政学观点的提出并不是为了另立门户，而是继承了“社会共同需要”“公共选择理论”和“公共价值理论”等理论内核，以期不断完善发展现有理论。此外，在期刊的核心概念的英文翻译中，我们使用“Neo-Public Finance”作为新市场财政学的英文名称。使用“Neo”而非“New”是因为前者更准确地表现了新市场财政学对欧洲大陆学派的传承和对当代主流财政学理论的反思，更重视市场的作用，反映了更为自由的政治经济主张。

二、新市场财政学：缘起、创新与传承

从西方财政学理论发展的历史来看，通常将财政学理论分为两派：盎格鲁-撒克逊学派（英美学派）与欧洲大陆学派。在当今世界学术界，盎格鲁-撒克逊学派的财政理论占主流地位，被称为所谓的“主流财政学派”，现代主流财政理论的理论基础实际上是现代西方宏观经济学的市场失灵理论。按照盎格鲁-撒克逊学派对财政理论的概述，财政学就是研究政府干预经济以便达到自

身目的的科学，而政府作为独立于社会之外的自治体，就是财政理论的研究核心。政府需要在市场失灵的领域内发挥干预者的作用，从而对财政现象进行解释和观测。但是究其根源，政府财政并不是以市场失灵为起点，政府财政最初并不是为了解决市场失灵问题才建立的。因此，“以市场失灵为政府财政的起点”的观点并不能完全科学地反映历史进程。

基于此，我们提出“新市场财政学”的理论体系。“新市场财政学”以社会共同需要作为理论源泉，以公共选择作为方法论的基础，以利润最大化作为私人部门经济活动的市场表现形式，以公共价值最大化作为政府财政活动的市场表现形式。公共部门和私人部门之间产生的经济活动都是在市场中进行的，因此，市场是包括政府、企业和私人等众多参与者的一个交易平台，这从根本上改变了传统市场财政学中市场与政府的对立关系。以政府作为代表的公共部门与以企业为代表的私人部门作为交易平台中的平等成员，通过市场博弈行为来调整约定控制权及剩余控制权，实现公私部门“双赢”，从而达到资源的有效配置，进而不断完善新的市场环境体系。具体说来，新市场财政学可以概括为一个核心概念和四个基础概念。

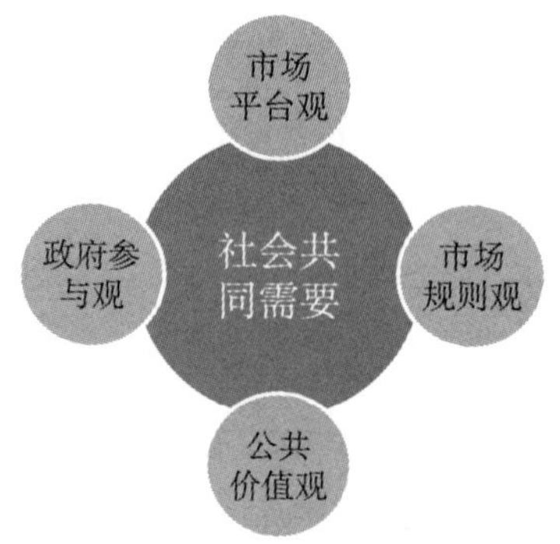

“社会共同需要”作为财政理论体系的核心概念首先回答了财政的来源问题。该概念从历史和逻辑的角度回答了财政是人类社会为了满足一定范围的“社会共同需要”而由社会集中性地支配一部分社会资源（在当代社会表现为“财政”）的现象。社会共同需要是导致财政活动产生的根本原因，明确了“财政”是用于满足社会共同需要的经济手段。按照这个逻辑，政府作为公共部门的代表，其职能和目标便在于满足“社会共同需要”。同时，“社会共同需要”也解释了市场的本质——一种在不确定环境下进行有规则竞争以满足人的需要的过程。市场的本质就是通过资源的配置与交换满足人的需要的，这里的“需要”包括人的“个体”的个别需要，也包括人的“群体”的社会共同需要。

以市场的本质问题为起点，财政科学必须回答：“市场满足人的需要的基本方式是什么？谁来满足人的需要？通过什么方式来满足人的需要？如何确定人们的需要的类型？满足社会共同需要财政活动和满足社会个别需要的经济活动各自在市场上的表现形式如何？”等一系列问题。为了回答以上这些问题，新市场财政学提出了四个基础概念。

（1）市场平台观。新市场财政学首先从物理学的角度出发，将市场视为一个“平台”，进而将市场上的一切行为主体（包括政府以及以政府为代表的公共部门）都视为“市场地位”相同的客体，这样的“市场平台观”符合我国以及其他国家市场经济的客观实际，在逻辑上是合理的，实践上也是可行的。“市场平台观”作为新市场财政学核心概念体系中的基础性概念环节，对近期出现的例如新公共管理运动、PPP等财政现象提供了全新的解释视角，因而构成了新市场财政学强大解释力的重要因子。

（2）政府参与观。作为与市场平台观相对应的、具有逻辑上的承上启下功能的另一个基础性核心概念环节——“政府平台观”概念的引入意味着财政学不再将政府视为站在市场对立面的、居高临下的干预者，而是将其视为市场的参与者，视为市场平台上的有机构成部分之一，因而“政府参与观”与“市场平台观”相辅相成，共同构成了新市场财政学核心概念体系中的基础性概念环节。

（3）市场规则观。我国和世界上其他国家的经济与社会发展实践证明，任何市场规则的确立首先都是由市场行为者基于各自在市场中的利益与竞争对手和合作伙伴相互博弈、相互妥协的结果。市场规则观认为，立法机构是市场规则的重要制定者，但不是市场规则的唯一制定者，应该将所有市场活动参与者都视为立规者，他们会基于各自的目标与利益诉求不断地重塑或扭曲规则。

（4）公共价值观。新市场财政学将公私部门在市场中的互动作为一种广义的交易：其中公共部门以创造公共价值、满足社会共同需要作为组织目标和财政活动的市场表现形式，私人部门以实现私人价值、满足私人或者企业个别需要作为目标和经济活动的市场表现形式。新市场财政学力图通过引入“公共价值”概念来解释和描述在市场经济条件下政府以及公共部门财政活动。在这里，公共价值并不是各类使用价值的集合体，而是市场经济条件下政府以及公共部门财政活动结果的理论表现形式。

三、主办单位

《新市场财政学研究》由新市场财政学研究所和中国财政发展协同创新中心共同主办。新市场财政学研究所是依托中央财经大学中国财政发展协同创新中心为平台，由中央财经大学学术委员会主席、新市场财政学研究所所长、中国财政发展协同创新中心首席专家李俊生教授及其带领的财政基础理论团队致力于建设新市场财政学理论范式的研究机构。中国财政发展协同创新中心是在财政部的直接领导下，由中央财经大学牵头，以六所原财政部直属高校以及三家国家会计学院为基础，联合国家税务总局、社科院等所属科研机构以及相关国际著名财税科研机构，于 2012 年共同组建的财政领域的国家级“智库”。中心拥有 14 支一流水平的跨学科、跨专业的团队，拥有完善的硕博研究生人才培养机制，汇聚多方优势资源，以实现“国家亟须、世界一流”为目标。

2016 年 11 月，中国财政发展协同创新中心成功举办了“新市场财政学”理论创新学术研讨会暨“新市场财政学研究所”成立大会。来自中央财经大学、中国社会科学院、中国财政科学研究院、国家税务总局、中国财经出版传媒集团、中国人民大学等多个合作院校的财经专家就财政基础理论的发展，中国财政学科的建设等问题进行了深入的讨论。会上，李俊生教授正式提出“新市场财政学”的理论并宣布成立新市场财政学研究所。中心和研究所学科带头人李俊生教授积多年潜心研究之成果汇聚形成的“新市场财政学理论”被确定为本研究所工作的核心要素，也是本中心今后学术研究、平台设立的灵魂与方向。

经过几年的快速发展，中国财政发展协同创新中心和新市场财政学研究所在理论研究、平台建设、人才培养和学术交流等方面取得重大进展，在学科带头人的领导下，形成了包含知名学者、教授、海内外财政领域优秀青年教师在内的专业研究团队。作为“新市场财政学”的阵地，新市场财政学研究所致力于推进中国财政实践与财政理论的融合，为中国学者对财政学基础理论建设提供平台和保障。为了实现这一目标，研究所在大力开展相关研究工作的同时，也希望为国内有志于投身财政基础理论研究的学者提供沟通和学习的平台。

《新市场财政学研究》期刊便是出于此目的而创立。在未来，我们希望学者能以《新市场财政学研究》期刊为桥梁，以新市场财政学研究所为平台，共同推动财政学基础理论建设，增强财政理论的预测力和解释力，更好地指导我国财政实践。

征稿启事

《新市场财政学研究》是一份综合性的财政学理论刊物。主要刊登财政基础理论及理论创新方面的论文，同时也欢迎对我国财政现实问题的分析。《新市场财政学研究》的编辑出版流程对接国际惯例，并按照技术标准规范出刊。

本刊采取网络在线投稿和邮箱投稿的方式。作者须在《新市场财政学研究》期刊的官方网站：http：//jnpf. cufe. edu. cn/上进行实名注册，完成相关的在线投递事宜，并同时抄送邮箱：inpf@ cufe. edu. cn。成功投递后，作者可直接在官网上的“投稿查询系统”追踪稿件的投审稿状态。本刊的稿件初审时间为 3 个月，如超过期限，可来电咨询。

1. 投稿须知。

稿件应是作者自己完成的原创文章，且坚决反对一稿多投，欢迎广大读者来信监督举报。来稿需注明：“专投《新市场财政学研究》”字样。编辑部收到稿件 3 个月后未接到本刊通知者可另投他刊。

文章需论点明确、论证充分且逻辑严谨。文章须对研究问题的理论和现实背景有清楚的描述，对相关领域现有的研究进展有必要说明，围绕中心话题展开严密详尽的讨论，并指出论文的创新之处。

研究方法不限。本刊在推动发展财政思想、财政基础理论的基础上，鼓励作者在财政学研究中采用多种研究方式，包括理论分析、数理建模、计量分析方法、案例分析方法等，特别是与新市场财政学理论的交叉科学研究，但更看中的是论文所阐释的财政学思想。

来稿须遵守学术道德规范。《新市场财政学研究》对来稿是否为原创和专投进行审查，一经查实由于作者原因导致剽窃行为或稿件重发等学术不端行为而影响《新市场财政学研究》声誉，《新市场财政学研究》将在第一时间将情况通报给作者所在单位的学术管理机构，并保留在《新市场财政学研究》公开情况的权利。

2. 投稿内容及格式要求。

论文封面。学术论文需加封面，标注中英文标题、作者姓名、工作单位、通讯地址、电话和电子信箱、基金项目等，基金项目需注明基金项目的名称和编号。此外，正文部分不出现作者姓名、通讯地址及电话、工作单位等与稿件内容无关的私人信息。

论文写作要求。论文正文需要在 10000 字以上。论文的中英文摘要 500 字左右，简要阐述所研究的问题、方法与结论；关键词 3—5 个。

外国人名和专业术语的翻译。外国人名的翻译必须附原文或直接采用原文。专业术语的翻译要规范化，较为生僻的情况下需附原文。

注释与参考文献。注释以脚注形式放在当前页下，参考文献放在文末。文中出现的参考文献标注要与文末列出的一一对应。中文在前，外文在后，按拼音或字母顺序排列。引自期刊，应给出该期刊的名称及期号；引自著作，应列出该著作的出版年份、出版单位、版次及地点；引自某一论文集要列出该论文集的名称及编者姓名、出版时间和地点。

本刊真诚希望广大学者踊跃投稿，优秀的文章我们会优先录用和发表。本刊不收版面费。对于采用的文章，本刊将电话或邮箱直接联系作者。

《新市场财政学研究》编辑部